T0334000

Brand Management in a Co-Creation Perspective

This book articulates a new theoretical approach to branding, labelled the Communication as Constitutive of Brands (CCB) approach. This approach combines understandings from the CCO (Communication as Constitutive of Organization) perspective with the branding literature.

The author outlines the evolution of corporate branding theory that has developed from an identity approach rooted in signalling theory to an understanding of brands as co-created by multiple stakeholders. She then develops and elaborates the latter approach by formulating and explicating the CCB approach, within which a brand is conceptualized as a discursive brand space, grounded in a performative and interactional ontology. Brand discourses are produced in a number of conversational spaces inhabited by both human and non-human actors. Seeing that non-human actors have agency, notions of hybrid agency and ventriloquism are key in the CCB approach, and the role of the brand manager is to function as a practical author. The CCB approach is presented and sustained by five chapters that each elaborate on a certain aspect of CCB and demonstrate the theoretical points in a number of analyses (i.e. the process of brand creation, the set-up of conversational spaces, the role of materiality and macro-actors, frame games, and the brand manager as a practical author). The data in the analyses originates from a business case that is used throughout the book.

Written for scholars and university students within the field of branding and organizational communication, this book represents an area of developing interest within the field of marketing.

Heidi Hansen is an Associate Professor within the Department of Language and Communication at the University of Southern Denmark. She conducts research on branding, organizational studies, and communication and media.

Routledge Studies in Marketing

This series welcomes proposals for original research projects that are either single or multi-authored or an edited collection from both established and emerging scholars working on any aspect of marketing theory and practice and provides an outlet for studies dealing with elements of marketing theory, thought, pedagogy and practice.

It aims to reflect the evolving role of marketing and bring together the most innovative work across all aspects of the marketing 'mix' – from product development, consumer behaviour, marketing analysis, branding, and customer relationships, to sustainability, ethics and the new opportunities and challenges presented by digital and online marketing.

Decoding Coca-Cola
A Biography of a Global Brand
Edited by Robert Crawford, Linda Brennan and Susie Khamis

Luxury and Fashion Marketing
The Global Perspective
Satyendra Singh

Building Corporate Identity, Image and Reputation in the Digital Era
T C Melewar, Charles Dennis and Pantea Foroudi

Corporate Heritage Marketing
Using the Past as a Strategic Asset
Angelo Riviezzo, Antonella Garofano, and Maria Rosaria Napolitano

Brand Management in a Co-Creation Perspective
Communication as Constitutive of Brands
Heidi Hansen

For more information about this series, please visit: www.routledge.com/Routledge-Studies-in-Marketing/book-series/RMKT

Brand Management in a Co-Creation Perspective

Communication as Constitutive of Brands

Heidi Hansen

Routledge
Taylor & Francis Group

LONDON AND NEW YORK

First published 2021
by Routledge
2 Park Square, Milton Park, Abingdon, Oxon OX14 4RN

and by Routledge
605 Third Avenue, New York, NY 10158

Routledge is an imprint of the Taylor & Francis Group, an informa business

British Library Cataloguing in Publication Data
A catalogue record for this book is available from the British Library

Library of Congress Cataloging-in-Publication Data
Names: Hansen, Heidi (Marketing researcher) author.
Title: Brand management in a co-creation perspective : communication
as constitutive of brands / Heidi Hansen.
Description: 1 Edition. | New York City : Routledge Books, 2021. |
Series: Routledge studies in marketing | Includes bibliographical
references and index.
Identifiers: LCCN 2021002595 (print) | LCCN 2021002596 (ebook)
Subjects: LCSH: Branding (Marketing) | Communication in organizations.
Classification: LCC HF5415.1255 H3686 2021 (print) | LCC HF5415.1255
(ebook) | DDC 658.8/27--dc23
LC record available at https://lccn.loc.gov/2021002595
LC ebook record available at https://lccn.loc.gov/2021002596

ISBN: 978-0-367-50489-2 (hbk)
ISBN: 978-0-367-50497-7 (pbk)
ISBN: 978-1-003-05010-0 (ebk)

DOI: 10.4324/9781003050100

Typeset in Bembo
by Taylor & Francis Books

For Laura and Sofie – my heart, my soul, my pride and joy

Contents

Figures

Tables

Preface

The present book seeks to answer a call for further development of a 'communication as constitutive' approach to branding. I have been teaching and researching branding since 2002 and it is striking how profoundly the field of branding is grounded in a transmission-based view of communication when other fields, such as communication theory and organizational communication research, recognize communication as performative and constitutive.

The field of branding only recently started to discuss the negotiated and political nature of a brand (see for instance, Iglesias, Ind, & Alfaro, 2013; Ind, 2014; Ind, Iglesias, & Schultz, 2013; Kornberger, 2015; Melewar, Gotsi, & Andriopoulos, 2012; Merz, He, & Vargo, 2009), and the development of this new line of theory is still in its nascent stages. Accordingly, there is a call for further development of a 'communication as constitutive' approach to branding.

In my PhD dissertation, I set out to look at branding from a communication perspective rather than a marketing one, and I found inspiration in the field of CCO (Communication as Constitutive of Organization). I argue that 'a brand' shares many of the same features as 'an organization'. Both 'brand' and 'organization' are generally talked of as entities. Each is a noun, even though neither exists in a bound, physical form. They both have physical features, such as a product or a building, but just as an 'organization' is not defined by the building in which it is housed, a 'brand' is not defined by the product or service it markets.

In this book, I will present an overview of the evolution of the field of branding and, building on that overview, I will articulate a new theoretical approach, labelled the CCB (Communication as Constitutive of Brands) approach. Drawing on data and analyses from my PhD dissertation, I will demonstrate how the CCB approach allows the process of branding (i.e. doing branding) to be viewed from a new perspective, and how it can be fruitful to think of a brand as a discursive brand space rather than an entity or object.

Introduction

Branding is an immanent aspect of the 21st century. Everything – products, services, experiences, people, places, and politics – is branded and branding is at the epicenter of everyday organizing processes (Mumby, 2016). Branding organizes consumer activities (Kornberger, 2015), and it has the potential to instruct organizational members (Kärreman & Rylander, 2008). Yet, even though brands are much exploited, they are little explored (Kornberger, 2015; Vásquez, Del Fa, Sergi, & Cordelier, 2017b), and scholars call for an exploration of the intersection of branding and organizing (Kärreman & Rylander, 2008; Mumby, 2016). Tentative studies of branding and organization have started to emerge (see for instance, Kornberger, 2015; Kärreman & Rylander, 2008; Mumby, 2016; Vásquez, Sergi, & Cordelier, 2013), but still the emergence of the brand has been overlooked. As noted by Vásquez et al. (2017b), brands and branding seem to be taken as a given and the ontological status of brands has rarely been touched upon.

As a scholar of branding, I have often been confronted with the fact that – due to its roots being in marketing and consumer research – the vast majority of research within the field of branding is conducted from a functionalist perspective.[1] This is an observation supported by various scholars (see for instance, Cornelissen, Christensen, & Kinuthia, 2012; Ind, 2014; Kornberger, 2015; Kärreman & Rylander, 2008; Mumby, 2016; Simmons, 2009; Vásquez et al., 2017b; Vásquez et al., 2013). The majority of existing research in branding is thus grounded in sender-oriented conduit models of communication dominated by a transmission-based view on the production of brand messages based on signalling theory (Cornelissen et al., 2012). A brand is viewed as an entity that can be designed, molded, and controlled by brand management. At a time when communication is increasingly understood as constitutive (see for instance, Ashcraft et al., 2009; Putnam & Nicotera, 2009; Robichaud & Cooren, 2013), it seems paradoxical that theories about branding are still so strongly rooted in the conduit metaphor of communication. Indeed, Cornelissen et al., (2012) argue that the field of branding could certainly enrich its theoretical vocabulary and strengthen its research and explanations by borrowing from other social fields, such as communication and organization.

Clash between textbooks and perceived reality

The majority of research in the field of branding has been conducted from a position that perceives the brand as a manageable phenomenon (Cornelissen et al., 2012; Edlinger, 2015; Edwards & Edwards, 2013; Wilden, Gudergan, & Lings, 2010). This is also the predominant view on branding in textbooks and teaching material, and it creates a clash between textbook prescriptions and the messy real-life of 'doing branding'. The way a brand is conceptualized in theories and educational material affects how students expect to encounter branding in their professional life, and thus how people will work with branding in their daily business of making decisions and launching initiatives (Melewar et al., 2012).

Gabriella Edlinger (2015) performed an empirical study of how employer brand managers think of their job, concerning the creation and management of a brand. Her research shows how the brand is thought of as an idea, formulated and controlled by management and transmitted to employees. However, Edlinger's research also reveals that everyday work experience is dominated by dynamic, non-linear, and interactional processes, which result in "frustration over or aggression against instances of uninvited co-creation of the employer brand" (Edlinger, 2015, p. 455). The brand managers see themselves as the creators of the brand and they describe the creation as a step-by-step process that is structured by them. Only few, strategically selected participants are invited to contribute to the creation of the brand. But when the brand leaves the sheltered environment, it is exposed to criticism and decodings divergent from what the brand managers intended. In those situations, the brand managers try to keep control of the brand by intervening and securing alignment with the "ideal" brand. They actively try to guard the brand against criticism and undesired interpretations by "policing it against unauthorized contributors and undesired, illegitimate contents and meanings" (Edlinger, 2015, p. 451). Edlinger's study illustrates the clash between theory, based on a sender-dominated understanding of branding assuming the possibility of consistency and alignment, and the actual experiences of brand managers in the context of a dynamic environment with messy and spontaneous interpretations of the brand. Another study suggests that the clash between textbook prescription and the real life 'doing' of branding also creates a dissonance between what brand managers think consumers do and the reality of how consumers live, use brands, and build relationships (Ind, 2014).

Based on her study, Edlinger (2015) suggests conceptualizing the brand as a *boundary-object*. While it is the job of brand managers "to provide direction for the brand, they must also be willing to accept that brand meaning is constantly negotiated with many other stakeholders" (Iglesias et al., 2013, p. 671). In today's society, where social media affects most people, not least companies and brands, the communicational arena is open for anyone to participate. It does not make sense to talk about who is allowed to author or affect the brand because people will discuss and affect the brand anyway. It therefore poses a challenge when textbooks continuingly conceptualize a brand as an entity and present numerous 'how to' steps of handling brand creation and brand management. It leaves students without the necessary knowledge to understand a brand as co-created and without the appropriate tools to engage in these co-creating processes.

The purpose of this book is, therefore, to articulate a Communication as Constitutive of Brands (CCB) approach that highlights the negotiated and performative character of brands and conceptualizes the brand manager as a practical author. The CCB approach is grounded in social constructivist and actor-network theory that recognize the negotiated character of meaning and the importance of non-human actors.

Note

1 "shorthand for positivist or empiricist approaches to organization science, aimed at the prediction and control of variable relations" (Ashcraft, Kuhn, & Cooren, 2009, p. 8).

1 The evolution of branding

Branding is a ubiquitous part of the 21st century. From its tentative beginnings in consumer and product marketing in the late 19th century, it has become an omnipresent aspect of today's modern society. Everything from products, companies, and places, to people and political parties is branded. The theoretical foundation of the field of branding originates from a marketing literature that is dominated by a sender-oriented perspective of communication in line with the conduit model. The conduit model reflects a one-way view of communication in which the brand manager is the one to initiate the communication process and the consumer is passive and defenceless, meaning that the consumer will be affected by brand messages as intended by the company. From such a perspective, the brand manager is in control of the brand and its meaning – or put differently, the brand is owned and controlled by the company.

This traditional perspective on branding and brand management was in line with similar perspectives on (mass) communication and management at that time. But even as new perspectives emerged in the fields of communication and management that recognized the active role of the recipient and the co-constitutive role of communication, the field of branding continued to exist as a rather guarded and somewhat restricted field, where theory development was quite consensus driven. The exposure to insights from other academic fields within social science has been selective, and scholarship on branding has carved out a niche for itself that has insulated the field from important findings in related academic fields that could enrich the understanding of branding and brand management (Cornelissen et al., 2012). However, this long-established research tradition in branding has been challenged by recent exceptions that orient towards a dialogical notion of communication and thus take a co-constructive approach to branding research (see for instance, Cornelissen et al., 2012; Hatch & Schultz, 2008, 2010; Iglesias et al., 2013; Ind, 2014; Ind & Schmidt, 2019; Leitch & Richardson, 2003).

This chapter provides an overview of the evolution of branding theory from its tentative beginnings in the late 19th century with a focus on product branding, to new ideas about corporate branding in the early 1990s and the newly developed ideas about co-creation and the constitutive role of communication. The chapter offers an understanding of the main concepts and theory developments that the CCB approach will build upon.

DOI: 10.4324/9781003050100-1

1.1 The origin of branding

The word *brand* is both a noun (a brand) and a verb (to brand). When *brand* is used as a noun, it refers to some kind of entity that has a physical existence in the world (e.g. product, company, people, places), or it can refer to a mental idea or construct, whereas as a verb, *brand* refers to a process - the act of branding something or someone (Stern, 2006).

The use of branding dates back many centuries, but the modern usage of the concept is related to the beginning of mass production (Hart & Murphy, 1998). The essential meaning of branding is to mark something by burning (Jevons, 2005), normally to show who owns it or produced it, and we are familiar with the practice of branding from the marking of cattle in which the brand is a proof of ownership and a sign of quality. In modern marketing, branding is used to differentiate similar products from one another as signaled in the definition by the American Marketing Association (2021): "A brand is a name, term, design, symbol or any other feature that identifies one seller's good or service as distinct from those of other sellers". Consumers can claim the brand values as their own and use the brand's symbolic meaning in their self-presentation and their efforts to stage themselves in a certain way. The phrasing of this American Marketing Association definition is very product oriented, and it reflects the original understanding of what a brand is and does.

Until the 1880s the vast majority of commodities were produced and sold locally as generic items, indistinguishable from one another. Since products were anonymous, consumers oriented towards the retailer, and most products were sold on a personal basis. The Industrial Revolution changed this. Mass production and new methods of packaging allowed (and forced) manufacturers to distribute their products more widely, and the development was spurred by improved infrastructure and the rise of mass media. As the supply of products grew in quantity and variety, manufacturers encountered a need to claim ownership of their products in order to differentiate their products from those of their competitors, and an essential means to this end was the introduction of brand names.

Early brand names

Most early brand names reflect the names of the founders, with some examples being: Thomas Twining, Sampson Lloyd II, John Cadbury, John Boots, Charles Heny Harrod, Levi Strauss, Louis Vuitton, Thomas Burberry, Gerard Adriaan Heineken, Henry John Heinz, Dr. John Harvey Kellogg and William Keith Kellogg, King C. Gillette, Henry Ford, and Charles Stewart Rolls, and Sir Frederick Henry Royce.

Naming a product with the founder's name is a strategy which demonstrates that the manufacturer takes pride in his product, seeing as he lends his name and thus his reputation to the product, and implicitly guarantees the quality of the product. William Keith Kellogg is known to have signed all packages of

Table 1.1 A selection of early brand names and the years they were established

Twinings – 1706	Burberry – 1856	Ivory soap – 1886
Lloyds Banking Group – 1765	Macy's – 1858	Kelloggs – 1900
Cadbury – 1824	Bloomingdales – 1861	Gillette – 1901
Boots – 1849	Heineken – 1864	Ford – 1903
Harrods – 1849	Sears – 1866	Carlsberg – 1904
Levi's – 1853	Heinz – 1869	Rolls-Royce – 1906
Louis Vuitton – 1854	Coca-Cola – 1886	

corn flakes with his original signature, thus signing off each package and vouching for the content (a feature of the brand name that is still reflected in the font used today). The original use of brand names was thus a way to signal product quality, and today such founder brand names add a certain heritage to brands and give them a vintage quality (Danesi, 2013).

The introduction of brand names and logos transformed goods into products. The original use of branding is rooted in the idea that a brand is created by the manufacturer, reflecting an inside-out perspective (i.e. the brand is developed inside the company and then broadcast to a wider audience). The overall purpose of the brand is to establish trust by guaranteeing a consistent quality, and thus create brand preference. Branding became a tool to distinguish one product from another, and brand names enabled consumers to make repeat purchases based on recollection. Accordingly, a brand name ought to be memorable in order to facilitate brand recall (Keller, Heckler, & Houston, 1998).

How brand names re-organize buying and selling

The introduction of brand names marks a significant shift in the way goods are sold. Generic goods are produced and sold locally, and consumers are primarily oriented towards the retailer. Brand names shift the focus from the retailer that sells the commodity, to the product itself or the manufacturer that produces the commodity. The development of branding initiatives thus signals an attempt to strengthen the importance of the product and its manufacturer and decrease the importance of the retailer (Lury, 2004). The brand became a tool for distant manufacturers to communicate directly with the end-consumer, and trade evolved from being a local activity to being a national and later, international business. In response to the weakening of the sales outlet, retailers started to develop their own store brands, and accordingly, the period also saw the emergence of branded retail outlets, such as Harrods and Macy's, which can be seen as some of the first attempts at branding a service.

Early branding theory reflects a stimulus and response perspective, where the success of branding is dependent on the brand manager's ability to select signals that appeal to the target group in order to build a strong and favourable brand (Merz et al., 2009). Such signals can either aim to communicate a core benefit of the product, known as a *unique selling proposition*, or to communicate some kind of immaterial, emotional added value, known as an *emotional selling proposition*. Differentiation is thus not simply a question of different, functional product qualities, but is as much about an imagined, immaterial differentiation in which brand names function as important cues.

Unique selling proposition: the brand as a sign of product quality

In the early days of mass production, brand communication focussed primarily on communicating superior product quality. Superior product quality relates to tangible product attributes, such as the taste, shape, size, fabric, weight, durability of the material, and its fragrance, which are all functional benefits of the product. Functional benefits are referred to as *unique selling proposition* (USP).[1] The USP is often related to innovativeness; that is, the ability to develop new and improved products with features unmatched by competitors. For instance, Levi's produced hardwearing trousers that could withstand a hard day's work in the goldmines, and Levi Strauss patented the process of putting rivets in the overalls for strength (Superbrands, 2021), thus Levi's USP was strength and durability. King Gillette introduced the safety razor in 1901 to compete with the shaving knife. Gillette's USP was sharpness, safety, and convenience. In other trades, such as the beer and soft drink industry, production processes could be challenging to handle (e.g. fermenting the beer or controlling the carbonic acid), and the ability to deliver a uniform product of a standard quality was, thus, a competitive advantage. In order to be competitive on USP, the product has to perform better on a functional benefit than similar products in the market; and the essence of USP thinking is that every advertisement has to propose a specific benefit that competitors cannot match or simply do not offer (Kippenberger, 2000).

The emphasis on unique product qualities is appropriate as long as the product truly stands out in the market, but as technology improves and supply increases, more and more products imitate functional benefits, and it becomes increasingly difficult to stand out on USP alone. Moreover, branding based on USP relies on the notion of the *economic man*. The economic man, or Homo economicus, is an abstraction developed by economists and usually attributed to the British philosopher and political economist John Stuart Mill. It is a philosophy that assumes that man is rational, acts with complete knowledge, and seeks to maximize personal satisfaction. The economic man is careful about how he spends his money as he seeks to attain his goals at the lowest cost possible. With such a perspective, the consumer will scrutinize the market in order to find the best product at the best price. Consumers will look to get the most out of their money, and thus the evaluation of product value will be based on rational product features alone. However, the consumer is often not as rational as the concept of the Homo economicus prescribes, and the rise of branding has given way to a new form of competitive advantage, namely the emotional benefit, known as *emotional selling proposition* (ESP).

Emotional selling proposition: the brand as a sign of symbolic value

When a product is semiotized into a brand, it becomes a *sign* that can hold multiple meanings, and product value is no longer simply a question of the functional quality of the product, but also its symbolic value. Maslow (1943) explained how humans experience a hierarchy of needs. When people live a comfortable life, focus shifts from fulfilling basic needs, such as hunger and shelter, to living 'the good life'. When the basic needs for material goods are fulfilled, consumption becomes increasingly value laden. Numerous products can deliver the requested functional benefits which means that brands can no longer compete solely on USP. Rather, the symbolic value of a brand becomes increasingly important. This symbolic value is referred to as an emotional selling proposition (ESP), and the notion of the ESP builds on the idea that the scope of a product is not limited to its physical characteristics. ESP refers to immaterial added value, such as brand imagery, brand personality, or symbols. Importantly, it makes the consumer feel a certain way about the brand (and themselves for using the brand), and the consumer can use the brand as a prop to stage themself. When brand value becomes symbolic, the consumer's interpretation of the brand (meaning) becomes of central importance.

Brand names communicate USP and ESP

A brand, then, is not simply used to identify the manufacturer of a product – a brand also adds meaning and value to the product. Brand names serve as important cues when consumers form perceptions about products (as do packaging and color). For instance, Mason & Batch (2009) report how sales went up significantly, when a brand name was changed from *Snow Pup* to *Snow Master*. *Snow Master* sounds significantly more powerful and masculine than *Snow Pup*, and the example illustrates that the consumer infers cues about the product's USP and its ESP based on the brand name. Accordingly, a brand name has perceptual implications, as it can spur connotations. This feature can be used to choose an inherently meaningful brand name that accentuates a particular product attribute which constitutes the USP (e.g. *Coca-Cola*[2]) or reinforces the product category (e.g. *Joe & The Juice*). Choosing a suggestive brand name can facilitate marketing communication and the initial positioning of the product in that it spurs immediate understanding of what the product can do or offer; it has been suggested that brand names that explicitly convey a product benefit also achieve higher brand recall among consumers (Keller et al., 1998). Seeing that consumers often do not invest much time and resources in examining the market, instant brand recognition and recall is an important advantage (Mason & Batch, 2009). Moreover, consumers tend to develop heuristics, which can enhance brand loyalty. If consumers learn to associate a certain brand name with a specific consumption habit, their buying decision becomes characterized by inertia, which is where the consumer buys the same brand out of routine.

A well-known, early brand name is *Ivory* soap. The soap had two primary functional benefits, but only one of them made it into the brand name. One of the benefits was that the soap would float. This may seem a trivial benefit, but in the late 19th century, when people would bathe in local rivers with murky water, the ability of the soap to float was a genuine functional benefit that made the soap superior to competing products. However, it was not this ability that was highlighted in the brand name, but rather the purity of the product. Procter and Gamble report on their webpage that Harley Procter had been struggling to come up with a suitable brand name for months, one that would signal the exceptional purity of the soap. As the story goes, Harley Procter was inspired by a passage in the 45th Psalm that he heard in church a Sunday morning: "All thy garments smell of myrrh, and aloes, and cassia, out of ivory palaces, whereby they have made thee glad" (Ivory, 2021) . The name *Ivory* was thus supposed to communicate the USP purity. However, it is evident that the name of the soap communicates something more than purity. Ivory is a valuable material that connotes prosperity or even exclusivity, so by using *Ivory* soap, the consumer can stage themself as quality-conscious, and maybe even as part of an elite or exclusive club. The notion of ESP builds on the assumption that people are not simply rational consumers. They do not only buy products for what products can do (as suggested by the notion of Homo economicus) but also for how the product makes them feel (Levy, 1959). In a marketplace, where many products are similar to one another if one looks only at USP, ESP becomes the main tool of differentiation, and ESP is often more important to the consumer than the physical product itself.

Possessions play a part in positioning a consumer in society, and people use brands as conspicuous consumption in order to stage themselves and signal their personal values, goals, and aspirations. Brands function as identity markers and become part of the consumer's extended self and, as such, products are essentially psychological things, and the meaning of the brand is ultimately symbolic. It thus becomes paramount for the brand manager to focus not only on the functional benefit of the product, but also on the emotional appeal of the brand and thus its symbolic meaning seeing that, "[a] symbol is appropriate (and the product will be used and enjoyed) when it joins with, meshes with, adds to, or reinforces the way the consumer thinks about himself" (Levy, 1959, p. 119). ESP is arbitrary to USP in the sense that the emotional benefit is not given by the functional benefit of the product. Taking mobile phones as an example, Apple (*iPhone*) and Samsung (*Galaxy*) provide essentially the same core product (USP), but the two brands add a quite a different ESP to their products, and that is why some consumers show intense loyalty to either one or the other brand.

Though, there might be some initial benefits to choosing a suggestive brand name, there are also drawbacks to consider. More often than not, manufacturers will later need to develop and reinvent their product, and thus reposition the brand. When a suggestive brand name is used, one that conveys strong associations with the original benefits claimed for it, it can be difficult to link it with new associations later on. Considering the possibility of being able to reposition the brand, a nonsuggestive brand name might therefore be a better choice. A nonsuggestive brand name is more flexible, and it can more readily accommodate new benefit claims. In this relation, it is also worth considering that since the ESP is arbitrary in relation to the USP, a suggestive brand name may limit the possibilities of developing the emotional selling proposition.

There is more to branding than just a brand name (e.g. logo, packaging, imagery, advertisement), but this account serves to demonstrate that a brand was understood as a concrete, manageable object, and that brand communication was a matter of selecting the most appropriate signals which would be transmitted to the consumer in a process of one-way communication. In other words, the brand was owned and controlled by the company, and this perspective is still somewhat dominant today.

From initial focus on branding a product to branding a service

Throughout the first part of the 20th century, the focus of the exchange process was the exchange of goods, and the moment of purchase was seen as the end of that exchange. Attention focused on the tools available to the manufacturer to develop and control the brand, and the marketing mix known as the 4Ps became popular. The 4Ps tool pinpoints four central areas of attention to consider when positioning a product: Product, Price, Place and Promotion. Naturally, attention centers on the *product* itself. A product can be positioned by focussing on product attributes, packaging, brand name, assortment, guarantee, color and design. *Price* can be used as a marketing tool since a high price is often understood to signal superior quality. A high price can make the product seem more exclusive, whereas a lower price can be a tool to gain a higher market share. *Place* relates to the sales outlet. Stores are branded as well and there is a spillover effect between product brand and the brand of the sales outlet. A high-end sales outlet adds to the exclusiveness of the product brand and vice versa. Place is also significant in relation to access to the product. The marketer must decide whether the product should be easily obtainable or whether it should only be sold in specialty stores or own stores. Lastly, *promotion* is brand communication, and whereas USP is adjusted in the product design, ESP is adjusted in the promotion. As it is evident from the 4Ps, a brand was understood to be created and controlled by the company in the same way a product was. The 4Ps gradually evolved as scholars suggested adding more Ps until the 7Ps became widely accepted as a way to deal with the aspect of services.

Branding a service: the 7Ps

Though it can be argued that *services* played a pivotal role in the relation between buyer and seller long before the concept of branding, it was not until the 1960s that the concept of *services* started to gain attention in the literature. The original ideas about branding were grounded in a dominant logic about the exchange of physical goods, and accordingly, the first conceptualizations of services described them as something that accompanied a tangible good in order to enhance its value. Such services could be sales personnel's ability to explain product benefits and differentiation and thus, guide the consumer in the decision-making process. It could be accommodation of a product to the customer's special requirements, or it could be after-sales services, such as maintenance and repair.

Gradually, society evolved into a service economy, where the service industries became the main generator of jobs (Kotler & Keller, 2006). Services were no longer add-ons to a physical product, but rather the product itself. Today these services include the government sector with all its public services, such as hospitals, schools, childcare, elderly care, police, courts, fire departments, military services, and tax regulation. They also include the private non-profit sector, such as charities, churches, and museums. Finally, they include the private for-profit sector, such as travel agencies, hotels, restaurants, banks, law firms, insurance companies, consulting firms, fitness centres, hairdressers, beauticians, and the entertainment industry. In the service industries, the main offering is pure services, these being acts or performances that do not result in the ownership of anything.

Such services brought about new management challenges because they were characterized by intangibility, inseparability, perishability, and heterogeneity (Merz et al., 2009). *Intangibility* refers to the lack of materiality. The purchase of a service does not result in ownership of a physical product. It is not possible to evaluate the quality of a service beforehand because a service is produced and consumed simultaneously. A service is *inseparable* from the employee who performs the service, as a service is characterized by the application of specialized competences, skills, or knowledge. Therefore, a service is also characterized by *heterogeneity* as the human factor makes it difficult to reproduce a service in the exact same manner. Lastly, a service is *perishable* as it cannot be stored, and it is consumed the moment it is produced. These new challenges led to the development of the 4Ps into the 7Ps, where people, processes and physical facilities were added. *People* addressed the employee, such as, proper training, dress codes, behaviour, and appearance. In service branding, employees are understood to play a crucial role. They have the power to make or break the brand. *Processes* addressed the codification of work processes to secure consistency in the service delivery, handling of customers, and service manuals. Lastly, *physical facilities* relate to the settings that the service takes place within, for instance, the decor of a room, sounds and light or the materiality of contact points, such as stationery, tableware, or furniture.

Marketing of services developed as a new subdiscipline, independent from product marketing, and a new paradigm emerged, termed the service-dominant logic (Vargo & Lusch, 2004).

The service-dominant logic

The service-dominant logic argues that the branding of goods and services should not be treated as two separate disciplines but rather as an integrated perspective. The proposition is based on the observation that, "focus is shifting away from tangibles and toward intangibles, such as skills, information, and knowledge, and toward interactivity and connectivity and ongoing relation-ships" (Vargo & Lusch, 2004, p. 15). In this perspective, goods are identified as vehicles for service provision rather than ends in themselves. Goods remain important, but it is ultimately a question about value creation, and a company cannot deliver value, but only make value propositions (Merz et al., 2009). A key point in the service-dominant logic is that value creation is always a ques-tion of co-creation as value is defined by the consumer rather than embedded in output. Resources *are* not; they *become* (Vargo & Lusch, 2004). It follows that the understanding of communication changes from one of one-way mass communication to one characterized by dialogue, acknowledging the value of asking and answering questions. The service-dominant logic thus emphasizes the negotiated and networked character of market exchanges.

However, the service-dominant logic is a quite recent development, and it does not yet dominate theory building. By contrast, ideas about corporate branding have had significant impact.

1.2 Corporate branding

In the early 1990s, the thinking around corporate branding prompts a new understanding of branding. Branding is no longer solely seen as a tool to market a product or a service; *corporate branding* is understood as a multidisciplinary man-agement discipline. Rather than focusing on a specific product or range of pro-ducts, branding activities are centered around the positioning of clear values; and a corporate brand can span a plethora of product categories and services. Initial conceptual work was centered around defining how a corporate brand is different from a product brand as well as determining key elements in the corporate branding process, as illustrated in Table 1.2.

In corporate branding, differentiation requires positioning the whole cor-poration and not just the product(s) (Hatch & Schultz, 2003). Focus changes from the imaginative and creative marketing of a product to the possibility of using the culture of the company as part of its unique selling proposition. In fact, Hatch and Schultz (2003) state that "a blending of corporate and cultural values with marketing practices is the hallmark of corporate branding" (p. 1047). Consequently, branding is no longer the responsibility of the mar-keting department; it becomes the responsibility of top management, since corporate branding requires a holistic approach to brand management, seeing that it is multidisciplinary in scope. Hence, the composition of the brand management team will typically be broadened, which requires a greater co-ordination of activities (Harris & De Chernatony, 2001; Hatch & Schultz, 2003). Corporate branding requires an organization-wide commitment and consequently, employees are viewed as important brand ambassadors. Employ-ees as important brand ambassadors is an insight already adopted in the litera-ture about service brands, as employees are the ones who literally perform the service. In corporate branding, the lens changes to focus on minimising and reducing gaps between the brand promises and the lived brand. To cope with

Table 1.2 Differences between a product brand and a corporate brand

	Product brand	Corporate brand
Scope and scale	One product or service, or a group of closely related products	The entire enterprise, which includes the corporation and all its stakeholders
Origins of brand identity	Advertiser's imagination informed by market research	The company's heritage, the values, and beliefs that members of the enterprise hold in common
Target audience	Customers	Multiple stakeholders (includes employees and managers as well as customers, investors, NGO's partners, and politicians)
Responsibility	Product brand manager and staff, Advertising and Sales departments	CEO or executive team, typically from Marketing, Corporate Communication, Human Resources, Strategy, and sometimes Design or Development departments
Planning horizon	Life of product	Life of company

Source: Hatch & Schultz (2008, p. 9)

the increased complexity of corporate branding, new conceptual models are developed. A recognized and much quoted model that pinpoints the importance of reducing gaps, is the VCI model developed by (Hatch & Schultz, 1997, 2003, 2008).

The VCI model

Hatch and Schultz (2001, 2003, 2008) argue that the scope of branding ought to be broader than viewing corporate branding as giant-sized product brands. Consequently, they have developed one of the most influential conceptualizations of corporate branding, where they seek to emphasize the *corporate* (or organizational) element of corporate branding. They conceptualize a corporate brand as an interplay of Vision, Culture, and Image (the VCI-model) (Figure 1.1).

Vision is the strategic vision or the brand vision behind the company. The vision expresses top management's aspirations for the company, and it includes decisions such as which lines of business to focus on, change initiatives, corporate symbolism, and partners and alliances. *Culture* is organizational culture, which, to Hatch and Schultz, is internal beliefs, values, and basic assumptions. Culture encompasses decisions made by organizational members, such as decisions to work hard and be loyal, and the way they choose to represent the company. In a corporate brand perspective, employees are understood to constitute the interface between a company and its external

Decisions made by top management:
- Lines of business
- Partners and alliances
- Location
- Change initiatives
- Corporate symbolism

Decisions made by organization members:
- Work hard
- Be loyal
- Seek challenge
- Resist influence
- Represent organization in a positive light

Decisions made by external constituencies:
- Buy product/service
- Seek employment
- Praise/criticize company
- Invest in company
- Seek to regulate
- Agree to supply

Figure 1.1 The VCI-model
Hatch & Schultz (2003, p. 1046)

environments (Foster, Punjaisri, & Cheng, 2010; Harris & De Chernatony, 2001; King & Grace, 2005), and employees are thus recognized as important brand ambassadors. They are the ones to deliver the brand promise (Balmer, 2006; Foster et al., 2010; Harris & De Chernatony, 2001), and therefore, employees have the potential to make or break the corporate brand (Foster et al., 2010; Iglesias et al., 2013). Accordingly, employees are seen as "key to building relationships with all the company's stakeholders as well as contributing to the meaning of the brand" (Hatch & Schultz, 2003, p. 1043). Employee behaviour is central in building emotional value (ESP). Emotional values are communicated through employees' interactions with stakeholders, hence each employee represents a source of customer information and "[e]mployees are thus becoming central to the process of brand building and their behaviour can either reinforce a brand's advertised values or, if inconsistent with these values, undermine the credibility of advertised messages" (Harris & De Chernatony, 2001, p. 442). The last component of the VCI model is *Image*, which is the outside world's overall impression of the company. Image is a term that competing academic discourses seek to invest with meaning in their own particular way (see for instance, Hatch & Schultz, 1997 for different definitions). In the VCI model, *image* is understood as "a holistic and vivid impression held by an individual or a particular group towards an organization and is a result of sense-making by the group and communication by the organization of a fabricated and projected picture of itself" (Hatch & Schultz, 1997, p. 359). Image is formed on the basis of Vision and Culture as well as press coverage and overall reputation. The point made by Hatch & Schultz (2001, 2003) is that a corporate brand is constituted by these three components – vision, culture, and image – and these must be in concordance with one another. If a gap occurs between any of the three components of the model, the brand will face a serious challenge that must be handled properly. Gaps can emerge if employees do not live the brand as promised, if employees cannot recognize the communicated vision in the daily life they encounter in the organization, if the brand has not succeeded in conveying its core values in its external brand communication, or if stakeholders do simply not view the brand as reliable – to name a few examples.

The authors claim that the model applies a constructivist approach to branding, and it recognizes the role of stakeholders in interpreting the brand. But the early days of corporate branding were still very much influenced by a transmission-based view of communication, reflecting a normative approach where brand management was in control of the brand and alignment of branding activities was a key focus.

Alignment of the corporate brand

Ideas about brand alignment dominated the early years of theory development within corporate branding and this is evident in the recognized contributions of theories such as, Balmer's 6Cs of corporate branding, Balmer and Soenen's corporate identity mix, and the ACID test. All of these contributions reflect a heritage from product branding based in *signalling theory*, where the corporate brand is built inside the company and disseminated to a wider public.

Balmer's corporate marketing mix, *the 6Cs of corporate marketing,* bears clear inspiration from the marketing mix. The 4Ps focused on positioning the product by paying attention to product attributes, place of sale, price, and marketing communication. The 7Ps added attention to the people aspect of services, the processes that guaranteed a uniform service delivery, and the physical facilities that embrace the service. The purpose of the 6Cs was to focus on the corporate level instead of the product level, and they encompass Character, Culture, Communication, Conceptualisations, Constituencies, and Covenant. According to Balmer et al. (2006), the 6Cs focus on aligning the brand in multiple exchange relationships with multiple stakeholder groups. *Character* is the organizational identity, "What we indubitably are", and includes organizational activities, corporate ownership and structure, corporate philosophy and history, as well as markets served. *Culture* is the organizational identity, "What we feel we are", and includes values, beliefs, and basic assumptions. Culture provides the context in which employees engage with each other and it offers an organizational membership that may, in part, define the employee. *Communication* relates to how the organization communicates with customers and other stakeholders, "What we say we are". In its most comprehensive definition, it also encompasses product performance, and how external stakeholders talk about the brand, such as word-of-mouth, media coverage and competitor commentaries. *Conceptualizations* refer to the corporate reputation, "How we are seen to be". It refers to the perceptions that the stakeholders hold of the brand, and therefore, conceptualizations can differ according to the different stakeholder groups. *Constituencies* refer to stakeholder management, "Whom we seek to serve". Constituencies take into account that the same people can be part of different stakeholder groups (or constituencies) and acknowledges that license to operate depends on meeting the expectations of salient stakeholder groups. *Covenant* recognizes that the emotional ownership of the brand lies with stakeholders, and the covenant is thus a quasi-bilateral informal contract between organization and stakeholders, "What is promised and expected". Balmer argues that the 6Cs should be seen as an organization-wide philosophy implemented by every employee, rather than a function orchestrated by a marketing department. Even though the 6Cs recognize the role of stakeholders as, for instance, in *Conceptualizations* and *Constituencies*, the philosophy of the 6Cs is still grounded in an inside-out perspective. The organization must make sure that every employee practices the brand values in order to send the right signals and thus secure a stable corporate brand. Initial theory development thus reflects a static perspective on the corporate brand that emphasizes the need for continuity, consistency, and coherence. The ideal is further explicated in the notion of *corporate communication,* which prescribes that the company speak with one voice.

However, writings on corporate branding agree that corporate branding is multidisciplinary, and that competitive advantage is no longer to be found in the 4Ps but in the people or the personality of the organization. Hence, concepts like culture and organizational identity become key notions.

1.3 Identity

A key promise made in corporate branding is the uniqueness of the company's *identity* (Harris & De Chernatony, 2001; Mosley, 2007) as the distinctiveness of corporate branding is the incorporation of corporate and cultural values into marketing practices (Hatch & Schultz, 2003). The concept of identity is ambiguous as it is informed by different disciplines, and definitions vary. In the following, I will highlight three common (and different) ways of understanding identity, namely via corporate identity, brand identity, and organizational identity.

Corporate identity

In the marketing literature, there is the convention of understanding *corporate identity* as a (visual) representation of the organization (Hatch & Schultz, 1997) or, as put by Balmer and Balmer (2001), "the mix of elements which gives organizations their distinctiveness". An example of a strong corporate identity is McDonald's. Its Golden Arches, Ronald McDonald, the design of their restaurants and food packaging, all ensure instant recognition of the brand.

Brand identity

Brand identity is conceptualized as "a unique set of brand associations that the brand strategist aspires to create or maintain" (Aaker, 2002, p. 68). The latter conceptualization of brand identity is a way to work with positioning the brand. Aaker (2002, 1996) argues that brand identity tends to be understood too narrowly, and so he broadens the concept by identifying four brand identity perspectives: 1) Brand as Product, 2) Brand as Organization, 3) Brand as Person, and 4) Brand as Symbol. Aaker believes that the reason why many brands fail is because brand managers do not understand the full scope of the different elements in a brand identity, and he supplies the *brand identity planning model* to aid brand managers in finding the full potential of the brand (ibid.).

Another way to work with brand identity is to consider the relationship between corporate brand and sub-brands as expressed in the brand relationship spectrum (Aaker & Joachimsthaler, 2000). The brand relationship spectrum is a brand architecture that seeks to optimise the synergy between corporate brand and sub-brand by structuring the brand portfolio and in specifying the roles and the nature of relationships between brands.

Organizational identity

In the organizational literature, there is a convention of understanding *organizational identity* as the way in which employees behave, think, and feel about their organization.

Identity in the branding literature

In the corporate branding literature, the term *identity* is frequently used without further specification, and often to embrace all three of the definitions listed above. For instance, Balmer and Soenen (1999), Balmer and Greyser (2002), and Balmer (2006) introduce five types of identity. These are 1) the *Actual Identity* (what the organization is), 2) the *Communicated Identity* (how the organization communicates), 3) the *Ideal Identity* (the optimum positioning of the organization), 4) the *Desired Identity* (the identity that management wishes to acquire), and 5) the *Conceived Identity* (how the organization is perceived) (Balmer & Greyser, 2002).

Balmer and Soenen (1999) introduce the notion of a *corporate identity mix* that consists of 'Soul', 'Mind', and 'Voice'. A company's *soul* is seen to be its culture, core values, internal images, and employees' affinities. *Mind* is related to managerial aspects such as strategy, vision, performance of products and services, brand architecture, ownership, and corporate performance. *Voice* is all forms of communication, both direct and indirect, controlled and non-controlled. Balmer and Soenen (1999) point out that the different types of identity must be in congruency, that is, "Organizations must manage their multiple identities to avoid potentially harmful misalignments" (Balmer & Greyser, 2002, p. 78), and Balmer and Soenen (1999) develop the ACID test to identify gaps between identities in order to enable management to act upon them. The ACID test has been refined several times (Balmer et al., 2017) but common to the ACID framework is that is has been developed for consultants to understand the importance of the different types of identity and to handle the process of managing the multiple identities in order to avoid potentially harmful misalignments.

A common theme in the corporate branding literature is thus, to understand *identity* as a tool to position and differentiate the organization; alignment of the different identities is seen as a central concern. The understanding of the importance of alignment, or the need to avoid potentially harmful misalignments, is in line with the focus on gaps as presented by Hatch and Schultz in their VCI-model. The VCI-model stands out in the corporate branding literature because it is grounded in an interpretative and social constructivist orientation (Hatch & Schultz, 1997). The VCI model therefore, bridges some of the early branding literature with the 'communication as constitutive' approach that I seek to further. I will therefore focus on the work by Hatch and Schultz to further explicate the notion of identity.

Identity as an interplay of internal and external interpretation

Branding theory is initially dominated by an inside-out perspective in which a brand is viewed as an entity, but gradually branding theory shifts from seeing the brand as an entity to seeing the brand as a process in which it can take on other meanings (Brodie, 2009). Hatch and Schultz use George Herbert Mead's notion of the 'Me' and the 'I' to explain this process. It is first important to have a look at how the authors explain the interplay between identity, image, and culture.

Hatch and Schultz (1997) explain identity as the way in which an organization perceives and understands itself. These interpretations are influenced by cultural assumptions and values, and by activities and interaction. To illustrate this dynamic interplay, Hatch and Schultz (1997) developed the following model (Figure 1.2).

Figure 1.2 is grounded in a social constructivist focus on interpretation and sensemaking. Hatch and Schultz (1997) demonstrate how organizational self-understanding (organizational identity) is used to produce messages

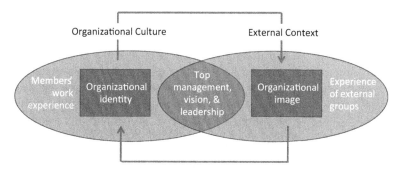

Figure 1.2 Relationships between organizational culture, identity, and image Hatch & Schultz (1997, p. 361).

targeted at external audiences in order to produce a desired organizational image. Organizational image is understood as externally produced meaning-making about the organization. The authors pinpoint that employees play a central role in the production of these messages as organizational image is also formed on the basis of direct experience and interaction with the organization. However, organizational image acts back, affecting identity, because organizational members mirror themselves in the comments and talk about the organization (Hatch & Schultz, 1997). These mirroring processes are also recognized by other scholars, and, for instance, Simmons (2009, p. 690) states that the "external image can form part of a feedback loop whereby stakeholder perceptions result in the organization revising components of its corporate brand". Hence, Simmons (2009) argues (in accordance with Hatch and Schultz) for an integrated approach to corporate branding. He believes that external and internal branding activities ought to be viewed synergistically and therefore, managed holistically. Hatch and Schultz (2002) explicate this dynamic understanding of identity in a later paper by incorporating George Herbert Mead's notion of the 'Me' and the 'I' into their theory of organizational identity.

George Herbert Mead

George Herbert Mead explains individual identity as a conversation between the 'I' and the 'Me' (Hatch & Schultz, 2009). The 'Me' forms as a result of how others respond to us. For instance, if a child is being praised for tidying up his or her room, he or she will form the idea that being a good boy or girl involves keeping the room tidy. That is the forming of the 'Me'. The 'I' is formed as a reaction to the 'Me'. When the child learns that he or she can resist the role, he or she is being fashioned into, the 'I' will produce an answer that either accepts the role or rejects it. The rejection needs not be complete; it can be a re-fashioning of the role. The 'I' can thus conform to, resist, or negotiate with the 'Me', and it is in this conversation between the 'I' and the 'Me' that identity emerges (Hatch & Schultz, 2009). Hatch and Schultz (2002) apply the concept of the 'I' and the 'Me' to explain how organizational identity is negotiated and thus the product of a dynamic process. An organizational 'Me' is formed, when organizational members engage in a *process of mirroring*, where they register how the organization is being perceived by external audiences. The 'Me' informs the members about the appropriateness of organizational behaviour and initiatives based on how positive or negative this behaviour is evaluated by external audiences. The 'Me' thus functions as a way to find (what is believed to be) the right direction. However, an organization also forms an 'I' that responds to the 'Me', and Hatch and Schultz (2002) believe the organizational 'I' to be analogous to organizational culture. Organizational identity is thus, a result of a conversation between the organizational 'I' and 'Me', and it follows that "just as individuals form their identities in relation to both internal and external definitions of self, organizations form theirs in relation to culture

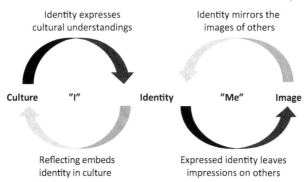

Figure 1.3 The dynamics of organizational identity
Hatch & Schultz (2002, p. 995)

and image" (Hatch & Schultz, 2002, p. 997). This is illustrated in their revised model (Figure 1.3).

The dark gray arrows in Figure 1.3 illustrate the organization's efforts to communicate and express cultural understandings in identity claims, and the light gray arrows illustrate how external audiences affect organizational self-understanding through processes of mirroring. If there is a discrepancy between organizational self-understanding and the way others understand the organization, organizational members will be motivated to change either their identity claims or their self-understanding in order to align the two interpretations. What they choose to do depends on the outcome of the conversation between the 'Me' and the 'I'. The 'Me' may convince the 'I' that the organization needs to change its behavior in order to conform to external expectations and requests, or the 'I' may argue that organizational behavior is legitimate and desirable and convince the 'Me' to continue as usual or with minor adaptations. The mirrored image will thus be interpreted in relation to existing organizational self-definitions, and "organizational identity occurs as the result of a set of processes that continuously cycle within and between cultural self-understandings and images formed by organizational 'others'" (Hatch & Schultz, 2002, p. 1004).

Hatch and Schultz (2002) also discuss how effects of power are represented in Figure 1.3. If, for instance, powerful managers refuse to listen to or recognize a report presented by market researchers, the processes of mirroring and reflecting will be distorted towards an 'I' that is more powerful than the 'Me'. Such a state is referred to by Hatch and Schultz as an instance of *narcissism*.

Narcissism and hyper-adaptation

If an organization falls prey to *narcissism*, its identity construction will primarily be informed by culture or the 'I'. As mentioned above, narcissism can be the result of powerful organizational members, who reject external input, or it can be the result of self-referential *auto-communication*. Auto-communication is an integral part of organizational culture, since all cultures communicate with themselves in order to confirm the culture's specific characteristics and remind themselves who they are (Christensen, 1997). Auto-communication is found in communication material such as strategy documents, annual reports, and politics, as well as advertising and public relations (ibid.). In fact, all communication is in a sense auto-communication, since employees are often the ones most interested in communication stemming from their workplace. Based on the idea that organizational members use the external environment to mirror their own performance, auto-communication can be mistaken as external input, and thus, the identity construction tends to close in on itself as it is primarily informed by input from the existing culture. A narcissistic organization runs the risk of losing support from external stakeholders or even being seen as irrelevant as it fails to produce a behaviour that appeals to the public. The organization is self-absorbed and seduced by its own claims, but the outside world is not. Narcissism is an instance of displacement of power towards the 'I'. The opposite situation would be one of *hyper-adaption*.

A *hyper-adaptive* organization is an organization that is too responsive to external input. It happens, when the 'I' is not able to balance the 'Me' (inputs from external stakeholders), and the 'Me' gains too much power. The organization is in risk of losing its distinctive culture as it loses its sense of who it is, and once it loses that it becomes difficult to decide which inputs it ought to react upon and how. It is therefore essential that there is a healthy balance between the 'I' and the 'Me'. If the 'Me' gains too much power, the organization loses itself in the effort to meet stakeholder requests. If the 'I' gains too much power, the organization may be perceived as overtly self-centered, and it risks being deemed superfluous or illegitimate due to a failure to respond to external demand. It was argued earlier that auto-communication can lead to narcissism, but auto-communication can also be used to counter a dominating 'Me'.

On the basis of Mead's notions of the 'Me' and the 'I', and the role of internal and external stakeholders, Hatch and Schultz produce a revised edition of Figure 1.3. The revised model (Figure 1.4) illustrates more clearly how identity is a

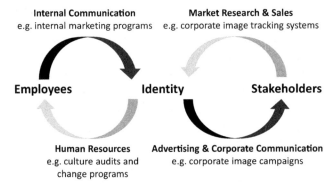

Figure 1.4 Communicative tasks of different corporate functions
Hatch & Schultz (2009, p. 126)

dynamic concept, one which is the result of representation practices and the interpretation activities of people internal and external to the organization.

'Culture' (in Figure 1.3.), seen as the internal perspective of an organization, is translated into 'employees' in Figure 1.4 (Hatch & Schultz, 2008). 'Image' (in Figure 1.3), seen as the external perspective, is translated into 'stakeholders' in Figure 1.4. In summary, the more abstract notions of 'culture' and 'image' are translated into people, 'employees (and managers)' and 'stakeholders' respectively, in Figure 1.4, which emphasizes the *agency* of the people that constitute the organization and its immediate surroundings.

With results from an empirical study, Knox and Bickerton (2003) confirm the interplay of vision, culture, and image, as suggested by Hatch and Schultz in the VCI-model, but they suggest that *competitive landscape* ought to be added as a fourth variable. Hatch and Schultz (2008) respond to this criticism by merging the above understanding (i.e. of identity as a dynamic construct based on representation practices and interpretation activities) into the VCI-model (see Figure 1.5).

When the dynamic identity model is incorporated into the VCI-model, the question of competitive environment (and other external influences) becomes a question of mirroring processes. The organizational 'Me' will be formed on the basis of information about competitive environment as well as other external influences, thus the question of competitive environment is indirectly built into

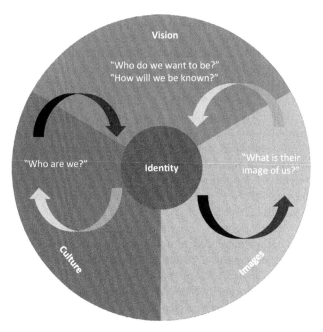

Figure 1.5 The dynamics of organizational identity incorporated into VCI
Hatch & Schultz (2008, p. 68)

the new edition of the VCI-model. A corporate brand is thus, the result of meaning-making by those who engage with the brand (Hatch & Schultz, 2009). Accordingly, the VCI-model can be understood to combine the outside-in perspective typically applied in an image-management approach, with the inside-out perspective typically applied in an identity-based approach (see Burmann & Zeplin, 2005).

Although, the VCI-model claims a social constructivist orientation, the elaboration of this position is very limited. The focus of the VCI-model is the mirroring processes, where inputs from external stakeholders are negotiated in a conversation between the 'Me' and the 'I' and, as such, the model implies a 'negotiated brand'. But the scholars do not account for *how* these processes of negotiation unfold. However, once a dynamic relationship between brand and stakeholders have been recognized, *co-creation* becomes of interest.

1.4 Co-creating brands

The notion of co-creation recognizes consumers and other stakeholders as key players in the creation of value. As suggested by the service-dominant logic, companies cannot produce and deliver value, they can only offer value propositions. Value is derived and determined in the use and consumption of a brand, not determined by the design and production. Prahalad and Ramaswamy (2004) point out that consumers are not passive recipients of a company's offer, but knowledgeable and skilled users that become increasingly aware of their power to negotiate. Networks and consumer-to-consumer (or stakeholder-to-stakeholder) communication provide consumers with new sources of information, and consumers today are active, informed, networked and empowered and they want to interact and exercise their influence. Consumers are perceived to be highly effective innovators, capable of delivering original and valuable ideas (Ind et al., 2013). Co-creation spans a continuum from *co-creation as a tactical market research tool* to *co-creation as a strategic collaborate innovation tool*, including testing of ideas, co-creation of brand identity, user-generated product innovation or market development, and development of competitive strategy and marketing program (Ind, Iglesias, & Markovic, 2017; Payne, Storbacka, Frow, & Knox, 2009; Schau, Muñiz Jr, & Arnould, 2009).

Co-creation often originates in networks, and a classic example of a consumer network is the brand community, which is " a specialized, non-geographically bound community, based on a structured set of social relations among admirers of a brand" (Muniz & O'Guinn, 2001, p. 412). Members of a brand community come together based on shared passion for a brand, and they are usually eager to share their experiences with and ideas about the brand. The internet and Social Media facilitate online brand communities, which means that members do not necessarily meet physically. Accordingly, brand communities are to some extent imagined communities as they represent a sense of shared human interaction situated within a consumption or user context. A brand community may be facilitated by the brand itself or it can be founded by brand enthusiasts. Regardless of the organization of the brand community, interaction cannot be controlled as community members engage in many forms of social interaction and networking practices (Schau et al., 2009), where they tell stories about the brand and brand experiences. Storytelling is found to be a central mechanism of creating and maintaining a brand community. Accordingly, a company can seek to influence the conversations about its brand by supplying stories (myths) or story inputs as well as to engage in conversations about the brand, but brand community members will also share their brand experiences and thus, invest the brand with meaning. Hence, brand communities play a vital role in the social construction of brand meaning in a broader perspective as brand communities become active carriers of brand meaning. Muniz and O'Guinn (2001) highlight the fact that brand community members may define successful interaction with the brand differently than the brand manager, and that community members may feel that they understand the brand better than the manufacturer does. Some theorists talk about brand hijack. Brand hijack happens if stakeholders outside the organization succeed in creating a dominant brand meaning which is quite different from the meaning intended by the company. However, the notion of brand hijack is rooted in the belief that a brand is owned by the company. Theories about brand communities point to a contested ownership of the brand, or rather, the social construction of brand meaning and value, and thus acknowledge the social nature of brands.

Though membership of a brand community is not restricted to include only consumers, there is an underlying assumption in the literature about brand communities that consumers are predominant in the membership composition, and thus in the co-creation of brand meaning. But co-creation is not limited to taking place in brand communities. Brand meaning is co-created in every interaction consumers and other stakeholders experience with different brand touchpoints. Accordingly, brand managers should consider how, not only consumers, but all stakeholders interpret and create brand meaning – what could be termed a multi-stakeholder approach to brand management (Iglesias & Bonet, 2012). Hatch and Schultz (2008) proposed a third wave of branding called *enterprise branding* (the first wave being product branding and the second, corporate branding). Enterprise branding encompasses the interests and expectations of *all* the company's stakeholders, and more time and attention must be given to engage the full range of stakeholders in the creation of the corporate brand. In enterprise branding

> many voices will shape and inform the corporate brand through myriad forms of communication – direct and indirect, face-to-face, and virtual – and through traditional channels as well as new media such as text messaging and Web sites like MySpace and YouTube.
>
> Hatch & Schultz (2008, pp. 206–207)

However, theories about co-creation and brand communities are generally quite vague about *where* and *how* co-creation of brand meaning happens. Ind et al. (2013) suggest that co-creation takes place in a *connected space*. A connected space is a space that allows a company to meet with individuals through face-to-face or online interactions, and the notion is further developed in the *organic view of the brand*.

The organic view of the brand

The *organic view of the brand* has been proposed by Iglesias et al. (2013) as an attempt to articulate a new approach to branding that builds on the idea of brands as co-created by multiple stakeholders. In the organic view, brands are understood as social processes, and "brand value is conversationally co-created by many different stakeholders in a fluid space subject to constant negotiation and often develops beyond the strategic aims set by brand managers" (Iglesias et al., 2013, p. 670). Brand value is thus dynamically constructed through social interactions between different stakeholders and accordingly, a brand is understood as a continuous social process where brand value is being co-created through stakeholder-based negotiations. The organic view of the brand challenges the traditional idea that the brand covenant and value proposition is developed and articulated by brand management; rather, the organic view of the brand suggests that while brand managers seek to provide direction for the brand, they must also realize that brand meaning is conversationally co-created by multiple stake-holders and thereby, constantly negotiated (Iglesias et al., 2013).

When a brand is conversationally co-created, it becomes of interest to iden-tify the settings, where these conversations unfold. The organic view builds on the idea of a *connected space* that allows for brand interactions to take place, and the authors denominate such a connected space, a *conversational space*. A con-versational space is a space where consumers and an organization can come together and interact through brand interfaces and frontline employees. Brand interactions may be planned or unplanned, and interactions can be shared with other people. Accordingly, new conversational spaces may form and arise beyond the reach of the organization. Brand interfaces are understood as all the non-human interfaces through which stakeholders interact with the brand, such as the product, packaging, logo, and points of sale. These non-human interfaces serve to make the brand promise tangible.

Although brand managers can still try to form and influence brand meaning by instruction of frontline employees and the production and distribution of brand interfaces, many parts of the branding processes are beyond their control. The organic view of the brand thus proposes that brand managers must accept a loss of control because the logic of brand management has shifted from the conceptualization of brands as firm-provided to brands as a collaborative, value co-creation activity of firms and all their stakeholders (Iglesias et al., 2013). Accordingly, brands become fluid – an observation that breaks with the understanding of a brand as an object or an entity. Hence, the organic view of brands calls into question long-established traditional assumptions in the branding field, and it certainly demands a new managerial style.

Whereas the organic view of the brand emphasizes the notion of conversational spaces as the place where brand meaning is negotiated and created, other authors have looked further into the idea of brands as conversationally constructed and framed the brand as a *discursive construct.*

1.5 Brands as discursive constructions

A discursive lens to brand management is rooted in the assumption that use of language is a social practice that constructs aspects of social reality in a certain way. The way we talk about things affects how we and others understand (i.e. make sense of) these things. From a discursive perspective, brands have no intrinsic meaning or substance, rather brands are created by the discourses produced about them. Leitch and Richardson (2003) conceptualize brands as "discursive constructs that occupy discursive space, which is the space in which meaning is created" (p. 1068). Hence, a brand is constructed according to the discourses produced about it, and "brands acquire meaning through a constantly evolving interaction and interpretation process involving multiple stakeholders" (Vallaster & von Wallpach, 2013, p. 1506). Discourse theories distinguish between macro and micro or what is also called capital D-discourse and small d-discourse. Macro discourses or D-discourses are discourses that are shared and accepted by a larger social group, in that they might exist at a societal level and express a 'truth' accepted by this social group. Micro discourses or d-discourses are small discourses produced in everyday talk and interaction.

Initial research looking at brands from a discursive perspective focused on macro discourses. For instance, Leitch and Richardson (2013) highlight how business partners, such as joint venture partners and co-branded products, as well as retailers and competitors, may feed into each other's 'brand webs'. Their metaphor of a brand web is supposed to illustrate how different brand discourses, such as discourses from competitors, retailers, or suppliers, may intertwine; the brand becomes entangled in a network of discourses that all add to the brand's meaning as the brand's "[d]iscursive space is made up of multiple discourses that compete with one another for dominance" (p.1068). A brand is thus constituted by multiple discourses that may collide and overlap or even be in opposition to one another. As an example of colliding discourses, Leitch and Richardson (2013) point to the tobacco industry where the brand discourses are entangled with the health D-discourse that state the risks and danger of using the product on the packaging. The health D-discourse is a macro discourse which exists at a societal level. Seeing that the health D-discourse has gained momentum in recent years, tobacco brands must observe this D-discourse in order to defend their legitimacy. Different discourses compete for hegemony or what we could call a provisional dominance of a particular perspective (Jørgensen & Phillips, 2002), and when the health D-discourse succeeds in establishing the truth that smoking is unhealthy, then it affects brands operating in the tobacco industry. In this particular case it has led to a legal demand to declare the harmful effects of the product on the consumer's health as part of the branding discourses. From a discursive perspective, stakeholder salience becomes a question of succeeding in creating a dominant discourse, and as expressed by Vallaster and von Wallpach (2013, p. 1506), "[c]hanges in discursive resource allocation strategies over time lead to shifts in stakeholder salience and add to the stakeholder network's dynamic nature". It is a built-in assumption in the brand web metaphor that it reflects power relations, in that the company can exert less and less control the further away from the hub it gets. Yet, as expressed by Vallaster and von Wallpach, power relations and stakeholder salience are questions of discursive resource allocation.

In another study that explored brands from a macro discourse perspective, Kärreman and Rylander (2008) conducted a longitudinal study in a consultancy firm with the aim of investigating how branding can be understood as *management of meaning* by looking at how different discourses create brand meaning. The scholars identify two discourses that are seen to manage brand meaning. One discourse is the external brand communication discourse, which they term the total corporate communication 'branding discourse'. The branding discourse includes advertising slogans, TV commercials, corporate website, mission, and vision statements. The other discourse they identify is the 'internal discourse', the one that expresses self-understanding (identity). Though, the 'branding discourse' is meant for an external audience, the authors find that the 'branding discourse' also has internal effects; in fact, it may even be more important internally than externally as the brand is seen as an indicator of a common identity. Vásquez et al. (2013) suggest that corporate branding is one of the core mechanisms through which organizational members make sense of who they are. Interestingly, Kärreman and Rylander (2008) found that employees tended to use words and expressions from the 'internal discourse' when they explained the brand, instead of using words and expressions from the 'branding discourse'. This suggests that discourses intermingle and that the 'internal discourse' affects how the employees act as brand ambassadors (i.e. how they represent the brand).

The 'branding discourse' was seen to change considerably, while the 'internal discourse', about who they are, remained relatively stable. This finding leads the authors to suggest that the 'branding discourse' and the 'internal discourse' represent two complementary but different discourses that serve different purposes for organizational members, and that branding can be understood as a practice for the management of meaning. The 'branding discourse' may not be crucial to the social construction of identity (i.e. the 'internal discourse'), but the brand can function as a symbol that provides elite confirmation of belonging to 'the best and brightest' (ibid.). If brand can manage meaning, it can potentially display organizing features.

The organizing features of branding

Looking at brands from a discursive perspective highlights the *organizing features of branding,* seeing as discourses organize and constitute reality. Kornberger (2015) suggests that a brand functions as a valuation practice that organizes demand and supply. He argues that the price of a product is a social construction and thus is not indicative of value. Rather, the value of a product is co-created through the consumer's meaning-making activities. A product can have, for instance, cultural, scientific, aesthetic, and social value, and this value can evolve and change over time. The brand is a signifier, but the signified is produced by the consumer. A brand is thus a space where consumer activities become productive. Things are made valuable through a multitude of evaluation devices, such as rankings, reviews, awards, guides, and expert opinions. As such, a brand can be understood as a *floating signifier* (Mumby, 2016). The meaning of a floating signifier is established through signifying processes that are never finally fixed. A floating signifier is, therefore, continuously open to contestation and appropriation by different actors (or discourses); the term 'floating signifier' thus, articulates "the unstable and arbitrary character of the relationship between signifier and signified in the construction of meaning" (ibid. p. 894). The creation (organization) of brand value is thus, a dynamic and messy process outside the control of the brand manager. If the brand exists in the eye of the beholder, then brand management becomes a question of turning internal and external audiences into co-authors of an evolving brand narrative (Kornberger, 2015).

In an organizational communication perspective, brands can potentially instruct and direct organizational members, and as such they can be understood to exercise a form of normative control (Huzzard, Benner, & Kärreman, 2017). Vásquez et al. (2013) have studied branding as *processes of representation*, that is, the day-to-day communicative practices of *doing branding.* The authors studied a rebranding process of a university department, and they found that organizational members reacted to some of the representation practices used (e.g. the website), as they were opposed to the way they were being branded. A website can be viewed as an *incarnation* of the brand and, in this case, it triggered identity issues in relation to how the 'we' was represented. The authors suggest that the brand is mobilized as a *frame* and a practice of *boundary setting* in order to structure *who* and *what* is being branded. While the brand is an outcome of interaction and negotiation, the brand is, at the same time, what orders these interactions and processes of negotiation. Thus, there is a dialectic relationship between the brand and the organizational actors. Accordingly, a brand is not a stable entity, but an ongoing accomplishment, and branding is seen to be a much more mundane activity carried out in everyday interaction, rather than a strategic process carried out by a marketing department as traditionally suggested in the branding literature. Another important observation is that the brand-as-object is perceived to have agency, seeing that it can structure interaction.

In another study, Vásquez, Del Fa, Sergi, and Cordelier (2017a) demonstrate how students are being utilised to *embody* the university brand, thus commodifying the student, and turning the student into a brand. The authors demonstrate how the brand is being negotiated by organizational members. The first draft, produced by an advertising agency, is being rejected by the dean and board of directors who also mobilize incumbent students to reject the campaign. In the creation of a new draft, former students are invited to conceive a piece of art to be part of the campaign. The process is documented and used as part of the campaign. The student is thus not only a targeted audience, but also a producer of the university brand, a spokesperson, and a product. The authors find that the marketing discourse (i.e. the marketization of the university) is masked by a discourse of creativity, and the organizational members easily accept the idea of the student as a prosumer while rejecting the idea of the student as a consumer. Macro discourses operating at a societal level are thus at play when organizational members negotiate the brand (i.e. in micro discourses). As pointed out by the authors, the D-discourse of creativity is a universally accepted discourse, and thus a core value in our western society, and it sways organizational members to embrace the idea of the student as a prosumer. In another study, by the same authors, they conclude that the D-discourse about creativity succeeds in achieving an internal truce. It is, therefore, seen that branding efforts do not refer to the university as it intrinsically is, but rather on larger social discourses that are able to gather support from important stakeholders. Such capital D-discourses function as resources that actors can draw upon to prioritize ideas and suggest brand value (Vásquez et al., 2017b). The authors conclude that the *doing of branding* both organizes, de-organizes, and re-organizes actors as well as means, ends and meanings. Accordingly, brand value is not an end result but a process.

A discursive approach to branding is thus grounded in a performative and interactional view of branding processes because it highlights the importance of language use (i.e. how the brand is being performed) as well as the negotiation of meaning. It does not necessarily see organizational members as more privileged than external stakeholders in the negotiation of brand meaning.

1.6 The evolution of a new brand logic

I have demonstrated in this chapter that branding theories have evolved from a focus on product branding. Product branding is rooted in a transmission-based view of communication, based on signalling theory, that focuses on communication *from* the organization *to* stakeholders. In product branding, brand identity is understood to be constructed internally to the organization (i.e. by management) and transmitted to relevant stakeholders (Burmann & Zeplin, 2005). Accordingly, employees and other stakeholders are conceptualized as passive receivers of pre-defined brand messages in agreement with the conduit metaphor of communication (Salzer-Mörling & Strannegård, 2004). Product branding has dominated the field for many years, but gradually new perspectives, such as *corporate branding,* the *service-dominant logic, co-creation,* and *the organic view of the brand* have emerged, where brands are recognized as co-created by multiple stakeholders. However, the majority of branding literature still applies a managerial perspective, where brand management is assumed to have a certain amount of control (Vallaster & von Wallpach, 2013). This perspective is based on a conduit metaphor with a sender-dominated view of communication and an objectivist assumption of the possibility of alignment and consistency. It misses out on the negotiated character of brand meaning and the understanding that phenomena (e.g. brands) are shaped by human sources rather than being "natural" or "genuine". Christensen and Cornelissen (2011) argue that such sender-oriented conduit models operate with a limited understanding of what an organization is or should be.

However, in recent years there has been a movement away from an organization-centric approach to branding in favour of one that sees communication as constitutive of branding and thus, branding activities as highly participative (Ind, 2014).

The need for further development of a 'communication as constitutive' approach

Cornelissen et al. (2012) stress the importance of continuing the nascent development away from the sender-dominated conduit models of branding towards a constitutive model in order to recognize the constitutive character of communication. The scholars argue that branding has existed in its own "bubble" rooted in the transmission-based view of communication for many years, and consequently theory development has been rather consensus-driven and, to a certain degree, guarded and restrictive. Exposure to, and borrowing from, other social fields has been fairly selective with the main inspiration deriving from marketing literature. Due to this historical development of the branding field, communication and management literature has only played a minor role in theory development. Cornelissen et al. (2012) suggest that the field of branding could certainly enrich its vocabulary and strengthen its explanations by incorporating intellectual developments around discourse and processes of communication.

Embracement of co-creation requires a new approach to brand management. Most brand managers are restrained by the belief that they can and need to be in control of the brand. Successful co-creation requires a participatory approach where the brand manager is willing to listen and able to value the contributions stakeholders bring to the table (Ind et al., 2017). Hence, there is a call in the branding literature to both explore the constitutive model of branding in greater depth as well as to enrich this new perspective with empirical research

In a response to this call for further development of a 'communication as constitutive' approach to branding, I will, in the next chapter, present a CCB (Communication as Constitutive of Brands) approach. In this approach I incorporate the language of communicative constitution to explicate brands as a communicative construct.

Notes

1 USP was defined by Rosser Reeves in 1960 (Kippenberger, 2000).
2 The name *Coca-Cola* refers to the original main ingredients, namely Coca leaves and Kola nuts.

2 A communication as constitutive approach to branding

The aim of this chapter is to further the understanding of brands and branding as communicatively constituted. An endeavor toward developing such an understanding has been commenced (see for instance, Ashcraft, Muhr, Rennstam, & Sullivan, 2012; Cornelissen et al., 2012; Kärreman & Rylander, 2008; Mumby, 2016; Vásquez et al., 2017b; Vásquez et al., 2013), but the venture is still in its infancy, and "the ontological questions of what brand and branding are have up to now rarely been touched upon" (Vásquez et al., 2017b, p. 1). In order to more fully explicate the understanding of brands as communicatively constituted I will turn to the CCO (Communication as Constitutive of Organization) approach. The CCO approach examines the communicative constitution of organization, and I argue that 'organization' and 'brand' share some common features that makes this approach appropriate to use as a springboard for theory development.

Appropriateness of the CCO approach to branding

Ontologically speaking, a 'brand' shares many similarities with an 'organization' as they are both usually conceptualized as an object even though neither has any intrinsic materiality. Taylor (2013, p. 214) states that an organization can be said to be "an entirely fictitious, totally immaterial construction". Yet, an organization is usually associated with a building or a group of people in the same way a brand is often associated with a product, a company, or a service. Both a brand and an organization are associated with materiality even though they are clearly not a material "thing" (Nicotera, 2013). Rather 'organization' and 'brand' emerge in communication and are conceptualized as discursive spaces. Based on these onto-logical similarities, I will argue for the legitimacy to use the vocabulary of CCO to explain the ontology of a brand, as has also been done by other researchers (see for instance, Ashcraft et al., 2012; Cornelissen et al., 2012; Kärreman & Rylander, 2008; Mumby, 2016; Vásquez et al., 2017b; Vásquez et al., 2013). Vásquez et al. (2017b, p. 4) suggest that transposing the CCO approach to branding "offers a theoretical framework to study branding as a communicative process through which people, things, bodies, artifacts, symbols, values, emotions, work, organize and get organized".

DOI: 10.4324/9781003050100-2

The understanding of a brand as a discursive space, where multiple discourses compete for hegemony resonates very well with the understanding of organizations as polyphonic. I find that the CCO approach can be used to explicate the idea of brands as discursive spaces, which so far has only been addressed at a very general level in the existing literature. Before I introduce the CCB approach, I will briefly present some core elements of CCO thinking.

2.1 A brief presentation of CCO

CCO (Communication as Constitutive of Organization) is an acronym that consolidates a number of ideas spurred by the *interpretive turn*, and it was coined by Putnam and Nicotera in 2008 (Ashcraft et al., 2009; Bisel, 2010). CCO is a collection of perspectives that concur in locating communication as the key factor in constituting organization (Putnam & Nicotera, 2010; Schoerneborn, Blaschke, Cooren, McPhee, Seidl & Taylor, 2014). CCO perspectives put forward a performative and interactional view of organizations as grounded in action, since it focuses on what is happening *in* communication (Cooren, Matte, Benoit-Barné, & Brummans, 2013; Fairhurst & Putnam, 2004; Vásquez et al., 2013). Putnam and Nicotera (2010) explain CCO as an effort to unpack the idealized abstraction of an organization that is rarely questioned. CCO embraces a communicational ontology of organization that invites users to "start *from* communication in order *to* explain organization and organizing and not the other way around" (Cooren, 2012, p. 4 italics in original).

Ontologically speaking, an organization is brought into being as it is performed or acted out (Robichaud & Cooren, 2013). Organization happens through social interactions, conversations, and co-orientations that produce different types of texts (Putnam, 2013). If these activities are no longer performed, the organization will come to a halt (Latour, 2013). An organization exists in communication, is made present in interaction, and incarnated by human and nonhuman agents who act in its name (Nicotera, 2013). It is important to bear in mind, though, that organization can never be reduced to the practices of any single conversation. Organization is not a here and now, but an imbrication of many heres and theres, nows and thens that produces a constellation of people, practices, and technologies (Taylor & Van Every, 2011).

Cooren, Kuhn, Cornelissen, and Clark (2011) lay out six CCO premises in order to sketch out what the CCO perspective entails as well as to invite other scholars to test and expand upon these premises. The six premises include the view that CCO should be as inclusive as possible about what is understood by organizational communication. Agency is not restricted to human beings; nonhumans, such as documents, technologies, furniture, clothes, and architectural elements, are recognized as having agency. Therefore, the question of who or what is acting is always an open one. Communication is co-constructed and "any performance is as much the product of the agent that/who is deemed performing it as the product of the people who attend and interpret/respond to such performance" (Cooren et al.,

2011, p. 1152). The co-construction of communication is further elaborated in the notion of *ventriloquism*.

Ventriloquism

Summarized in one sentence, Cooren (2012) explains 'communicatively constitutive' as "noticing that a variety of forms of agency are always in play in *any* interaction, a phenomenon that I propose to call, metaphorically, *ventriloquism*" (p. 4, italics in original). In an organizational context, ventriloquism is the ability to reconstruct or invoke the voice of another author or even the many voices of several authors (Cooren & Sandler, 2014). Ventriloquists are able to "throw their voice" and thus make other beings *say* or *do things* on their behalf (Cooren, 2016; Cooren, Matte, Benoit-Barné, & Brummans, 2013). The common way to think of ventriloquism is that of a human actor animating a non-human dummy and thus, making it speak and act. In an organizational context, this form of ventriloquism would correspond to a human actor speaking through a non-human actor, like, for instance, a text (or some other kind of materiality). Ventriloquism can thus be seen as a way of tele-acting since the dummy does not speak with a voice of its own, rather it is transmitting the voice of the ventriloquist (Cooren, 2016). But what is noteworthy is that not only are we, as humans, able to animate a dummy (or a figure) and make it say or do things, it works the other way around as well, in that human actors are animated by a number of different figures. Cooren et al. (2013, p. 263) argue that, "ventriloquism provides a useful metaphor for reconceptualizing communication, as human interactants do not only ventriloquize specific figures but are also ventriloquized (animated) by them". Everybody is both a ventriloquist and a dummy. When we enter into interaction with the dummy, we respond to it and thus not only is the dummy animated by a human, but the human actor is simultaneously animated by the dummy, because he or she responds to it. Clearly, the dummy gains an agency of its own and the effect of ventriloquism is therefore bidirectional (Cooren, 2012), in other words, ventriloquism is an instance of *hybrid agency*.

Hybrid agency

Cooren (2004, p. 376) re-conceptualizes action and agency by scrutinizing eight lexicographic definitions of "action" and concludes that action is "*a transformation of state operated by an agent*" (italics in original). It is therefore possible to talk about non-human agency, as material objects can transform a state of being by reminding, providing structure or making visible, for instance. However, materiality cannot communicate without a partner (Leonardi & Barley, 2011), thus non-human objects do not operate on their own. They operate in co-operation with a human actor, and their agency thus becomes an agency of *hybridicity*. The concept of hybrid agency was introduced by Bruno Latour in the field of actor-network theory and Latour has been a key inspiration in the material turn (see for instance, Latour, 1996).

Latour believes that hybridization of the subject and the object world is inevitable, and when two agents are combined, the result is a hybrid. For example, we can imagine $Agent_1$ being an HR manager and $Agent_2$ being an employment policy. If $Agent_1$ (the HR manager) refers to a decision stated by $Agent_2$ (the employment policy), a new form of hybrid agency emerges in the form of $Agent_{1+2}$. $Agent_1$ can draw on his or her personal authority as well as on the authority of $Agent_2$ that is being ventriloquized. $Agent_{1+2}$ can thus be seen as an imbrication between human and material agencies (Fayard & Weeks, 2014) and humans and the nonhuman are co-constitutive. This example also demonstrates how the understanding of ventriloquism can be broadened to not only refer to a situation, where a human actor speaks through (animates) a dummy (a material thing), but also the reverse. A material object may animate a human actor and thus speak through him or her. "Texts supply motives and obligations *to* actors and thus 'speak through' them" (Kuhn, 2012, p. 554), when organizational members are mouthing a text. One could also imagine a situation where a human actor, such as a CEO, speaks through another human actor, such as a middle manager. In this case, the hybrid would be an imbrication of different human agencies.

Multiple forms of agency can thus be said to be at work in any given situation. In an organizational context a written policy may *act out* a certain sort of authority, an artifact may *remind* an organizational member about a certain brand value or a setting of furniture may *encourage* interaction and cooperation. However, materiality does not possess a certain kind of agency per se, rather the agency is co-constructed in the interplay or relation between $Agent_1$ and $Agent_2$:

> As soon as we realize that many different voices can be recognized in a given text or discussion, we have to acknowledge that no priority in terms of expression should be given to the human beings over the other figures.
> Cooren & Sandler (2014, p. 238)

Non-human actors

In light of the discussion of ventriloquism and hybrid agency, it becomes apparent how the CCO approach recognizes the agency of non-human actors and thus the importance of text and materiality, which are key concerns in the CCO literature.

A text can function as a nonhuman-actor as it can act in the name of an organization or a brand. An employment policy can inform employees about expected and desired behavior as well as their rights and obligations. It may stipulate brand values in order to enable employees to live the brand and function as brand ambassadors. When the employment policy is read by an organizational actor and spurs a certain behavior, a hybrid agency is produced, and thus the employment policy becomes a non-human actor. Texts (or materiality) "participate, like other agents, in the daily production of organizational life" (Cooren, 2004, p. 374).

When decisions and directives are written down and the texts are published in the organization, the original author vanishes from view and a 'naturalization' of the text takes place. The text no longer expresses what one person – or a limited group of persons – knows; it expresses what *everyone* knows (Taylor, 2011), and "[a]uthority is now attributed to the textual abstraction itself rather than any particular individual" (Koschmann, 2013, p. 67). When the original author vanishes from view, the text is 'distanciated' from its site of production, and it is this 'distanciation' that creates a 'naturalization' of text. It is thus a combination of vanishment of authorship and distanciation from production that ascribe authority to the text. The text comes to be seen as reflecting the collective rather than an individual (Koschmann, 2013), meaning that the text can be understood as a *macro-actor*.

Macro-actor

A macro-actor is an actor that acts as a 'we' (Taylor & Cooren, 1997) hence, a macro-actor speaks on behalf of a collectivity and thus speaks with an enhanced authority: "When an actor speaks for more than him- or herself […], such an actor speaks with an enhanced authority because it is the voice of more than one person, and thus has an extra weight" (Taylor & Van Every, 1999, p. 159). Speaking as a 'we' or 'on behalf of' a collectivity multiplies the sources of authorship, which amounts to multiplying the sources of authority and hence legitimacy.

Cooren, Fairhurst, and Huët (2012) illustrate the power of a macro-actor by referring to the US constitution. The US constitution represents a 'we', consisting of the 55 delegates of the Philadelphia convention who drafted it. Anyone who animates the constitution thus animates the power of the delegates. The authors refer to Barack Obama's inauguration, and demonstrate how Chief Justice Roberts could legitimately swear Barack Obama into office, because Roberts was acting as an agent in the name of the US constitution. It was not Robert (i.e. the person) who had the power to inaugurate Barack Obama, it was the network in which he acted on behalf of that held that power.

Apart from illustrating the function of a macro-actor, the example also illustrates an act of ventriloquism in that the US constitution spoke through (or animated) Chief Justice Roberts.

Materiality

In the light of non-human actors, materiality becomes a key concern. While the *linguistic turn* addresses the discursive construction of our social worlds, the *material turn* contends that discourses alone are not enough to explain the world we live in. Rather, discursive practices need to be considered side by side with other forms of social and material activity (Nicolini, 2012), and the importance of materiality has been re-theorized in a number of ways in what has been labelled *the material turn*. Hence, the ongoing discussion about the organizing properties of text and conversation is now reframed or extended to include not only text (understood as written text) but all kinds of objects or materiality.

All communication is grounded in the material world as there is no communication outside the context of activity (Taylor & Van Every, 1999). Interaction is always related to some kind of materiality or embodiment, where thoughts and ideas are incarnated or reified. Consequently, materiality is not an appendage to discourse; materiality is an integral part of discourse, actively participating in constructing it (Cooren et al., 2012). The material turn is thus based on a relational and performative ontology in which "there is no divide between the world of materiality and the world of discourse and communication" (Cooren et al., 2012, p. 302), and the attempt is to articulate and push forward a dialogue about the ways in which social and material agencies configure each other (Fayard & Weeks, 2014).

Material agency is something that the interactants implicitly or explicitly orient towards (Cooren et al., 2012). Cooren (2004, p. 375, italics in original) illustrates this point by referring to an example of a pilot and his checklist:

> The airline pilot's checklist before takeoff *structures* talk with the copilot, navigator, and ground crew; *enacts* directives from the legal and regulating bodies overseeing flight; *establishes* a record of action taken by the flight crew; and *provides* a task-oriented frame for interpreting other recordings of conversation and instrument readings. Further, the checklist *regularizes* and *structures* the procedure of the takeoff, the perception and inspection of instruments and the physical environment, and the manipulation of the aircraft and its control.

As seen here, communication tasks can be delegated to non-human actors, and such a delegation of communication to the material can be a powerful way to guide the production of meaning (Leonardi & Barley, 2011). Organizational objects are seen as having both material and ideational qualities, and a characteristic of all elements in the material world is the capacity to lead an existence independent of where it was originally produced because of the properties of durability and thus transportability (Ashcraft et al., 2009; Taylor, 1999). Materiality and text have *restance*, that is, 'staying capacity'. Objects' (and texts') actions last as long as the materiality remains intact or recognized (Cooren, 2004), and thus objects may function to coordinate and control (Ashcraft et al., 2009). Materiality helps hold together an organizational order because "[o]bjects embody the constancies of organizational life in that they endure beyond the time and place of a given interaction, yet they are present to mediate future conversations" (Fairhurst & Putnam, 2004, p. 18).

The agency of material objects is conditional upon their (human) construction, but once they have been devised, they may take on a life of their own, 'act back' and become part of (new) hybrid agencies. Materiality works as a delegate, it speaks on behalf of someone, but materiality also put its own spin on messages (Leonardi & Barley, 2011). Producers of non-human actors inscribe their vision of how the artifact should be used in its material features, but "the translation of intents into artifacts always escapes the control of their creators" (Robichaud & Cooren, 2013, p. xvi). There is always a gap between the construction of an artifact and its possible (mis) uses (Nakassis, 2013).

Discussions of materiality are often arranged around the three elements: objects, sites and bodies (Ashcraft et al., 2009; Putnam & Nicotera, 2010). It is however important to notice that such distinctions between categories are only for analytical purposes, in that "the different types of material are not mutually exclusive but rather coexist, coevolve, can be mutually generative and can create concurrent impact" (Dameron, Lê, & LeBaron, 2015, p. S2). As Cooren (2008, p. 12) puts it: "we live in a world full of various agencies […] where many different 'things' can be said to be doing things: companies, technologies, societies, machines, texts, paintings, architectural elements, artifacts, etc.".

A ventriloquist approach not only recognizes the agency of material things as they are able to animate us, but also of immaterial things, like emotions, attitudes, and beliefs, which can animate us to act in a certain way. Hence the emotion, attitude or concern becomes the ventriloquist and the human, responding to or acting on behalf of that emotion or attitude, becomes the dummy (Cooren, 2012). Many different things can thus be identified as literally and figuratively expressing themselves in any given form of communication, and these can thus be acknowledged as partly constituting that situation (Cooren & Sandler, 2014). Accordingly, one ought to ask oneself who or what is speaking at a given moment.

When we speak, we orchestrate the many different voices in our utterances, and we can thus be said to articulate a doubled-voiced discourse. The speaker is not always able to control the voices that he or she brings into the talk (ibid.). A ventriloquist can mobilize a wide variety of texts or materiality to speak for them, but it will always – to a certain extent – be unpredictable how other actors "materialize" those texts (Kuhn, 2012). If a voice is introduced and the legitimacy of that voice is questioned or it is suggested to be saying something else than first ventriloquized, the person who introduced that voice may not achieve what he or she hoped for by introducing that voice. Hence, "figures do not always end up saying what people initially thought they would say" (Cooren & Sandler, 2014, p. 237). The ventriloquist and the dummy are entangled and mutually constitutive. The meaning of the dummy is not defined a priori and it "can be made to say many different things depending on who is giving them a voice" (Cooren et al., 2013, p. 264).

Polyphony

In the recognition of human and non-human actors, acts of ventriloquism and hybrid agency, organizations can be conceptualized as polyphonic. The concept of polyphony is inspired by the work of Mikhail Bakhtin, who was among the first to insist on the polyphonic and heteroglot nature of discourse (Belova, King, & Sliwa, 2008; Cooren & Sandler, 2014; Kornberger, Clegg, & Carter, 2006). Today the term is used to imply that organizations are discursive spaces "where heterogeneous and multiple voices engage in a contest for audibility and power" (Belova et al., 2008, p. 493). In this sense organizations can be seen as "discursive spaces which are shaped by a multiplicity of voices, dominant and peripheral, which together make up a contested and ever-changing arena of human interaction" (Belova et al., 2008, p. 495). The concept of a polyphonic organization thus refers to an understanding that organizational reality is constituted by a variety of discourses (or voices) (Kornberger et al., 2006). Voices are to be understood more broadly than the voice of a human actor. Voices encompass discourses, cultural meanings, and historical, social, and economic circumstances; polyphony can be understood as the interplay between human voices and discourses (Belova, 2010; Kornberger et al., 2006). As it should be clear from the presentation of ventriloquism, hybrid agency and non-human actors, many different voices can be appropriated in an instance of hybrid agency and thus be made to speak through or on behalf of someone.

Cooren and Sandler (2014) see a close relationship between ventriloquism, polyphony and authority or power and believe a voice will often be invoked in order to sustain authority as "[b]eing right or justified means, by definition, being able to position himself or herself as *not the only one* who says what he or she says" (p. 234). In order to back one's arguments or argue a case, other human or non-human actors are animated, and this practice adds voices to the conversation, which adds to the polyphony of organizational life. The concept of polyphony can thus be used to problematize relations within organizations as well as relations between organization and external stakeholders. External partners come to have a voice in the organization when they are being ventriloquized by internal members. This is where "[t]he boundaries between inter- and intra-organizational distinction blur: in fact, instead of the simple inside-outside divide, boundaries multiply" (Kornberger et al., 2006, p. 8). As organizational boundaries are seen to be enacted in different ways at different times, boundaries ought to be conceived in an elastic way, embracing the idea that "what makes up the organization in one moment may not making it up in the next" (Cnossen & Sergi, 2017, p. 2).

Kornberger et al. (2006, p. 4) state that "polyphony is always present, even though it may be silenced by a dominant discourse". As such, an organization is constituted by complex webs of sensemaking activities, which David Boje explains using the metaphor of the organization as a *Tamara play*.

Tamara play

Tamara refers to a play in Los Angeles where the characters move from stage to stage and the audience is able to move around as well. Since the audience moves in different directions, following different actors and listening to different dialogues, every member of the audience will leave the play with a different impression of plot and characters. According to Boje (2001) the organization can be viewed as a *Tamara* play. Organizational members move from stage to stage as they chase multiple story lines, or they are limited to certain stages and never get the full picture of what is going on in the organization. Rather they listen to fragments of stories – *antenarratives* – and they play the role of both actors and audience. Organizational events are thus constituted by polyphonic rather than univocal sensemaking (Belova et al., 2008), since "people are only tracing story fragments, inventing bits and pieces to glue it all together, but never able to visit all the stages and see the whole" (Boje, 2001, p. 5). Kornberger et al. (2006) supplements this by saying that while organizations may well be scripted through missions and strategies, there are too many executives for only one script to be followed.

Polyphony is the condition of the modern organization. Therefore, Kornberger et al. (2006) suggest viewing management as a discursive practice. They explain that "[o]ne can conceptualize managing the polyphonic organization as a discursive practice circumscribed by the processes of *deconstructing* existing language games and *translating* between different language games" (p. 16, italics in original). Translation is to be understood as the process of moving from one language to another, that is, a process of becoming, since the etymological origin of translation is 'to bring or to carry over'. Kornberger et al. (2006) believe "management should encourage the deconstruction of dominating narratives and languages and provide space for new languages" (p. 15) in order to be able to grasp organizational reality in another way or guide a new form of sensemaking. Translations will never be perfect. The essence is to acknowledge the existence of a different language that enacts a different reality, and translation thus becomes about exploring the opportunities of communicating one's ideas or understandings in the realm of another language to enact a new way of making sense.

Based on this brief and condensed presentation of the CCO approach, I will now move on to explicate how the language of CCO can enrich the emerging understanding of brands as communicatively constituted. The CCO approach will be further elaborated as theory is incorporated into the account of branding being grounded in communication.

2.3 Communication as Constitutive of Brand (CCB)

The first steps towards a 'communication as constitutive' approach to branding have been taken (see for instance, Ashcraft et al., 2012; Cornelissen et al., 2012; Kärreman & Rylander, 2008; Mumby, 2016; Vásquez et al., 2017b; Vásquez et al.,

2013). However, as mentioned, the venture is still in its infancy. I propose to label the emerging approach CCB (Communication as Constitutive of Brand), and the aim of this chapter is to further explicate the CCB approach. Taking the contributions presented in Chapter 1 (especially sections 1.4 and 1.5) as my point of departure, I will substantiate the idea of a brand as a discursive space by incorporating the language of CCO. I will go on to demonstrate how the notions of *talk, text, materiality, macro-actor,* and *ventriloquism* can help to clarify how a brand is produced in communication.

Understanding a brand as a discursive brand space

As evident from Chapter 1, a brand has been conceptualized as a *fluid space,* a *conversational space* (Iglesias et al., 2013), and a *discursive space* (Leitch & Richardson, 2003). To add to the multiplicity of *spaces,* Kornberger (2015) has suggested understanding a brand as a *semantic space.* As I ascribe to the idea of a brand as a *space,* I will begin with an explanation of the notion of space and a clarification of concepts (see Table 2.1).

Vásquez et al. (2017b, p. 7) embrace the different conceptualizations of brands as space when they write that they consider branding to be "a communicative (semantic, discursive or conversational) process of organizing". The crux is the idea that a brand is constituted in communication, hence, it is *in communication* that brand value is created and negotiated.

I propose to define a brand as a *discursive brand space.* Discourse is to be understood as also embracing social and material activity, as suggested in the

Table 2.1 Clarification of 'space'

Type of space	Explanation by original author	Use in this book
Conversational space	A space where consumers and organization are able to come together and interact (Iglesias et al., 2013).	*Conversational space* will be used to discuss the set-up of spaces that allow for conversation and interaction (the *sites* of 'doing branding').
Discursive space	Multiple discourses that compete with one another for dominance (Leitch & Richardson, 2003).	A brand will be viewed as a *discursive brand space* where multiple discourses compete for hegemony.
Fluid space	A conversational environment or a *conversational space* (Iglesias et al., 2013).	The notion of a *fluid space* will not be used as I prefer to use *conversational space* for clarity reasons.
Semantic space	The total sum of visualizations and valuation practices that generate the values associated with the brand (Kornberger, 2015).	The notion of *semantic space* will not be used as I prefer to use *discursive brand space* for clarity reasons.

material turn. A *discursive brand space* is the sum of all discourses produced about the brand over time – oral as well as material. A brand is thus grounded in a performative, relational and interactional ontology. In principle, oral and material discourses are of equal importance but, seeing that oral discourses are elusive and transitory, there is a tendency for material discourses to dominate because they possess a "staying capacity" that oral discourses lack (we will return to the interplay between talk, text, and materiality). Accordingly, a discursive brand space is constituted by multiple discourses that intermingle and interact seeing that no discourse is a closed entity. A discourse gains meaning and is being transformed through contact with other discourses (Selg & Ventsel, 2008), while each discourse struggles for hegemony. Hegemony is obtained when one discourse comes to overpower the other discourses at a certain moment in time. When a discourse is established as hegemonic, it comes to be seen as the "truth" – at least temporarily. As such, hegemony can be understood as social consensus. It is a consensus that arises spontaneously (Selg & Ventsel, 2008) based on a current negotiation of meaning. Brand meaning is thus a matter of consent among various actors, and the illusion of a common understanding of brand meaning emerges, when a particular discourse comes to dominate. Accordingly, brand meaning does not exist in any absolute or definitive form; it emerges and is (re-)negotiated in an ongoing discursive struggle for hegemony. Brand meaning is, therefore, talked into existence, and it is negotiated in an ongoing discursive struggle. Hence, the discursive brand space is fluid and ever-changing as new discourses about the brand are produced. The meaning of the discursive brand space is therefore subject to constant negotiation because "branding is a process characterized by indeterminacy of meaning" (Vásquez et al., 2017b, p. 7). A brand is a boundary object (Edlinger, 2015; Vásquez et al., 2013), a contested space open to negotiation. Actors will seek to create and maintain social boundaries that separate and exclude the boundary object from other objects, and as an analytical perspective, boundary-work draws our attention to struggles for authority and reveals the inherently political nature of branding (Edlinger, 2015).

When a brand is conceptualized as *a discursive brand space*, working with brand meaning becomes a question of advancing desired discourses as well as questioning or counteracting undesired discourses. Consequently, guarding or demarcating the boundaries of the brand becomes an issue of inclusion/exclusion of discourses. Hatch and Schultz (2003) claim that a brand is both about belonginess and differentiation. A brand must claim its territory (Hatch & Schultz, 2008) or, as Selg and Ventsel (2010) put it, "something has to be *created* as an 'outside' in order to achieve systematicity on the 'inside'" (p. 454, italics in original). Hence, to influence the creation and development of a discursive brand space, it is necessary both to articulate what the brand is and what it is not. The boundaries of the discursive brand space are thus enacted in discursive struggles of sensegiving and sensemaking, including struggles over which discourses to include and exclude. Social interaction in the discursive brand space is an evolving process that will continue as long as the participants are able and motivated to engage in the discursive activities (see Dean, Arroyo-Gamez, Punjaisri, & Pich, 2016; Vásquez et al., 2017b).

Having discussed the ontological understanding of a brand as a *discursive brand space*, the next question that presents itself is how a discursive brand space can be analyzed.

Identifying discourses

Working from the ontological premise that a brand emerges in communication, the epistemological question is: How do we identify that communication and how can it be analyzed? (see Taylor & Van Every, 1999). In their presentation of various levels of constructionist research Holstein and Gubrium (2008) state that some constructivist researchers pay attention to the face-to-face or micro-interactional activities, such as talk and situated interaction, whereas others pay attention to the macro level, such as Foucauldian inspired discourse analysis or media discourses. Thus, in the academic literature there are researchers adhering to *text* as the unit of analysis and there are researchers adhering to *conversation* as the unit of analysis. Taylor and Van Every (1999) refer to the two approaches as a *text-world* and a *discourse-world*, but Taylor (1999) calls the split an uncomfortable division, in line with Boden (1994) who declares that "the world is of a piece, single and whole" (p. 5).

The separation of text and conversation as two distinct levels of analysis bears resemblance to the micro-macro split. However, it has been argued that 'micro' and 'macro' are not ontological givens and thus distinct levels of analysis, but rather linguistic constructions employed by analysts to frame their research (Kuhn, 2012). Accordingly, Taylor and Van Every (1999) suggest viewing the *text-world* and the *discourse-world* as complementary and suggest a *flatland view*. The metaphor of a *flatland* is used to suggest that all organization, in this case branding, must be found at a single level. Hence, communication is the *site* and *surface* of the emergence of a brand. With *site*, Taylor and Van Every (1999) think of the daily interactions as conceived in the conversation approach, and with *surface* they think of texts where the brand is made present to its members in a medium. Fairhurst and Putnam (2004) phrase it the way that talk-in-interaction is 'the doing' of organizational discourse, and text is 'the done', or the material representation of discourse. For an organization to transcend the boundaries of a single conversation, it must mobilize text as a way of keeping record and informing and guiding future conversations (Taylor, 2013). Taylor describes the relation between talk and text as a self-organizing loop. He explains that "[t]ext is the product of the conversational process, but it is also its raw material and principal preoccupation" (Taylor & Van Every, 1999, p. 210). It means that conversation is guided by text (e.g. minutes, policies, strategies) so text informs conversation. But these texts are the output of conversational processes and therefore talk and text form a self-organizing loop. Taylor and Van Every (1999) therefore suggest that "[i]f the finality of conversation is to sustain interaction, the finality of text is to produce a collectively negotiated interpretation of the world" (p. 40). Neither text or conversation should be foregrounded. Rather communication should be studied from a flatland perspective. Conversation is action, and text provide structure, and the two are co-determinative (Boden, 1994).

Applied to branding, it means that talk-in-interaction is 'the doing' of branding discourse, while text/materiality is 'the done' or the material representation of these brand discourses. Applying a flatland view, brand meaning is not to be found in a slogan, a commercial, or in the talk by employees, but rather in the bricolage of discourses about the brand and the imbrication of meaning that is thus created. This conceptualization of a brand is supported by Vásquez et al. (2013), who suggest that a brand can be said to be the result of *doing* branding, that is the day-to-day branding practices (communicative practices) as well as external discourses that becomes entangled with the organization's branding practices. It is thus important to remember that organizational members are not the only actors that engage in discursive practices. As argued, brand meaning is conversationally co-created by multiple stakeholders (Hatch & Schultz, 2008; Iglesias et al., 2013) – a point, I will return to in the discussion of polyphony in the discursive brand space later in this chapter. The purpose of this section is to argue that a *discursive brand space* is created in talk, text, and materiality, and can thus be studied as language in use in a local, situational context as well as texts and materiality that (re)present brand discourses. Accordingly, the study of a brand as a *discursive brand space* can be informed by CCO theories about the interplay between talk and text.

Talk, text, and materiality

A key concern in the CCO approach has been to look at the interplay between talk and text (see for instance, Cooren, 2004; Taylor, 1999, 2011; Taylor & Cooren, 1997; Taylor, Cooren, Giroux, & Robichaud, 1996; Taylor & Van Every, 1999; Taylor & Van Every, 2011). With the material turn, the notion of text is broadened to include all kinds of materiality, and the initial ideas about text and conversation were accordingly supplemented by thoughts about materiality and *presentification* (see for instance, Benoit-Barné & Cooren, 2009; Cooren, Brummans, & Charrieras, 2008; Cooren et al., 2012; Cooren & Matte, 2010; Fairhurst & Cooren, 2009; Iedema, 1999, 2003, 2007; Iedema & Wodak, 1999; Iedema, 2001). In the following, I will only distinguish between text and materiality if it is necessary in order to consider their heterogeneity. My main focus will be on the material aspect of both text and materiality and thus their similarity.

Conversation

If a brand is the result of 'doing branding', that is the day-to-day commu-nicative practices as suggested by Vásquez et al. (2013), an important part of branding activities is the daily conversations in organizations or among other actors – what we can term the 'doing of discourse' (Fairhurst & Putnam, 2004). When actors engage in conversations about the brand, they take part in authoring the brand. Based on their current understanding of the brand's meaning, they make a conscious or unconscious decision about how to express the brand in social interactions (Dean et al., 2016). The 'doing of discourse' happens in the here and now and is characterized by elusiveness as it only exists in the transitory moment of the present. Conversation is bounded by the specific circumstances of time, place, occasion, identity of the participants, history and purpose, and is enabled or constrained by the participants' knowledge of language and their ability to express themselves. Taylor (1999) refers to the last-mentioned as a person's *repertoire*, that is, a person's personal repertory of words, phrases, metaphors, and anecdotes, stored in memory, that functions as a resource for the production of talk. Conversation is thus highly contingent upon the actors present and their linguistic capacities, which resonates with the idea put forward by Golant (2012), that an important management function is to develop expressions of the brand that promote desired conversations. When actors express brand meaning, they engage in sensegiving activities because they make the brand present in a certain way. Yet, at the same time, they also re-evaluate brand meaning based on their social interactions with others, which highlights the co-creation of the brand (Dean et al., 2016). Conversations (talk) about the brand are thus both a matter of sensegiving and sensemaking, the two are co-constitutive.

Conversational space

Conversation, or the 'doing of discourse', is not only contingent upon the participants' repertoire but also upon the *conversational space* that is created. As mentioned in Table 2.1, I use the notion of *conversational space* to discuss the settings of spaces that allow for conversation and interaction. If we accept the premise that brand value is constituted when stakeholders interact and thus produce a *discursive brand space*, it should be a key concern how this interaction is enabled and who is invited or excluded, since "the creation of brand value depends on the interactions established" (Iglesias et al., 2013, p. 677). Conversations take place in a *conversational space*. A conversational space can be a physical setting that allows face-to-face conversation, like, for instance, a meeting room, a canteen, a sales outlet, or a brand event. Equally, it can be virtual, in the form of an intranet, a website, an online brand community, an anti-brand web site, an online forum, a weblog, or social media that allow for interaction. The *conversational space* is thus the space where interlocutors come together and interact. It can be *formally set up* by the organization in the form of a meeting, an event or a company Facebook group for instance, but it can also be *informal*, in the form of talk (gossip) in the canteen or by the hot drinks' dispenser. A conversational space can thus emerge spontaneously, which is often the case on social media, when actors start to discuss a brand. Sensemaking about the brand is thus not limited to taking place in the *established conversational space*; sensemaking will happen in conversations anywhere. The setup of virtual conversational spaces (formal and informal) can provide information and resources to stakeholders that they would not have had otherwise, and stakeholders may use these resources to actively co-create brand meaning (Vallaster & von Wallpach, 2013). Interaction in conversational spaces is also a vital source of information to the brand manager who can gain an insight into actors' discursive activities, and thus how they co-produce the discursive brand space.

It follows that one of the ways (brand) managers can try to influence interaction in the conversational space is in how the space is set up and how easily access is gained. The setup of a conversational space is related to the number of people invited to the conversational space and how these people are selected. (Brand) managers can choose to include everyone by using social media or in other ways invite thoughts and ideas. But (brand) managers can also choose to establish a limited conversational space, where only selected members are invited, such as an exclusive brand event. However, it is important to realize that the setup of a defined conversational space does not stop other actors from impacting the co-creation, as invited interlocutors can ventriloquize voices that are not (physically) present. Members that have been excluded from a formally designed conversational space can thus, teleact through ventriloquism or by taking part in discussions outside the established conversational space (informal communication) and hence, affect the sensemaking of actors participating in the official conversational space. The boundaries of a conversational space are thus impossible to control. (Brand) managers can try to set up boundaries, but these boundaries can be transcended and expanded.

Physical facilities, such as room and arrangement, can affect the 'doing of discourse' as different material settings put forward different affordances. Material settings influence "the resources available for interaction and, thus, conditions agency" (Ashcraft et al., 2009, p. 3 1). The physical world supplies a meaningful "infrastructure" to interaction, and it can assume cultural meaning (ibid.). Dean et al. (2016) suggest that employees develop brand meaning based on their brand interactions and experiences with management, other employees, and external stakeholders, and that "it is in the production and reproduction of these social interactions where value and meaning are co-created" (p. 3043).

As a (brand) manager it is thus important to pay attention to the material aspects of the conversational space as well as who is invited to participate in the conversational space, since the inclusion and exclusion of interlocutors (i.e. voices) will be highly formative in the conversations that are enabled, and thus the brand value that can be co-created. Conversations may also be affected by power relations and organizational hierarchy as well as organizational common practice or procedures. The task is to create a conversational space where participants or interlocutors can come together and discuss and hence, co-create and negotiate brand meaning. The conversational space can, to a certain extent, be influenced and molded (i.e. designed), since management can invite certain people to participate and exclude others; but the conversational space is also fluid and subject to constant negotiation as participants can withdraw from the space, and new participants can be invited or appear either in person or through ventriloquism. The boundaries of the conversational space are thus a discursive construction not a corporeal demarcation; hence, the boundaries are fluid and elastic (see Cnossen & Sergi, 2017; Ind, 2014). The 'doing of discourse' not only takes place in formal settings but also in informal conversations among organizational members or other participants. Organizations are characterized by a great deal of informal communication that affect organizational members' sensemaking (Mills, 2009; Nymark, 2000), so while managers can seek to provide guidance and direction for the development of brand meaning, they have to accept that the co-creation of brand meaning happens in a polyphonic arena with fluid boundaries.

The first theorizing in the CCB approach proposes that:

1 Brands are partly constituted in the 'doing of discourse' in both formal and informal communication and are affected by participants' repertoire.
2 The 'doing of discourse' takes place in a conversational space and is shaped by the material settings and its affordances as well as the participants.
3 The boundaries of the conversational space are not corporeal but constituted discursively.

The 'doing of discourse' is, however, only part of the communicative practices that constitute a brand and it is, therefore, necessary to also consider the 'done discourse' primarily in the form of text but also in the form of materiality more broadly defined. A common feature of text and materiality is that they have *restance* (Cooren, 2004).

Text and materiality

Text and materiality are the surface of the brand. Accordingly, the material and visual representation makes the brand present (see Cooren et al., 2008; Taylor & Van Every, 1999; Vásquez et al., 2013). For anything to be present to us, it must have been mediated, and Cooren et al. (2008, p. 1343) use the term *presentification* to "signify the activities involved in making something or somebody present to something or somebody else". The scholars argue that it is through various materialities – whether these are texts, bodies, architectural elements, or artifacts – that something is experienced as having a presence, and people's experience of the world is thus intimately tied to how something is made present to them.

In a study of the MSF (Médecins Sans Frontières), Cooren et al. (2008) describe how the organization is made present in Paris through the buildings in the neighborhood of the 11th arrondissement that represent its Parisian headquarters, representatives of the organization, emails, meetings, an official MSF card, and documents. In the Democratic Republic of the Congo, MSF is made present by other representatives: a white all-terrain Toyota vehicle bearing a flag with the MSF logo and the continuous use of the MSF logo on jeeps, hospital entrances and on the doors of the compounds that MSF rents to its members. This use of particular signs helped to show where

MSF was even though its presence was never fixed and, in this way, the signs served as documentary evidence of MSF's presence in the region. Human and non-human actors, such as physicians, surgeons, nurses, and medical equipment, coproduced MSF's presence by interacting in the organization's name, and the scholars conclude that MSF is literally what its members, documents, and instruments do in its name.

I argue that a brand needs to be made present in the same way as an organization does. A brand is thus experienced through various materialities as it is these materialities that give the brand 'staying capacity' (Cooren, 2004), and enable us to experience the brand. However, text and materiality serve not only to make the brand present; as already argued, text and conversation form a self-organizing loop (Koschmann, 2013; Kuhn, 2008; Taylor & Van Every, 1999).

Inspired by Michel Foucault and his work on how the discursive formations of language become the institutional bases of power, Taylor (1999) seeks to explain how language-as-text informs language-as-speech as well as how the interactive patterns of conversation come to be embedded in language as structure. Text/materiality is the raw material of conversations as it informs and guides them, but text/materiality is also the product of conversational processes and it allows conversations to move through time and space as materiality provides a record of past conversations (Putnam, 2013). Earlier it was suggested that conversations about brand meaning in the conversational space would be informed and constrained by the interlocutors' repertoire and their ability to call to mind different kinds of knowledge. We see now that conversations about the brand and the creation of brand meaning are also informed by texts about the brand (e.g. the written proclamation of brand values, a slogan, a brand promise or pay off) or the organization (e.g. strategies, policies, website), and it becomes clear what is meant by the proposition that text and conversation form a self-organizing loop. Texts feed into conversations about the brand, and at the same time such conversations about brand meaning will produce texts (e.g. minutes, decisions, action plans) that express brand meaning and inform future work. Organizational members will thus take on different roles as authors and readers, when they engage in branding activities (Dean et al., 2016; Golant, 2012), and brand meaning will constantly evolve on the basis of these activities. It also follows that

> the production of a text is inherently a social event (there must be a reader as well as an author, a hearer as well as a speaker, for it even to be a text), and so the production of a text-world is simultaneously the production of a discourse-world, realized in conversation.
>
> Taylor & Van Every (1999, p. 325)

The production of text and materiality is an important re-semiotization because it creates a *surface* to the brand (i.e., makes it present), but equally important, it provides attestation of initiatives and decisions agreed upon in conversational activities. When talk is re-semiotisized into print (text/materiality), it is formalized, and stakeholders show their commitment to the text by "'signing it off' as a true and accurate record of their concerns, wishes and agreements" (Iedema, 1999, p. 51). Therefore, meanings presented in printed written texts are harder to challenge than talk (Iedema, 2003), as the texts supposedly represent a decision already agreed upon. In this sense, the production of text/materiality produces imbrication. When conversation is written down (e.g., the minutes of a meeting), the account is frozen, and the freezing is a way of stitching conversations together (Taylor & Van Every, 2011).

As explicated earlier, a text can come to function as a non-human actor and thus produce hybrid agency. When, for instance, a brand pay-off is written down and published in the organization (and possibly to the outside world), the pay-off is removed from situated interactions (see Putnam, 2013) and distanciated from the original author(s). Therefore, it is no longer seen as the creation by a single person or by brand management. When the author of a text becomes invisible, it is now the text that becomes invested with authority (Koschmann, 2013; Taylor, 2011).The text then gains an existence of its own as a macro-actor that has the capacity to create "the 'rules of the game' to which actors orient" (Kuhn, 2008, p. 1234). A translation from an individual to a collective agency takes place (Putnam, 2013), and the pay-off is no longer seen as a text from someone. It is seen to act in the name of the brand hence it is the brand that speaks through that text (ventriloquism).

The production of a text is an abstraction, and abstraction bolsters the authority of the text (Koschmann, 2013) since it is more flexible and can accommodate multiple interpretations:

> Meanings presented in printed written text are generally harder to challenge, not only because the writer is often not present to answer questions, change formulations or accept additions, but also because written registers are generally more abstract and generalizing than spoken ones.
>
> Iedema (2003, p. 42)

Due to the 'staying capacity' of materiality, text and materiality can be transported and thus transcend the situation of production to become available for appropriation in different contexts (Kuhn, 2012). There is, however, no guarantee that a text (or another kind of materiality) is received, decoded, and used in the original intentionality of its author. Each reading of a permanent text constitutes a re-contextualization, and the meaning re-found in the text not only stems from the text itself but also from the new situational context that frames its reading (Taylor et al., 1996). Since a text is a non-human actor, it can never act on its own. It needs to be appropriated or ventriloquized in order to co-produce a hybrid agency.

The notion of a fluid *discursive brand space* that is constantly being re-constructed has now been explicated by a *flatland view*. The flatland view establishes that communication is both the *site* and the *surface* of branding. Branding is the day-to-day branding practices, which embraces talk-in-interaction or 'the doing' of discourse as well as texts and materiality that can be understood as 'the done' discourses or the representation of talk-in-interaction.

The first part of theorizing in the CCB approach can thus be supplemented with an understanding of the role of text and materiality. The second part of theorizing proposes:

4   A brand is made present through materiality.
5   Text and materiality are the outputs of 'doing discourse' in the discursive brand space, but they are also the inputs to these conversations.
6   Text and materiality are non-human actors that become part of different hybrid constellations, and hence their agency cannot be controlled.

From branding activities to brand

As suggested above, a text (i.e. a brand pay off) can be seen to ventriloquize the brand, and in order for a brand to act as a ventriloquist, it must have been constituted as a macro-actor. Drawing on insights from the CCO literature, collective identity or collective agency is typically associated with the conceptualization of an entity. A brand is more often than not conceptualized as an entity, even though it has no intrinsic materiality. For instance, Lury (2004, p. 1) writes that, "the brand is an object. What might this mean? An object surely, is something that is external, fixed, closed; something solid that can be touched. The brand is none of these things".

Nicotera (2013) has been looking into how we get from individual conversations to the understanding of something as an entity and, with reference to a framework developed by Taylor et al. (1996), she suggests that a critical step in the process of going from talk/conversation to entitative being is the re-semiotization of conversation into some permanent or semi-permanent medium. Inscribing an account in a permanent medium is the first step toward *distanciation* (Taylor & Van Every, 2011). When conversation is transcribed into text, it is objectified, and the re-contextualization of meaning from one discourse or practice to another is a cornerstone of how formality is constructed in organizational settings (Iedema, 1999). Text and materiality serve to materialize the brand as an entity in its own right. In order for brand meaning or brand value to be formalized, it is thus important that conversational discourses are re-contextualized into a permanent or semi-permanent medium to create *restance*. Text/materiality becomes a materialization and reification of branding activities, and the reification of branding activities in text and materiality ascribes object-ivity to the brand (Lury, 2004).

When the brand is constituted as an entity, it comes to function as a frame and a boundary setting device that orders and structures the branding practices (Vásquez et al., 2013). Lury (2004, p. 1) explains the brand as "a platform for the patterning of activity, a mode of organizing activities in time and space", and Vásquez et al. (2013, p. 140), explains the way "the brand acts as a frame that is mobilized to make sense of a situation, account for it, and decide what to do". The brand as macro-actor enacts boundaries to the discursive brand space by informing organizational members about which discourses are relevant to the brand, and thus which discourses ought to be included or excluded. Hence, understanding the brand as a macro-actor is closely linked to the idea of brand-as-entity.

Though the re-semiotization of conversations into material representation is an important step in the creation of entitative being, materiality in itself is not sufficient.

> A socially signified entity can be said to have *entitative being* (or to *be* an entitative being) when, by virtue of authority attributed to it, its identity *transcends and eclipses any human individual or human collective*. The entitative being, though it emerges from a human collective, is itself a nonhuman.
>
> Nicotera (2013, p. 68, italics in original)

In order for a brand to gain entitative being, it thus needs to establish an identity that transcends and eclipses any single discourses and any human actors or collectives.

Polyphony in the discursive brand space

The discursive brand space is not only constituted by discourses produced by the organization, but also by discourses originating from external stakeholders (Leitch & Richardson, 2003; Vásquez et al., 2013), and brand meaning is conversationally co-created by multiple stakeholders (Hatch & Schultz, 2008; Iglesias et al., 2013; Ind, 2014). Even though (brand) managers can design formal *conversational spaces*, and thereby try to influence access by enacting boundaries, these boundaries can be transcended and expanded, hence the boundaries of the discursive brand space are fluid and negotiated in discursive struggles. Accordingly, conversational spaces are polyphonic arenas with fluid boundaries, and the fluidity of boundaries is the focus of this section.

Leitch and Richardson (2003) illustrate how the health discourse intermingles with the advertisement discourse in the tobacco industry: "[I]n some countries the health discourse now overlaps with the marketing discourse in cigarette advertisements when advertisements promoting the consumption of tobacco products are overlaid with messages from the surgeon general advising the health risks" (Leitch & Richardson, 2003, p. 1069). The health discourse is what Alvesson and Karreman (2000) conceptualize as a capital D-discourse (i.e. a macro Discourse). A capital D-discourse is a universal, historically situated set of vocabulary about a certain phenomenon. Fairhurst and Putnam (2004, p. 7) describe Discourses "as general and enduring systems of thought" versus small d-discourse as "the study of talk and text in social practices". A capital D-discourse is a Discourse that you recognize (Cooren, 2015), and capital D-discourse is thus inspired by Foucauldian thinking, given that Discourses order and naturalize the world in particular ways

(Taylor & Van Every, 2011). Capital D-discourses signify the idea that it is possible to identify over-arching themes in everyday conversations (Alvesson & Karreman, 2000), and such overarching themes can be found both at the organizational level as well as societal level. D-discourses at the organizational level could, for instance, be Discourses about customer service, management style or cultural assumptions. Examples of Discourses at societal level could be professional Discourses, Discourses about CSR, or a legal Discourse.

Capital D-discourses will inform the interlocutors about what is deemed right or wrong, and good or bad, or how things ought to be done, because invoking a capital D-discourse can be understood as invoking a frame. Activating a frame creates expectations about what is important, as the frame represents a prototypical way of understanding the issue (Christensen & Cornelissen, 2011). A frame can also be referred to as an idealized cognitive model or script which organizational members use "to make inferences in context, to make default assumptions about unmentioned aspects of situations, and to make predictions about the consequences of their actions" (Christensen & Cornelissen, 2011, p. 399). In their research of the rebranding of a university, Vásquez et al. (2017b) demonstrate how different Discourses are at play in the micro meaning negotiations taking place. Their analysis revealed that at each turning point in the branding process "a different Discourse was drawn on and mobilized to bind elements in order to establish the university's identity. In other words, in each instance, this Discourse shaped the construction of the brand" (p. 24). As such, Discourses function as non-human macro-actors in the discursive brand space.

D-discourses as macro-actors

A Discourse is a macro-actor, because a Discourse does not belong to a single person, but rather a society or a profession. Hence, Discourses express collective agency. By invoking a Discourse, interlocutors can invoke the authority of, for instance, the institution or profession from which the Discourse originates or is seen to ventriloquize (see Cooren et al., 2013). Since Discourses are loaded with a certain worldview, perspective or way of understanding the world, they can be used to argue for the relevance or the rightness of something (or the opposite) as "[i]ssues do not simply arise, but are defined by certain parties, confined within a certain linguistic frame of reference, and, most powerfully, identified discursively" (Kornberger et al., 2006, p. 13). When one ventriloquizes a Discourse, one does not just speak in the name of oneself, but rather on behalf of the collectivity associated with that Discourse. Macro Discourses can be invoked by organizational members as part of the brand discourses, but they may also be invoked by other interlocutors as a way of making demands on the brand. Leitch and Richardson (2003) mention how a health Discourse has become part of the branding discourses in the tobacco industry. Another example might be CSR Discourses that can be invoked by both internal and external members of the organization in order to demand social or environmental responsibility. Yet, macro-actors may be macro-acting, but it always happens in a micro-world of interaction (Taylor &

Van Every, 1999). Capital D-discourses cannot invoke themselves; they need to be appropriated by interlocutors who ventriloquize the Discourse and thus bring into play the worldview and authority embodied in that Discourse. That is, the person who ventriloquizes a Discourse, invites a new macro-actor into the conversational space, and it becomes even more clear why the boundaries of the conversational space are not corporeal, but linguistic.

In the study of discourse – the everyday conversations and interactions – it will be possible to identify a number of Discourses when, for instance, technical terms are used, since these words have what Bakhtin refers to as the "taste" of their profession and thus invoke a particular Discourse according to how the world is understood in this profession (Cooren et al., 2013). Every discourse is polyphonic and heteroglot since "[a]ll words have the 'taste' of a profession, a genre, a tendency, a party, a particular work, a particular person, a generation, an age group, the day and hour" (Bakhtin 1981/1975, in Cooren & Sandler, 2014, p. 225). To understand what is going on in the daily communicational activities, and hence the meaning of discourses, it is necessary to examine which Discourses are invoked and how they inform discourse because "[m]eaning is not present in the single sentence or statement (message) but in how it ties together with other elements in the discursive formation of which it is a component" (Taylor & Van Every, 1999, p. 30).

As soon as one starts to talk about the creation of a brand, a number of discourses are being interwoven; initial brand meaning is created on the basis of these discourses. When Discourses are invoked, external stakeholders, such as institutions, other organizations, legislators or even predominant Discourses in the media, become non-human actors in the conversational space. It follows that it makes no sense to talk about 'internal' versus 'external' stakeholders as external stakeholders function as ventriloquists when Discourses are ventriloquized by internal organizational members, and thus speak through them. No man is a tabula rasa and thus interaction will always comprise hybrid agency as actors are mobilized and enabled by different Discourses.

The *discursive brand space* is thus a bricolage of discourses produced by various actors, human and non-human alike. The production of discourses happens in a number of *conversational spaces*. The term *conversational space* relates to the setting of a space where discourses can unfold. It is relevant to consider the *conversational space*, when one is interested in how organizational members (or others) design such a space in order to promote (desired) brand discourses. Some actors are explicitly present in the form of materiality, whereas others are only present as Discourses (or other actors) that are being ventriloquized. It is clear that the boundaries of a conversational space can never be guarded. Brand management is thus not able to control who participates in the production of brand discourses. The brand emerges in a process of lamination where some discourses are repeated or referred to again and again in oral and written text. This produces a discursive closure (Putnam in Robichaud & Cooren, 2013), where these discourses transcend the pluralism of many voices and become central to the brand. Discursive closures ascribe meaning to the brand, but to establish a closure something must be positioned as part of the discourse and other things as outside, that is, a closure requires the establishment of limits (Selg & Ventsel, 2008). However, a brand has no intrinsic materiality, and thus no obvious limits. Accordingly, a brand becomes a boundary object, where different participants try to negotiate the limits of the brand (Edlinger, 2015; Vásquez et al., 2013), and any discursive closure will only be momentary. A brand does not exist outside its communicational *incarnations*,[1] but yet a 'brand' is an immaterial, abstract construction. A brand thus navigates between concreteness and abstractness. It is an idea or a value that materializes itself through various incarnations that make it (or parts of it) present in a certain moment for certain people (see Cooren, 2012).

Having explicated how a brand can be understood and studied as a *discursive brand space*, I will now turn my attention to the notion of the brand manager. A brand manager is usually portrayed as the one who makes decisions about the brand, and thus decides what the brand is. In the CCB approach, the brand is conceptualized as a discursive brand space, and I have argued that this space is fluid and open to negotiation, and thus impossible to control. The CCB approach thus radically alters the idea about what brand management entails. Iglesias et al. (2013) call for a new understanding of brand management one which is more humble, open and participatory, since managers will need to accept a loss of control. Alongside this, Golant (2012) suggests the need to understand the brand manager as a *practical author*.

Practical authorship

The notion of the manager as a practical author was first presented by Shotter (1993) and later discussed in Holman and Thorpe (2003). The concept of the practical author is inspired by the understanding that an author creates a text in a felt unity with his or her readers (Shotter & Cunliffe, in Holman & Thorpe, 2003). Accordingly, practical authorship "treats communication as a relationally responsive dialogical activity, where the production of meaning is negotiated through circuits of sense-giving and sense-making that creates for participants a unique sense of their shared circumstances" (Golant, 2012, p. 117). *Sensegiving* attempts to create a preferred definition of organizational reality (Gioia & Chittipeddi, 1991), and "*sensemaking* is about how people construct their own reality" (Nijhof & Jeurissen, 2006, p. 316). The essence of 'practical authorship' is that "meanings are created in the spontaneously coordinated interplay of people's responsive relations to each other" (Shotter & Cunliffe in Holman & Thorpe, 2003, p. 17).

When a brand is conceptualized as a *discursive brand space*, managers will need to give up the idea that a brand can be managed and controlled. What (brand) managers can seek to influence is the language that is used to discuss the brand. An important management task thus becomes to develop and promote a brand-language as well as brand-discourses. Managers can seek to promote desired discourses as well as counteract or contradict discourses that are conflicting with the desired hegemonic brand discourse. It is important to articulate the (desired) boundaries of the brand space. As argued by Hatch and Schultz (2008), a brand must claim its territory. Therefore, I find Golant's (2012) conceptualization of the brand manager as a practical author very useful in explaining the management of brands from a communication as constitutive perspective, and I will elaborate on Golant's work in order to extend it to embrace CCO thinking.

Golant (2012) suggests that the task of the brand manager becomes to "promote conversations that matter to the brand's audiences, and through which the corporate brand can be refined and elaborated in new and unexpected ways" (p. 117). Brand managers must work with sensegiving by creating intelligible formulations of organizational reality. The task is to produce stories that order the chaotic welter of impressions, and through this interpretation provide actors with a direction for action. Selg and Ventsel (2010) argue that in order to create a hegemonic discourse, discrete elements need to be translated into a non-discrete or a coherent whole. In relation to brand management, it means that discrete brand elements need to be translated into one or more coherent narrative that expresses the desired brand meaning and explain how the different brand elements are interrelated.

Employees can be recruited as co-authors of the corporate brand, especially if the brand positioning is based on a validation of organizational members' expertise. Such a positioning is based on a recognition of the fact that it is the on-going practices that create brand value. Therefore, in order to engage the employees as active co-authors, it is necessary to develop a language that is able to articulate this role and thus aid the employees in their sensemaking towards an understanding of themselves as brand authors. Brand value must be re-produced on a daily basis, and discourses about the brand can assist the employees to self-monitor their performance as well as to challenge and support colleagues. In his study, Golant (2012) demonstrates how employees were able to draw on the aspirational brand discourse as a resource to boost their morale and challenge conventions. He thus concludes that brand management depended less on the exercise of explicit directions by management, and more on the way and the extent to which aspirational brand discourses were appropriated by organizational members and understood as central to their work identities.

From a CCB perspective, brand management is a relational activity (Cunliffe, 2001). The *discursive brand space* is a contested space of sensegiving and sensemaking. Brand meaning is therefore "constructed *dialogically between* managers and others in everyday conversations" (ibid. p. 354, italics in original). To manage a brand is thus to provide a (new) language, one that is able to express existing or desirable brand values. Being a skillful brand manager is to be responsive and reflexive to the everyday use of (brand) language. Brand meaning cannot simply by constructed by the author, as "meaning depends upon the responsiveness of the listener(s)" (Cunliffe, 2001, p. 366). It is also important to bear in mind that the meaning of the brand is articulated as much in the informal conversations among employees as by customers and other stakeholders in different social networks, brand communities and online forums (i.e. different conversational spaces) (Golant, 2012). A brand manager should therefore be sensitive to the different discourses that feed into the *discursive brand space*. It means that brand management must pay attention to both the small d- and capital D-discourses that are articulated either directly or through ventriloquism. The establishment of (provisional) boundaries to the *discursive brand space* is a question of advancing discourses that express desired brand meaning and try to counteract discourses that conflict with this meaning. The *discursive brand space* can be enriched by embracing new discourses, as long as these discourses are compatible with the hegemonic discourse the organization tries to produce, as "any imagined reality can always be updated or renegotiated" (Cunliffe, 2001). But practical brand authorship is not only about promoting desired discourses. As pinpointed by Selg and Ventsel (2010), something needs to be created (constructed) as an outside in order to produce boundaries, and thus express the substance of the *discursive brand space* more clearly. Hence, constructing a *discursive brand space* is about promoting and sustaining desired discourses (as well as marking a stance) by counteracting undesired ones, and thus demarcating the *discursive brand space*. Authoring a brand is thus a steady process of sensemaking and sensegiving as organizational members continuously have to make sense of the multiple and diverse discourses that present themselves in the discursive brand space. Organizational members also need to consider whether these discourses ought to be adopted and integrated in the discursive brand space or whether they should enact a boundary by counteracting some of these discourses.

The notion of the brand manager as a practical author thus brings a new perspective to the traditional understanding of brand management that focuses on brand alignment, as presented in Chapter 1. In classic branding theory, the important role of managers and employees to communicate and act out brand values was recognized, but it was based on an understanding of communication of already established brand values. Practical authorship emphasizes that the brand is continually being scripted or authored, and the challenge for brand managers is then, to listen, to seek to coordinate and integrate, and to orchestrate brand discourses. The process of authoring involves all kinds of stakeholders, but employees are naturally ascribed a central role as they are members of the organization, and the ones to 'articulate the brand'.

Authoring brand meaning

As already suggested, brand managers are engaged in sensegiving, when they point out and label activities in order to help employees make sense of the chaotic welter of impressions (Cunliffe, 2001; Golant, 2012; Holman & Thorpe, 2003; Shotter, 2008). Sensegiving is achieved through linguistic resources such as stories, metaphors, labelling, archetypes, and contradiction.

> Metaphors and stories can provide ways of crossing the boundaries of discourse to create a sufficient common sense to allow us to act within a

context. They open up possibilities for connecting by creating images that strike the imagination of other participants in the conversation.

Cunliffe (2001, p. 365)

Sensegiving is thus about *identifying* and *promoting* key discourses as the discursive brand space is *talked into existence*.

Theoretically *sensegiving* and *sensemaking* can be separated as the way someone tries to create a preferred definition of organizational reality and the way people construct their own reality, but in practice the two are entwined, since *sensegiving* is contingent upon *sensemaking*. In order to participate in the deliberate production of meaning, one has to have first determined for oneself what reality is or ought to look like. But as will be seen in Chapter 6, sensemaking sometimes emerges in the course of conversation as organizational members discuss brand meaning. Efforts of sensemaking thus result in sensegiving when organizational members agree on a definition of reality. A brand is thus authored by everybody who participates in producing the *discursive brand space*, but not all voices are equally heard or recognized. Ways to produce authority include the production of hybrid agency for instance in the form of a textual macro-actor or by multiplying the sources of authorship for instance by the use of ventriloquism. Hence, it is not only managers that can function as practical authors, but (brand) managers ought to assume a certain responsibility to do so, and a central task of the brand manager as practical author is thus also to pay attention to the set-up of conversational spaces, as conversations about the brand are affected by who is invited to participate in the conversational space as well as the affordances put forward by different material settings (as explained earlier).

Skillful and practical (brand) authors are able to explicate vague understandings (see Cunliffe, 2001). Brand features are not real but imagined in discourse, and the role of (brand) management is thus to promote a language and a number of discourses that articulate these imagined features. Practical authorship focuses on the successful creation of a hegemonic brand discourse that expresses the desired brand meaning. The *discursive brand space* is continually being authored, and authorship always happens in living response to circumstances. Brand management is therefore an emerging and embodied practice (ibid.). The last part of CCB theorizing thus proposes that:

7   Non-human actors can animate other actors and thus participate by proxy in the conversational space.
8   Since brand meaning emerges as some actors succeed in creating a (provisional) hegemonic brand discourse, the brand manager ought to function as a practical author, seeing that the discursive brand space is continually being authored.

2.4 Summary

With this chapter, I hope to have explicated a 'communication as constitutive' approach to branding – what I propose to label the CCB approach (Communication as Constitutive of Brand).

In a CCB approach, a brand is conceptualized as a *discursive brand space* in which brand meaning emerges as a *bricolage of discourses*, and the task for brand managers is to create/promote a brand language and to influence discourses in order to produce a desirable hegemonic brand discourse. At the same time, the brand manager needs to acknowledge that brand meaning cannot be controlled as meaning is negotiated in interaction and co-produced by other participants in a number of *conversational spaces*. The term conversational space refers to the facilitation of conversation, that is, the settings of spaces that make interaction possible or the *site* of 'doing branding'. The task of brand managers is therefore, not only to influence discourses by paying attention to the use of language, but also by paying attention to who is invited to participate in (or excluded from) the conversational space. The inclusion of certain actors is a way to inspire the talk (the doing of brand discourse) in the conversational space but talk/interactions can also be influenced by the affordances of the material settings of the conversational space. However, access to the conversational space can never be controlled as the boundaries are not corporeal but constituted discursively. Actors may participate by proxy as people, Discourses or other actors can be ventriloquized by participants.

The study of branding thus implies the study of a discourse-world as well as a text-world, as suggested by the *flatland view*, since communication is the *site* and *surface* of branding. A brand is brought into being as it is performed discursively or acted out, hence branding happens through social interactions, conversations and co-orientations that produce different types of text and materiality. These materialities give restance to the discursive brand space and produce imbrication of meanings. Talk and text/materiality inform each other and are thus co-constitutive. If these activities are no longer performed, the brand will cease to exist. A brand exists in communication, is made present in interaction, and is incarnated by human and nonhuman agents. The propositions in the CCB approach can thus be summarized as:

1 Brands are partly constituted in the 'doing of discourse' in both formal and informal communication and are affected by participants' repertoire.
2 The 'doing of discourse' takes place in a conversational space and is shaped by the material settings and its affordances as well as the participants.
3 The boundaries of the conversational space are not corporeal but constituted discursively.
4 A brand is made present through materiality.
5 Text and materiality are the output of 'doing discourse' in the discursive brand space, but it is also the input to these conversations.
6 Text and materiality are non-human actors that become part of different hybrid constellations, and hence their agency cannot be controlled.

7 Non-human actors can animate other actors and thus participate by proxy in the conversational space.

8 Since brand meaning emerges as some actors succeed in creating a (provisional) hegemonic brand discourse, the brand manager ought to function as a practical author, seeing that the discursive brand space is continually being authored.

The CCB approach offers an enhanced understanding of what it entails when we say that a brand is 'communicatively constituted', and it suggests the notion of a *discursive brand space* and a *conversational space* as important entry points when we want to analyze a brand from this perspective. The eight points summarized above should not be understood as an exhaustive list of what a 'communication as constitutive' approach to branding entails, but as an invitation to engage in the dialogue and further explicate and discuss the emerging CCB approach.

Note

1 Cooren et al. (2008) argue that presentification is made possible through *incarnation*. In order for something to be made present, it must be embodied or incarnated in some way. Incarnation thus refers to "all the activities that make a given social collectivity present through interacting human and nonhuman agents" (p. 1343).

3 Case presentation

In this chapter, I will present a case study that functions as an example throughout the book. The case study originates from my PhD dissertation, in relation to which I conducted a longitudinal single-case study based on a method of *passing organizational ethnography*. The notion of passing organizational ethnography accepts the premise that an organization is a "Tamara play". It is impossible to observe everything that goes on as many things happen simultaneously, and, therefore, passing organizational ethnography rejects the traditional idea of 'total immersion' in favor of an ambition to seek as much context as can reasonably be obtained. I was interested in observing 'instances' of 'doing branding', and accordingly, I attended meetings about brand development and talked to employees at all levels about their engagement in the brand.

Documents and materiality

My observations included the collection of documents and materiality related to the brand, because text and materiality are ascribed fundamental importance in the CCB-approach. Documents are active agents with relational properties that participate in structuring relationships (Lee, 2012), and analyses of documentary evidence can provide an important contribution in broader ethnographic studies of organizational life.

The obvious documents to collect were the texts (e.g. emails, agendas, minutes, enclosures) related to the brand meetings, but Yanow (2012) reminds the researcher that organizational ethnography embraces all kinds of texts, including documentary sources and physical artifacts. I used *targeted sampling* (Linders, 2008) to collect the documents and artifacts that were used to consciously communicate the brand.

3.1 Presentation of organization and situational background

Globalco is a family owned, European conglomerate with companies in more than 120 countries and branches that cover a broad area. The case centers on the headquarters, where each branch is represented.

DOI: 10.4324/9781003050100-3

All subsidiaries were operated as independent and autonomous companies in their own name. In other words, Globalco employed a house of brands strategy (Aaker & Joachimsthaler, 2000) where the subsidiaries (subbrands) were positioned individually with a targeted value proposition to their niche customers. Globalco had solely functioned as a holding company and has only been present as a board of directors. In this sense, Globalco has not been visible in everyday organizational life. In 2017, the decision was made to launch "Kind2Mind" as a conglomerate wide corporate branding strategy. The name "Kind2Mind" (K2M) had existed for a number of years, but it was generally regarded as a brand positioning, stemming from the subsidiary Apparella, and K2M was also closely associated with Sam, one of the owners.

The history of K2M

The brand K2M had been coined by Sam in collaboration with a business partner, and since Sam held a position in Apparella at the time of the first promotion of K2M, K2M is generally understood to originate from Apparella. In the late 1990s and henceforward, Apparella embarked on a number of new branding activities, generally focusing on a social cause. According to the managing director of Apparella, these activities were not part of an overall branding strategy, but the management team found the activities cool and fun to do, and it turned out that they also created some awareness. The engagement was generally seen as a clear statement of Sam's Buddhist-inspired way of doing business, and he talked about "Kind2Mind" as a new way of doing business.

The use of K2M in Globalco

The concept of K2M is thus understood to originate from Sam (and his business partner), but it is also linked to Apparella. When Apparella formulated their 2020-strategy, they phrased their value proposition as "Springle kindness everywhere" and K2M became the overall branding strategy. The branding strategy was strengthened in 2018, when Dave was employed as Kindness Developer.

Due to the use of a 'house of brands' branding strategy, the Globalco brand had been more or less invisible, so even though there had been a strong link between K2M and Apparella, K2M had not been related to Globalco. Internally, K2M had been promoted at a couple of events, but K2M had not been employed by subsidiaries other than Apparella. However, in 2017 it was decided that K2M would be launched as a conglomerate wide corporate branding strategy.

Further development of K2M: establishment of a steering group

When the decision was made to launch K2M as a conglomerate wide corporate branding strategy, a steering group was appointed. The steering group was assembled with the aim to further develop K2M as a brand and execute the new branding strategy. The steering group comprised Sam (CEO and co-owner) and a middle manager from each of the five subsidiaries (the main branches). In the following section, I will sum up the brand development in a case description covering three years of organizational life and ten steering group meetings (SGMs).

3.2 Case description

At the first steering group meeting, the K2M branding strategy is presented to all of the subsidiaries with the aim of further developing the strategy. The brand K2M had been conceptualized in a chart that is presented at the meeting. The chart divides K2M into three legs or pillars named "CSR and sustainable growth", "Branding", and "Corporate Culture". With the chart as a point of departure, the discussion focuses on what K2M entails and how the brand can be implemented in all subsidiaries. The main purpose of "CSR and sustainable growth" is to identify a number of KPIs (Key Performance Indicators) that can feed into the CSR report that Globalco needs to publish once a year. "Branding" is about identifying a number of branding projects that can express K2M's core values, and the main purpose of "Corporate Culture" is to mobilize employees to do voluntary work and upload their Kind2Mind projects on a special subsite of the Globalco website.

At the meeting it is acknowledged that it has been challenging for everybody to understand the concept of K2M. There had been talk about engaging the managing directors of each subsidiary, but that idea has been abandoned in favour of first having a discussion in the steering group in order to reach a common understanding before involving the managing directors. The managing directors are repeatedly referred to as the main stakeholders and the ones to lead the process of incorporating K2M, but they have not been invited to the steering group meeting. The explanation given by Sam is that there would be "too many chiefs" at the meeting.

As a way of involving the managing directors, it is decided to leave the identification of KPIs to them. The managing directors get to define their own areas of concern and they get to formulate the goals. A deadline is proposed, and the middle managers are instructed to arrange a meeting with their managing directors. The meeting is concluded with a promise to work out a set of guidelines to ensure some kind of uniformity as to how the process is addressed in the subsidiaries, and Sam is encouraged to send out a director's email before the middle managers are to have their first meeting with the managing directors in order to "set the scene". However, the guidelines are never produced, and the director's email is not sent out until much later in the process.

Roughly three weeks after the first steering group meeting, Anna (a middle manager) summons a meeting in GoNuGa. The subsidiaries GoNutri and GoGastro market themselves jointly as the GoNuGa Group, and hence the meeting with the managing directors is arranged as a joint meeting. Two middle managers from the steering group are present. The director's email has not been sent out yet, so the managing directors have not been informed about any of the decisions made at SGM1 or what is expected of them. One of the middle managers initiates the meeting by setting out to explain the K2M chart which she has illustrated on a white board, and there is a discussion about how the notion of KPIs is to be understood in the context of the K2M chart. Due to many factors of uncertainty, they do not decide on any KPIs but they decide to work from UN Global Compacts with a special emphasis on environment.

A week later, the steering group meets again. The aim of this second meeting is to present the KPIs identified in each subsidiary and discuss objectives for improvement of the identified areas. However, it is evident that all subsidiaries have had problems identifying KPIs, never mind setting objectives. A middle manager initiates the meeting by telling Sam that they need some more information about the KPIs. The participants at SGM2 agree that KPIs ought to be identified according to UN Global Compact.

The discussion about how to set and measure KPIs takes up most of the meeting, but they also discuss the K2M projects each subsidiary needs to establish. The subsidiaries prefer to work with local projects in order to make them relevant to their employees, but Sam prefers high profile international projects that stand out at fairs and business meetings. In contrast to the subsidiaries, he is not concerned about employee involvement as he believes employee involvement is to be obtained via the "Corporate culture" part of the K2M chart. A key element in the "Corporate culture" part of K2M is the launch of a new webpage (MyK2M.com), where employees can upload their personal "My K2M project". A "My K2M project" can be anything from coaching a football team in the local club to raising money for the Red Cross. Sam, Lucy, and Dave believe that many Globalco employees are involved in voluntary work, and they want to showcase all the good initiatives on the MyK2M.com webpage in order to brand K2M via their employees and their acts of "doing good". When an employee uploads a "My K2M project" at the webpage, he or she participates in the competition to win €1,500 for the cause they are engaged in, and the money is sponsored by Globalco. The site will be launched at the upcoming Globalco event the following day, and the participants at SGM2 spend some time discussing how they can get employees to upload their projects, who should elect the winning project and how it should be done.

By the end of the meeting, Sam and Lucy promise that a director's email will be sent out to inform the managing directors about the decisions made at the steering group meetings and to inform them about the procedure of identifying KPIs.

The next day, a Globalco event is hosted. The Globalco event is a new initiative that is supposed to brand Globalco as an organization and spur a sense of collective identity. Every employee receives a gift certificate of five chickens that have been donated through a charity organization to a family in Africa on behalf of the employee. Globalco thus engages the employees in "doing good". The new upcoming MyK2M.com webpage is presented, and the participants at the event are asked to cast a vote in order to elect the winning "My K2M project" from among three. The winning project has been uploaded by an employee from GoTech, who volunteers at a local go-cart pitch; he receives a big cardboard check worth €1,500 for the go-cart pitch.

A week after the event, a middle manager summons another meeting in GoNuGa. The middle manager informs the managing directors that they have to present the KPIs at the business lunch in December. But the managing directors state that it is impossible since they need to gather information about energy consumption from the subsidiaries in order to identify a point of reference. They discuss the complexity of measuring energy consumption since it needs to be related to production.

The managing directors would prefer that the K2M (branding) projects are decided and run by Globalco since they do not feel that they have the expertise or insight to identify an appropriate project, even less so to run it. However, they agree to identify what the subsidiaries are already doing today and to compile that information in a CSR document. They reach the conclusion that they should write a letter to the subsidiaries asking for information about energy consumption and what CSR-related branding projects they are carrying out at the moment. But then they realize that they should not involve the subsidiaries until they have received the director's email in case it should contain information that would affect the plan they have agreed upon. They decide not to take further action until their focus areas have been approved and they have received the director's email.

Two weeks later, the steering group meets again (SGM3). The meeting starts rather informally, and the participants brainstorm about MyK2M.com and the social movement that Sam hopes to spur. After the informal brainstorming process, the meeting continues as a roundtable discussion where each middle manager presents the KPIs they have decided on.

The subsidiaries have succeeded in defining focus areas but they are still unable to supply any specific numbers about current energy consumption. Though GoTech, for instance, states that they will ensure a 20% reduction of waste and energy, they do not know what the current numbers are or how they are going to measure the reduction, and GoNuGa, GoDeliver, and Apparella are even vaguer on their KPIs. Sam requests that they document the current numbers before Christmas. Based on the complexity of setting realistic objectives for the KPIs, he sets a deadline four months ahead for when they have another meeting planned.

At the fourth steering group meeting (SGM4), Sam opens by establishing the importance of CSR, based on the fact that Globalco is required by law to produce a yearly CSR-report. He underscores the importance of the work they are doing in this group, stating that it is not just something they do because they find it fun and enjoyable, rather that it is required by law. Lucy has produced a Globalco code of conduct that establishes some guidelines for the work with K2M that she presents in a PowerPoint presentation. After Lucy has presented the elements of the new Globalco code of conduct, the participants move on to a roundtable, where each middle manager has to present their progress with the KPI-work. In general, the work with KPIs is still very hesitant.

The third part of the meeting concentrates on the launch of the new My K2M webpage. As an initiative to generate traffic to MyK2M.com, Lucy introduces an activity which she calls the "Buddha baton". The idea is to have a Buddha figure travel in the suitcase or briefcase of employees to visit Globalco sites all over the world. When an employee receives a visit from the Buddha, the employee is supposed to take some photos and write a story that tells of what the Buddha has experienced and post it on the My K2M webpage. The employee then passes the Buddha on to a colleague, who takes up the baton. Lucy hopes that the Buddha baton will create some interesting and different content to My K2M that will make it attractive for the organizational members to use the page.

The fifth steering group meeting is characterized by the presence of more people than usual. It has been a concern on Sam's part whether the participants in the steering group are the right people. Consequently, this time more people have been invited, including two people from a subsidiary that is only partly owned by Globalco, but renowned for its prominent work with CSR. As usual they go round the table and each subsidiary has to present a progress report. Some of the subsidiaries are able to present slight progress but Sam is still not satisfied with the speed of the process and he questions why it is so hard to produce the requested figures.

Sam initiates another roundtable where the participants argue whether they see themselves as the right person to be part of this group or not. A middle manager asks Sam what he and Lucy believe would be the right composition, since Sam's roundtable must have been motivated by this concern. But Sam says that it may differ from subsidiary to subsidiary whether it is a representative from HR, marketing, or someone else who should participate, but he wants a specific person from each subsidiary to be "the one responsible" in relation to K2M.

Up until now, the participants in the steering group have met rather frequently (five meetings in half a year), but from now on the steering group meetings are continued as biannual forums for the exchange of experience of K2M. When they meet again six month later, Sam is not present when the meeting begins. Lucy starts the meeting with a status update about participation in the Globalco event. All subsidiaries have enlisted more participants than the year before, which she is pleased about. Lucy describes how she and Sam are working to promote a paradigm shift. They want to promote Globalco as a group identity to make all employees feel part of something bigger, not just part of the subsidiary in which they work. The yearly Globalco event is seen as a key driver to promote this Globalco identity. Sam arrives, and as usual they go round the table to present a status update about KPIs. They also discuss how they can get more employees to engage in the "My K2M project".

Meetings 7, 8, 9 and 10 follow the same pattern. Each middle manager presents a status update about KPIs. The nature of KPIs is continually being discussed as it is still difficult for some subsidiaries to set them. At SGM7, GoNuGa's KPIs are being challenged by Sam, and the middle manager says that all she can do is bring the ideas back to her managing directors. The gifts for the winners of the Globalco awards are discussed and a Buddha figure is a preferred item because of its symbolic value. It is still difficult to engage the employees in MyK2M, but GoTech has completed a kindness project, where each employee has donated working hours. SGM8 reflects the appointment of a new Chief K2M Officer and a new CSR controller in Apparella. The meeting is thus a presentation of the appointees to steering group members and a discussion of the ongoing work with K2M. The CEO highlights K2M as the main platform for differentiation, stating that it is K2M that makes Globalco and the subsidiaries unique. He emphasizes the importance of representatives embodying K2M and, with this in mind, initiates another roundtable in order to decide on the right people for the steering group meetings. He further suggests using the color orange more extensively to embody K2M. They also discuss the strong embodiment of K2M that the CEO represents and the pros and challenges that come with this. The main topic at SGM9 is the forth-coming publication of the yearly CSR report as well as the usual update on the work with KPIs. At SGM10, the CEO is absent and the meeting is affected by a number of last-minute cancellations, which frustrates the people present.

At a Globalco event, a new Globalco corporate movie is launched, featuring the corporation's owners. In the movie Sam describes the interconnectedness of all the Globalco subsidiaries, which is illustrated by the image of a spider's web. Later at the event, Sam also presents a new logo and company signature. Globalco's logo has been updated and the color orange has been incorporated into it. The logo is inspired by Indra's net, which is a Buddhist symbol. Indra's net symbolizes the interconnectedness of everybody and how one action affects everybody in the network. Lucy presents the MyK2M.com webpage, which was launched six months previously, drawing attention to the Buddha baton and the "My K2M project". Three finalist projects are announced, with the winner an Apparella employee who raises money for children in the developing world.

The above case spans a period of three years, and it will serve as data material in the subsequent chapters where the CCB-approach will be elaborated by empirical analyses.

4 The process of brand creation

As explained in Chapter 2, I base my work on the premise that *a brand is a discursive brand space*. In the space metaphor, "a brand is viewed as a continuous social process" (Merz et al., 2009, p. 337), but this 'continuous social process' has yet to be examined in detail. Vásquez et al. (2013) argue that a brand is the result of 'doing branding' but the authors do not explicate exactly how we get from 'doing branding' (process) to 'a brand' (product). I acknowledge the authors for commencing the discussion about the ontology of brands and branding by explaining branding as representation practices, that is, the "actual day-to-day communicative practices through which people collectively engage in representing the organization, and by doing so participate in creating its brand(s)" (p. 136). But at the same time, the authors write that "before anybody can become branded, a brand has to be enacted, created, elaborated, or modified" (ibid. p. 136). The authors thus identify a dialectic relationship between doing branding and being branded, which creates a double nature of a brand as an outcome of negotiation interactions. But, at the same time, the brand is what orders these interactions as it is seen to function as a frame and a boundary. We are thus left with a puzzle about how a brand is first created. It is, therefore, relevant to examine the process by which we come to conceptualize a brand as an entity in order to understand the ontology of a brand.

The analysis in this chapter is inspired by Anne Nicotera (2013) who has conceptualized how an organization comes to be seen as an entity. A brand and an organization share some central characteristics in that they are both conceptualized as an entity even though neither has any intrinsic materiality. They both have physical aspects such as buildings, furniture, and machinery as well as logos, products and ads, but buildings, furniture and machinery do not make up an organization just as logos, products and ads do not make up a brand. Nicotera proposes a phasic model to the analysis of how we go from individual conversations (process) to entitative being (product) that transcends and eclipses the individual. In this chapter, I will use Nicotera's framework to illuminate the process of brand creation. I will briefly present Nicotera's model before I go through the phases one by one in order to create an overview of the process of constituting the brand Kind2Mind (K2M).

DOI: 10.4324/9781003050100-4

4.1 Nicotera's model

Nicotera's model (Table 4.1) is a stage model consisting of seven phases, and it builds on the assumption that "an organization (entity) is the product of organizing (process)" (Nicotera, 2013, p. 74). It is consistent with Vásquez et al.'s (2013) proposition that a brand is the product of branding processes. The purpose of using Nicotera's model is to shed light on the interplay between 'process' and 'product', or, as Nicotera puts it, to problematize the hyphen in the 'process-product' relation – how do we get from here to there? By using Nicotera's model I hope to be able to explicate how we come from 'branding' (i.e. doing branding) to 'brand'.

Nicotera's primary purpose is to provide a set of baseline concretized processes to ground the analysis of the process-product relation. As she comments, the use of a stage model immediately raises questions about the order of phases and their normativity. But Nicotera also argues that stage models historically have been used to concretize abstract processes and are abandoned when they fail to answer more complex questions. Since the discussion about the ontology of a brand is in its tentative beginnings, I argue that the inspiration from a stage model can be useful at this point in the discussion.

By using Nicotera's stage model, I emphasize the ontological similarities between an organization and a brand, as constituted in communication. There are, undoubtedly, also significant ontological differences. For instance, one can question whether a brand is a 'we' in the same way an organization is a 'we'. For the purpose of shedding light on the construction of a brand as an entitative being, I have chosen to background the discussion of possible differences in the present analysis in order to examine what we can learn by focusing on the similarities.

4.2 Phase 1 – Individual agency and human interaction

According to Nicotera (2013) the first step in the process of constituting an entitative being is individual action in the form of engagement in conversation. Taylor et al. (1996) explain conversation as interpretive activities, that is, interaction. The first interactions involving K2M took place years before I started my data collection, so I asked Sam about the first steps in the development of K2M:

Excerpt 4.1

SAM: Well, I can answer that relatively precisely. The thing, that I work in this way, stems from 2004.
INTERVIEWER: 2004?
SAM: Yes, because that was when we launched a number of new activities focusing on kindness and we started to work with … well, we had a lot of activities that people don't know about. 'Save the Children', 'Red Cross', and ehm … we continually did all kinds of projects in relation to K2M.
JACK: But the concept of K2M?
SAM: That's from 2008.

JACK: 2008.

SAM: That's when we came up with it, right. And it was in relation to the book. It was before the book actually. My business partner and I had a little forum for the exchange of experience…before the economic crisis, right. You know, the way business was carried out before the crisis was not exactly healthy due to an extremely short sightedness and all that. As you all know of course. And then we had this little group and started to give speeches about it and then we started to call it K2M, and then it turned into a book. But it started in 2004 […] but I will say that it was not until Dave was hired that we became more goal-oriented about it and tried to fit it into some boxes and so on. But it has been there since I started it in 2004 as a philosophy, you could say, even though it was not manifested, or structured may be a better word, until Dave came along four years ago.

Sam attributes the first interactions about K2M to talks in a group for the exchange of experience and public speeches which he gave. He also explains K2M as something that started at Apparella, so I found it interesting to also ask the managing director at Apparella about the background of K2M. The managing director (MD) explains the development of the brand in this way:

Excerpt 4.2

MD: I think the first … or the first step was actually … it is not an invention, you can say, it is rather a naming that took place some years ago. What we have always done … We have always been very careful to … it is a kind of an old-fashioned concept that I use "to behave decently" …

INTERVIEWER: Yes?

MD: You know, to behave decently in general and it all started back in … it began back in 1997, where we shipped stuff to a refugee camp. Back then we did not use it as marketing, we just did it in order to … well to behave decently in general, right! So, we have always had a broad foundation and commitment to doing the right thing in the market.

It appears that Sam and the managing director tell two different stories about the first interactions related to K2M. Sam ascribes the first conversations about K2M to talks he had in a group for the exchange of experience, and the managing director believes that the concept of K2M grew out of an underlying philosophy about behaving decently that has existed in Apparella since 1997. Looking at their narratives, it becomes evident that they construct two different starting points to the story of K2M. But they concur in the perception that K2M existed as a philosophy before it was named K2M. To Sam it is a philosophy about "a new way of doing business", and to the managing director it is a philosophy about "behaving decently". It was just something they did, and it was not something they used purposefully as marketing activities. It can thus be argued that as long as the activities are not named as part of K2M, they remain a diffuse, unrealized branding potential.

Table 4.1 Nicotera's phasic model

Phase	Element	Characteristics
Phase 1	Individual agency and human interaction	Human actors engage each other in goal-directed conversation.
Phase2	Construction of the social collective (a 'we')	Through a process of collective sensemaking, a social collective with agency emerges, when speakers are reconstituted as actors in a narrative. Groups and collective actors start to appear.
Phase 3	Construction of text	Transcription of conversation into a permanent or semi-permanent medium. Through the execution of its agency, the social collective generates enduring outcomes of conversation that become the ground for ongoing goal-directed interaction among the collective's members. Hybrid agency emerges.
Phase 4	Self-conscious collectivity	With the emergence of a speech community, the collective becomes conscious of its own col-lectivity as a distinct entity in itself. A sense of a professional collectivity emerges as shared mean-ings are embedded in practices. A nexus of prac-tices are used to construct the identities of actors. This sense of professional collectivity must pre-cede the birth of an organization-as-entity: there has to be a '*we*' before there can be an '*it*'.
Phase 5	Presentification	Text is being transformed into design. The exis-tence of material frames and artifacts are a sign of presentification, which may be a precursor to or simultaneous with organizational birth. A) Materialization may be a precursor to (but not a guarantee of) presentification. B) Materialization may be simultaneous with or the mode of presentification.
Phase 6	Birth	An organization is born in the moment '*it*' is incarnated by an individual or collective agent acting on its behalf or in its name. Making the organization present in interaction may be the most fundamental form of presentification.
Phase 7	Reification	The organization, once *it* exists as an *entitative being*, is recursively presentified and incarnated in standardized form as those forms are disseminated to broader publics and audiences external to the organizational boundaries. To be an organization, this form must be reified as an entitative being – an independent entity upon whose behalf and in whose name individuals and collectives con-tinually act, such that those interests remain pri-mary and the '*it*' transcends and eclipses the humans comprising its collectivity.

Source: Based on Nicotera (2013, italics in original) and Taylor et al. (1996)

According to Taylor et al. (1996) the key to organization is not in the activities as such, but in their interpretation. Applied to the field of branding, this insight means that the constitution of a brand lies less in the activities and more in how those activities are interpreted. As long as the activities are interpreted as random activities that the organization engages in because they are cool and fun to do, the activities are not processes of branding. But the moment that a brand name is superimposed, the activities become part of 'doing branding'. This suggests that 'the process of branding' requires a brand name (i.e. a common signifier) in order for activities to be organized and interpreted as a process of 'doing branding' because "Words make things exist for us by naming them: The name comes before (or at least simultaneously with) the thing" (Taylor & Van Every, 1999, p. 66). Hence it is with the coining of a name – a common signifier – that goal-directed conversations start to emerge.

The importance of a name

Naming brings into being. Brand names are an essential semiotic resource because the brand name allows the brand to become part of a system of meanings of equivalence and differentiation (Lowrie, 2018). Inspired by Saussure, the meaning of a sign is defined by its difference from other signs rather than on some essential, internal meaning in the sign or its external referent (Lowrie, 2007). Different brands make up a system of meanings (antagonisms), and without the logics of equivalence and differentiation, there can be no identity (Lowrie, 2018). A brand name does not possess a fixed, internal meaning (or identity). Saussure argued that the relationship between signifier and signified is arbitrary, which means that a brand name is not given by the product. It also means that a brand name (signifier) can point to multiple possible referents (e.g. a product, a company, certain values); a brand name is a floating signifier. Meaning is created through discourses that invest the brand name with meaning. Exclusion serves as a discursive point of difference, and this exclusion is needed in order to achieve identity (Lowrie, 2018). Hegemonic discourses about the brand serve to fix the meaning of the brand name and, as such, there is a narrowing of the field of possible brand discourses over time. Therefore, it can be argued that a brand name serves to create a nodal point of brand meaning (ibid.). Accordingly, a brand name is an organizing element. Naming is a linguistic investment that serves to create frontiers or boundaries to the brand by excluding certain elements (Lowrie, 2018). A brand name serves as a common signifier and thus a unifying element under which brand discourses can start to evolve and establish brand meaning. Therefore, I find that it is necessary to add *naming* to the process of brand creation.

The brand name become a nodal point that marks the establishment of a *discursive brand space*. Conversation does not become goal directed until there is a common signifier to talk about. But when a brand name is coined, the first discourses about K2M are produced and thus a discursive brand space start to form. The brand name functions as an organizing element. Prior to the coining of a brand name, discourses are able to shift and float and are not connected (as they are not seen as interrelated), but when a brand name is coined it serves to connect the different discourses. As pointed out by Lowrie (2018), the name is fixed but descriptors are contingent and can change. In relation to brand development, it means that the brand name becomes the nodal point around which multiple brand discourses can form. Branding discourses may change according to context and focus and some of the discourses may be in opposition to each other or contradictory. However, since the brand name is a nodal point, the brand name binds the discourses together, making them part of the discursive brand space in which brand meaning is negotiated. The finding that the act of naming the brand is an important step towards the creation of a brand as an entitative being is in line with Brummans et al.'s (2009) findings. Brummans et al. (2009) studied the constitution of a new political party and found naming to be a crucial step in establishing the party as a collective agent.

Hence, with the coining of K2M, the participants can start to engage in collective sensemaking about K2M, which leads us to phase two in Nicotera's model.

4.3 Phase 2 – Construction of the social collective

The second phase in Nicotera's model is the construction of a social collective based on collective sensemaking. In Chapter 2, it was stated that sensemaking is about how people construct their own reality. Sensemaking involves translating streams of experience into language. By naming, labelling, and categorizing, streams of experience are punctuated into events and talked into situations (Taylor & Van Every, 1999). Collective sensemaking takes place when events are turned into a narrative representation and participants are constituted as actors. It is when speakers are reconstituted as actors in a narrative that collective identity begins to take shape (Taylor et al., 1996).

Before the naming of K2M, the activities in Apparella had been about "behaving decently" and "doing the right thing", which could be understood as core values, but with the invention of a name, these activities were converted into conscious expressions of a specific brand value, or a narrative of K2M. Naming something is thus a significant step in creating the existence of something, because it is through a name that 'it' (the brand) can be made present (see Cooren et al., 2008; Selg & Ventsel, 2008). Naming K2M allows the philosophy to be re-presentified, and the name itself brings a certain materiality to the brand.

With its naming, K2M came into being as a brand because the organizational members collectively willed it to exist, "[b]y saying it exists, it exists" (Taylor et al., 1996, p. 28). When the name K2M was invented and superimposed, dispersed activities were unified in a narrative about K2M. We see how individual actors engaged in conversations about "doing the right thing" and "behaving decently" (phase 1) but these conversations remained an unrealized branding potential until the name K2M was coined. From the data and the analysis above, it becomes evident that in order to move from individual conversation to a sense of a social collective or *brand collective* (phase 2), *naming* is an essential activity. It is in the naming of K2M that we see a move from individual actors engaging in conversations about doing the right thing to the creation of a brand collective. The coining of K2M enables a retrospective sensemaking, where the participants are able to understand their past actions and conversations as part of the K2M philosophy and the activities can be seen as constituting a certain brand identity. Retrospective sensemaking is evident when K2M is explained as the 'courage' to engage in offbeat activities, which makes Apparella stand out from other companies.

My analysis thus demonstrates that *naming* is a central step in bridging phases one and two when it comes to the creation of a brand. It is the naming of the brand that enables the production of brand narratives, and thus the creation of a social (brand) collective. However, the naming in itself is not enough to create a brand as an entitative being that eclipses the individuals. According to Nicotera (2013) the next step towards the creation of entitative being is the construction of text.

4.4 Phase 3 – Construction of text

The third phase in Nicotera's model is the transcription of conversation onto a permanent or semi-permanent medium. As explained in Chapter 2, the production of a text gives *restance* to discourses about K2M. When ideas about K2M are re-semioticized into text, those ideas come to exist as a *surface* in the form of 'done' discourses. Vásquez, Bencherki, Cooren, and Sergi (2018) explain the importance of re-semiotization as the need for 'matters of concern' to be provided with endurance in order to allow them to travel through time and space.

The first text that is produced about K2M is a book. Sam refers to the book when I inquire about the origins of K2M in my interview with him (see excerpt 4.1). He explains how K2M is framed in relation to some ideas about a new way of doing business, which he presented with the publication of the book, *Kind2Mind*. The text is a result of ongoing conversations about K2M between Sam and his co-author, but the text will also feed into future conversations about K2M. The book is thus able to supplement the *repertoire* about K2M as the book is distributed to organizational members. When they read the book, they might be able to talk about K2M in new or more nuanced ways than before. The production of a text about K2M is also the production of a non-human actor because the book can *animate* someone to think about K2M or to act in a certain way. The text can be appropriated by different people and thus produce a hybrid agency. If the book is seen to be acting on behalf of a collective, it becomes constituted as a macro-actor. The book is accompanied by another initial text about K2M – a video presentation of K2M on Globalco's webpage supplemented with a written presentation. The next time a central text about K2M is produced is when Globalco publishes its first CSR report (which they call the K2M report) about six years later.

Nicotera (2013) suggests that the hybrid agency that is enabled by the construction of text sets the stage for self-consciousness and the emergence of a speech community. The ability of the above-mentioned texts to feed into future conversations about K2M is thus an important step towards the next step in Nicotera's model, namely the constitution of a self-conscious collectivity.

4.5 Phase 4 – Self-conscious collectivity

The fourth phase in Nicotera's model is the constitution of a self-conscious collectivity. The self-conscious collectivity emerges as shared meanings are embedded in practices and a nexus of practices constitutes a sense of a professional collectivity.

In an effort to boost and further develop the concept of K2M, Dave is hired as Kind Developer at Apparella. Different initiatives are enacted and activities undertaken, such as a number of events with book presentations and guest speakers. Yet it is still very difficult to establish a group of people who feel part of a self-conscious collectivity in which K2M can be discussed and further developed. This difficulty is expressed at a meeting in GoNuGa:

Excerpt 4.3

[The exchange follows a discussion about what K2M is, and a middle manager has listed his point of view]

MD: You just had to list your own opinion?

[everybody laughs]

MM5: I had to remind myself what I think about it, right! It is not completely obvious to me.

[everybody laughs again]

MM5: So, I figured, I have to write it down; then I might learn it.

[everybody jokes and laughs]

MM5: It is something about a concept, and I remember when we had that meeting in GoTech… do you remember? About a year ago, I think … you were there, right?
MM1: Yes.
MM5: Well, let me tell you. We had some discussion about what the fuck this thing is supposed to embrace. And what it is about. What is a part of it? What isn't? Is it marketing? Is it not marketing?
MM1: The problem was that Sam did not participate back then.

A middle manager expresses the common viewpoint that people feel insecure about what K2M is supposed to entail, and nobody experiences themselves to be in a position to talk about K2M with authority except the CEO. When the CEO is not present, it becomes difficult to talk about K2M as expressed by another middle manager. This can point to a limited repertoire about K2M or the fact that there is not yet a nexus of practices related to it, which hinders the constitution of a self-conscious collectivity that shares a sense of professional K2M collectivity. In the realization of this obstacle, a steering group is created with the clear-cut objective to further K2M. The creation of a steering group is the deliberate creation of a conversational space (which I will return to in Chapter 5), since the meeting is a connected space that renders interaction possible, but the establishment of a steering group can also be seen as an attempt to create a self-conscious collectivity by "brute force".

At the first meeting of the steering group a chart of K2M is presented. The chart is an example of *presentication*.

4.6   Phase 5 – Presentification

The fifth phase in Nicotera's model is presentification. This term was explained in Chapter 2 as, the activities involved in making something or somebody present (Cooren et al., 2008). The essence of the presentification phase is the transformation of the initial conversations' content into a design that becomes the basis for future conversations (Taylor et al., 1996). Presentification is found in material frames and artifacts, such as offices, manuals, and organizational charts (Nicotera, 2013). At the first steering group meeting, the participants are presented with the K2M chart. The chart is a visual metaphor that functions as a *map* of K2M, since it is an attempt to create structure and to provide an overview of K2M. In the practice-based approach to discourse analysis it is recognized that "any perception, thinking or acting, presupposes some structuration of the field of meanings that precedes any factual immediacy" (Selg & Ventsel, 2010, p. 447). The (immaterial) idea of K2M is difficult to comprehend, but the model illustrates the totality of K2M, or at least it gives the impression that it does so, and thus constitutes a map. A map can be used to imaginatively grasp the brand and thus facilitate action, since "maps are for going places, doing things" (Taylor & Van Every, 1999, p. 252).

The chart is a result of many conversations stitched together (the K2M chart is a *lamination*), thus learning about K2M is being indexed in the chart. It can be seen as summarizing the acquired understandings about K2M because it is a record of the understanding of K2M obtained so far. The K2M model has restance, that is staying capacity, and can be seen as a 'point of no return' (inspired by Iedema, 2003). The transposition of conversations about K2M into a chart constructs K2M as a fact due to the durability of the modality (inspired by Iedema, 2001). As described by Coffey (2014), documents will often conform to particular genres. The K2M chart conforms to the genre of a textbook model. It divides the concept of K2M into three pillars that each constitute one third of K2M. When the participants in SGM1 are presented with the K2M chart, they are able to imagine K2M as a demarcated space (territory), providing a common point of reference for discussions about K2M: "If there were no map, there would be no territory for the communication to be 'in'" (Taylor & Van Every, 1999, p. 280). As seen in excerpt 4.3, it had been difficult for Sam to demarcate K2M's territory, but with the chart, K2M was no longer an abstract idea, it was now an object consisting of three pillars with respective headlines. As such, the presentification of K2M is seen to *organize* the ideas about K2M differently than the book or the CSR report (text). A set of boundaries are enacted to the brand space, and the presentification of K2M via this model establishes a sense of K2M-ness (inspired by Brummans et al., 2009) or a *brand territory*. Vasquez et al. (2013) argue that a brand functions as a frame and thus a boundary to the discussions about branding activities and, as it will be seen, the K2M chart comes to play a central structuring role in subsequent talks about K2M.

The K2M model establishes a number of mandatory elements of K2M, such as the KPIs and a K2M branding project. When organizational members start to put K2M into practice by performing branding activities according to the design in the K2M model, a *set of practices* is established. Practices are essential in the constitution of a self-conscious collectivity because practices transcend individuals. The establishment of practices is more important than the establishment of relations between individuals (Czarniawska, 2013) because organizational members may be replaced, but practices endure. The K2M model thus spurs the development of a self-conscious collectivity (phase 4), which demonstrates that the relation between the phases is not temporal-linear but rather cyclical. As pointed out, the limited repertoire and the lack of a common language about K2M can serve to explain why it is difficult to establish a speech community and thus a self-conscious collectivity (phase 4). The *presentification* represented by the K2M model may also serve to develop the repertoire about K2M.

Another presentification is seen in the K2M code of conduct that Lucy presents at SGM4. The K2M code of conduct establishes some guidelines for the work with K2M. It can thus be seen as an attempt to re-enact K2M in a standardized form in co-operation with the K2M model. The Production of a K2M code of conduct is a presentification that functions as a material frame for brand meaning, because as Lucy says the code of conduct provides structure and stability:

Excerpt 4.4

> [...] we can follow up on each other, what we demand of the companies and what the companies can demand of Globalco. Ehm ... and how we can observe the processes [...] and if somebody calls and asks, "what is your policy?", well, then you can look it up say, "here you go, I know that".

Lucy states that the K2M code of conduct is an attempt to write down everything they need to report on; it is supposed to supplement the work initiated with the K2M chart. She also states that the initiatives stated in the K2M code of conduct are not new but "now they are on paper", signaling the importance of transposing talk into text. The participants at SGM4 all agree that the K2M code of conduct is a helpful macro-actor. From a theoretical perspective, the K2M code of conduct is an important step towards entitative being because it establishes a set of *practices* that transcends any individual being. Nicotera draws upon Czarniawska (2013) in order to argue that the crucial connections in the ontology of an entitative being are not between individuals but between their practices. A practice can endure whereas organizational members may be replaced. Practices are also crucial in order to distanciate a brand from individual actors. Once established, practices preexist any given individual, and a nexus of practices is a decisive factor in the creation of a brand as an entitative being.

Other central presentifications of K2M are Buddha as organizational artifact, the use of orange, Globalco awards, the MyK2M.com webpage, K2M screens, and Globalco events. These presentifications do not seek to establish a nexus of practices in the same way as the K2M chart or the K2M code of conduct, but they are pointed to by organizational members as something that makes K2M present to them.

The advantage of permanent mediums, like the K2M chart and the K2M code of conduct, is that "the representation, having been written down, can now become a reference for many, many people. It is no longer one person's idiosyncratic experience of a place. It claims objectivity: what *everybody* knows. It claims *authority*" (Taylor & Van Every, 2011, p. 54). The K2M chart is central to the establishment of the steering group as a self-conscious collectivity since it indicates practices related to the work with K2M. Presentification (phase 5) is thus seen to function as a constituting force to the creation of a self-conscious collectivity (phase 4), which indicates a cyclical correlation to Nicotera's phases rather than a sequential one. The next phase is the birth of the brand.

4.7 Phase 6 – Birth

Nicotera (2013) sees an entitative being as conceived somewhere between phase 2 and 4, with the emergence of a self-conscious collectivity; the entity is born somewhere between phase 4 and 6 "in the moment '*it*' is incarnated by an individual or collective agent acting on its behalf or in its name" (p. 80).

The K2M model is a *re-semiotization* (of earlier conversations) that materializes the K2M philosophy. As a non-human actor, it can be understood as an *incarnation* of K2M. It is also a *macro-actor* (or collective agent, to use Nicotera's phrase), because it is able to speak on behalf of the K2M department. The K2M chart is thus an important step towards the creation of K2M as entitative being because K2M (i.e. the 'it') is incarnated by a macro-actor able to act in its name. Other incarnations can be found in the K2M code of conduct and the CSR reports (K2M reports). There are thus a number of non-human actors that incarnate K2M but it turns out to be more of a challenge to have human actors acting in its name, with the exception of the CEO, who is seen as a strong embodiment of K2M.

K2M incarnated by the CEO

The CEO is recognized as the original author of K2M, and K2M is generally acknowledged to spring from his personal values. An Apparella employee identifies this personal link: "Clearly, the kindness-concept stems from Sam via his approach to Buddhism and his faith". A middle manager in Apparella agrees: "It is a philosophy that Sam practices because of his own religion and way of thinking". The level of Sam's backing is also recognized by employees in other constituent companies. An employee at GoNutri says: "There is no doubt that it is Sam's project", and a middle manager in GoGastro expresses the same view: "There is no doubt that Sam is behind this". When asked how big a part Sam plays in relation to K2M, a middle manager at GoGastro answers: "Very big. I will almost say, if he wasn't there, I don't think K2M would be there". The perception that K2M is Sam's project is shared by employees at all levels in the companies. Sam and the concept of K2M are thus inextricably linked; K2M is incarnated by Sam. The body is acknowledged to be a strong communicator because ideas materialize in bodies (Ashcraft et al., 2009), and Sam certainly is a conspicuous embodiment of K2M.

Sam is a person who stands out from the crowd. There are many pictures of him in the public domain in which he is wearing apparel from Apparella and distinctive glasses, in a setting different from the "management office". A middle manager recalls his first meeting with Sam at a board meeting and describes how Sam stood out:

Excerpt 4.5

> When we participated in a board meeting back then, we would dress up nicely in a suit wearing a tie, and then Sam arrived in an open shirt, with some jewelry around his neck and big glasses, looking peculiar – it was a silk shirt.

The middle manager recalls his first meeting with Sam in response to being asked when he had first heard about K2M. This vivid impression signals that Sam truly is a strong incarnation of K2M. Sam is generally described as behaving curious or hipster-like. Right from the beginning, Sam established his position in Globalco as a non-traditional company owner, and his conspicuous appearance incarnates K2M in a certain way. An employee at GoGastro describes a picture that is part of GoGastro's company presentation material:

Excerpt 4.6

> […] there is this picture of Ted [co-owner] who is dressed in a business suit and sits in the foreground and Sam sits in a sofa in the background,

casual, with his legs crossed, wearing sneakers and fancy glasses and very business casual and that contradistinction appeals to our customers.

It seems that Sam's conspicuous appearance is part of a deliberate branding strategy. In addition to his physical appearance, Sam is known to be a Buddhist even though he does not claim to be a Buddhist himself. He acknowledges that he has a great interest in and is inspired by Eastern philosophy due to his predilection for martial arts. He also acknowledges that he decorated his home with Buddha figures long before it trended in interior design. The introduction of the Buddha as an organizational artifact in Globalco stems from Sam but, even so, he claims that K2M is not a Buddhist philosophy. However, organizational members understand K2M to express Sam's personal values. The middle manager, heard from in excerpt 4.5, continues his story:

Excerpt 4.7

> Then we became acquainted with Sam's way of being – his philosophy. And that is the basis of K2M. It stems from his political point of view. That's what has been put into practice. It is very obvious that it is Sam's way of thinking, his philosophy, that is practiced, and he expects us all to take part in it.

Not only do the employees see Sam as an incarnation of K2M, but they also recognize him as the originator of the concept. They see the K2M values as Sam's personal values that have been applied in Globalco's branding strategy. Sam is thus an authentic author and a true embodiment of K2M, which makes it difficult for other organizational members to venture to incarnate K2M.

K2M incarnated by Lucy

The person who incarnates K2M most successfully (apart from Sam) is the Chief K2M Officer (Lucy). Chief K2M Officer is the first full-time position allocated to the work with K2M, and Lucy, in this role, is supposed to be the new driving force in the further development of K2M. Several employees see Lucy's appointment as an indicator that K2M is assigned a higher priority by the owners. This view is expressed by a middle manager:

Excerpt 4.8

> The fact that we now have someone employed, who is supposed to make K2M work 100% makes a difference. It signals to everybody that K2M is something that is taken seriously. So, I think that makes a significant difference.

Lucy is thus a successful incarnation of K2M, but she is not viewed as the original author in the same way that Sam is, as these employees explain:

Excerpt 4.9

INTERVIEWER: How would you explain K2M to me?
EMPLOYEE A: I would say: "Lucy will be back on Monday".
INTERVIEWER: What does Lucy know about K2M?
EMPLOYEE A: She IS K2M.
EMPLOYEE B: Yes.
INTERVIEWER: She IS K2M. What does that mean?
EMPLOYEE B: She shapes it.
EMPLOYEE A: Yes.
EMPLOYEE B: She works with it 100%.
EMPLOYEE A: Yes.
INTERVIEWER: So, she is the one, who decides what K2M is?
EMPLOYEE B: No, she does not. That is Sam.
INTERVIEWER: That is Sam?
EMPLOYEE B: That is without a doubt.
EMPLOYEE A: But she is the one, who does the work.

It is apparent from this extract of the conversation that Lucy is seen as an incarnation of K2M, but it is an incarnation that is controlled by Sam. Hence, Lucy is not seen as an incarnation of K2M in her own right, but rather as the right-hand woman of the CEO. The CEO is a *ventriloquist* that animates Lucy to perform or carry out K2M the way that he wants it to be carried out. This point of view is supported by other organizational members:

Excerpt 4.10

> Well, I will say, Sam is the pioneer. I know, Lucy is doing a lot of work, but it is Sam, who – if any – is the public face. He is the one who created the idea and set this rock in motion.

Excerpt 4.11

> It [K2M] cannot stand by itself. It is so young. I don't know if Lucy could carry it through if Sam wasn't behind her all the time. Lucy is very well-reputed in the organization. It is not that. She is a very likeable person, and she is skillful, so she is welcomed. But everybody knows that K2M is something that is very close to Sam's heart, hence it is treated accordingly.

Lucy is recognized as an incarnation of K2M, and as such K2M is incarnated by a human actor who acts in its name, but K2M is not being distanciated from Sam as he is seen as a ventriloquist who controls the way that Lucy performs K2M. This lack of distanciation is one of the core challenges because managers at the operational level ought to embody the brand spirit and act as role models

(Punjaisri, Evanschitzky, & Rudd, 2013). Another challenge comes from the fact that Lucy is employed as Chief K2M Officer. K2M is seen as something that is now based in a K2M department with Lucy as the one responsible for carrying out K2M activities, and this becomes a legitimate reason for other organizational members not to engage in K2M on a daily basis. So, in a sense, incarnation by Lucy becomes an excuse for others' non-engagement with the incarnation of K2M.

Lack of authority to incarnate

The fact that Lucy is seen as a dummy that is animated by Sam suggests that Lucy is not seen as authorized to author K2M in her own name. A similar lack of authorization to author is expressed by other employees, who find it difficult to speak in the name of K2M:

Excerpt 4.12

> I just think it would kick in stronger if you [Sam] were the one to communicate it instead of little me.

Excerpt 4.13

> I just think it would have a stronger effect if it is coming from Sam. If you write it, then it is something you have been given from Sam, then it is something that has been fobbed off on you by the CEO. Whereas if it is Sam and the K2M department that write it then it is something that we want in Globalco.

Such examples illustrate the fact that the CEO is the original author and that K2M is inextricably linked with his person. The middle managers do not perceive of themselves as being in a position to incarnate K2M effectively. If K2M is to become more than Sam's personal philosophy, it is necessary that a *naturalization* of K2M takes place.

Hence, although there are glimpses of a self-conscious collectivity and incarnation of K2M, the phases are not successfully completed. Even so, it has been possible to move K2M to the last of Nicotera's phases, *reification* (phase 7), which is the recursive presentification and incarnation of K2M.

4.8 Phase 7 – Reification

Reification refers to the incarnation and presentification of the entitative being in standardized forms that are disseminated to broader publics, and audiences external to the organization (Nicotera, 2013). Reification serves to reiterate K2M in the same way from one communication event to another (Vásquez et al., 2018). Reification is important because the brand needs to be made present again and again in order to produce endurance to the brand. The "it" (the brand) must transcend and eclipse the humans that comprise its collectivity.

Every year Globalco publishes a K2M report, which is Globalco's CSR report. Other reifications of K2M are the *Kind2Mind* book, the presentation of K2M on the Globalco website, the MyK2M.com webpage, and the Globalco logo inspired by Indra's net. Internally in Globalco there are other more or less standardized re-enactments of K2M, such as K2M newsletters, K2M screens, Globalco awards, Globalco events, the use of orange and Buddha as organizational artifact that function as reifications of K2M. This shows that it is possible to work with reification in the form of materiality even though a self-conscious collectivity has not yet been successfully constituted.

4.9 Discussion of Nicotera's 7 phases

Nicotera's 'process as a model' creates a useful overview of the organizing of brand elements that ultimately come to constitute the brand as an 'it'. The model identifies important stepping- stones in the process, from the first conversations about K2M to the constitution of the brand as an "it". This is an appropriate model because it applies a flatland perspective, thus embracing both the discourse-world (talk-in-interaction) and the text-world. In my data, I found two additional aspects to be of central importance in the creation of a brand, namely *naming* and *distanciation*.

The importance of a name

My analysis demonstrates that *naming* the brand is a prerequisite for the discursive brand space to evolve. To create a name is to create a common signifier that makes the brand exist and makes it present. Based on the explanations offered by Sam and the managing director of Apparella, the underlying activities of K2M have been going on for years, but it is not until the name K2M is coined that the activities are seen as strategic branding activities. To *name* K2M is to *bracket* and *label* activities as branding activities as the creation of a common signifier makes it possible to group activities under the name K2M. A *name* is also a prerequisite for the branding process to move forward and construct a social collective. The essence of a social collective is collective sensemaking, which is spurred through narrative representation where participants are reconstituted as actors. The brand thus needs to be named in order for "it" to be able to perform as an actor in a narrative and in order for other actors to be able to relate to that actor.

Even though a brand name is created, the meaning of K2M is not fixed yet. The name K2M becomes a reference point for the people that participate in conversations about K2M, and the discursive brand space evolves as different discourses seek to invest K2M with meaning. K2M is therefore a floating signifier, seeing that a floating signifier is a sign that "different discourses struggle to invest with meaning in their own particular way" (Jørgensen & Phillips,

2002, p. 28) (see also Mumby, 2016; Vásquez et al., 2017b). The understanding of a brand name as a floating signifier underscores that a brand is always in a state of becoming because different discourses struggle to fix its meaning.

Another finding in my analysis is the importance of *distanciation*. In the analysis of phase 6, "Birth", it became evident that K2M is very much seen as Sam's personal philosophy. This makes it difficult for other organizational members to incarnate K2M because they do not feel that they have the authority to author K2M, given that Sam is the original author. I therefore argue that a *naturalization* needs to take place.

The importance of distanciation

According to CCO theory, an important step towards *naturalization* is the production of texts since text is supposed to *distanciate* the discourses from the original author. Even though a text about K2M (the *Kind2Mind* book) is created quite early in the process, the book does not serve to distanciate K2M from Sam.

The *Kind2Mind* book is written as a record of conversations between Sam and his co-author. Throughout the book their names are stated in order to indicate, who is talking. The book is thus not presented in a conventional book format with a cut-and-dried presentation of K2M, rather it is presented as conversations written down. The book provides the reader with a window onto a *conversational space*, where Sam and his co-author air their personal thoughts about management, and the two of them seek to approach a common understanding of what K2M might be. The book is thus a discussion "frozen in time" – an invitation to observe Sam and the co-author interacting in a conversational space rather than a text that distanciates K2M from its original context of production. In order to succeed with the distanciation and naturalization of K2M, the original author needs to vanish from view or at least take a step back. Yet the *Kind2Mind* book does the opposite. It positions Sam and his co-author as the inventors of K2M and moreover they seek to position talk about K2M as a new D-discourse.

K2M as D-discourse

To Sam and the co-author, K2M is a new way of doing business, and given their statuses as a recognized businessman and his business partner, K2M is promoted as a new business D-discourse. They talk about K2M as if it is a new theoretical concept. For instance, Sam mentions at the first steering group meeting that students are writing college papers about K2M in Japan. The promotion of K2M as a D-discourse hinders the activity in the conversational space, since only people with the right qualifications are deemed legitimate to speak about a theoretical concept. In order to be able to participate in a D-discourse, one needs to be familiar with the D-discourse.

If one does not recognize a D-discourse, one needs to be able to familiarize oneself with it in order to participate in the conversation. Even though Sam and his co-author seek to explicate the underlying ideas of K2M in the

Kind2Mind book, the explication is given in broad and general terms, such as, "K2M is about realizing that we have a universal responsibility – that our actions have a universal dimension" or "It is a philosophy, a conscience about the fact that we leave a footprint. The understanding that we are all connected". K2M is explained as, "not just something you do in the marketing department. It is deeply grounded in the emotions and realization of managers and employees"; it is a way of thinking, "a mindset for the company, the leader, the employee and the individual". These discourses do not really explicate the content of K2M, and thus it is not exactly clear what is signified by the signifier K2M. The problem is not that different discourses struggle to invest K2M with meaning, but rather that the discourses are devoid of specific meaning.

The promotion of K2M as a new business D-discourse works contrary to achieving distanciation of K2M from Sam since it prevents other people from authoring K2M with authority. If K2M is to succeed as a D-discourse, the D-discourse about K2M needs to be established, but the discourses in the book operate at a very general level. This openness of the concept could potentially be an affordance that would invite many different contributions, but there is the risk that the concept of K2M becomes so abstract that it is too difficult for people to participate in the conversational space, and the latter seems to be the case. This finding is supported by organizational members of Globalco, who repeatedly refer to K2M as "fluffy".

Instead of opening up the conversational space and inviting in different voices, the abstractness of K2M narrows the conversational space down so that it is only Sam and his co-author who are really able to participate. Since K2M has been coined by Sam and his co-author, they are the *authors,* the ones who have the authority to articulate K2M. They are the ones with the authority to decide what K2M is and what it is not and that makes it challenging for other actors to participate in developing the discourses about K2M.

According to Nicotera's (2013) phases, the production of text (phase 3) should spur the emergence of a speech community (phase 4). But the *Kind2Mind* book does not succeed in doing so. Rather it limits the speech community to just Sam and his co-author, which hinders the constitution of a larger self-conscious collectivity. As a consequence, I see the lack of distanciation as the main obstacle to creating a broader speech community. Hence, the production of text does not itself suffice to bring about a self-conscious collectivity (phase 4). This case suggests that distanciation of text from the original authors is an essential step in bridging phases 3 and 4, and the lack of distanciation and naturalization can serve to explain why it is difficult for organizational members in Globalco to incarnate K2M.

Nicotera sees the elements as succeeding each other in a linear fashion. However, I found it was possible to move to phases 5 and 7 even when phases 4 and 6 were not successfully accomplished. I propose that this arises from a cyclical relationship between the elements, where the process of 'doing branding' moves back and forth and where later phases, such as *reification* (phase 7), may serve to push the constitution of a self-conscious collectivity (phase 4) as well as making it more accessible for organizational members to incarnate the brand (phase 6). An explanation of this finding can be found in the difference between "organization" and "brand".

Difference between "organization" and "brand"

Nicotera developed her phasic model to discuss the construction of an organization as an entitative being. I chose to background the discussion of possible differences between an organization and a brand in order to focus on the similarities, so as to use Nicotera's framework to discuss the construction of a brand as entitative being. However, I have found an important difference between "organization" and "brand". It is the fact that the creation of a brand partly takes place in an already organized environment with preexisting structure and power relations, and this turns out to be important in relation to the constitution of a self-conscious collectivity (phase 4). As explicated, the constitution of a self-conscious collectivity does not emerge spontaneously, but since Globalco already exists as a macro-actor, it has the power to delegate responsibility and grant power.

The phases that are seen to be most troublesome to complete successfully are phase 4, the constitution of a self-conscious collectivity, and phase 6, birth in the form of incarnation. The constitution of a self-conscious collectivity does not evolve spontaneously therefore a steering group is put together, which I argue is an attempt to create a self-conscious collectivity by "brute force". Therefore, the existing power structures at Globalco turn out to be of central importance in the constitution of K2M as an entitative being. The pre-existence of structure enables the K2M department to put together a steering group that is to further the work with K2M, which is a way of trying to force the establishment of a self-conscious collectivity (phase 4). It is, however, important to notice that even though, a Globalco "we" in the form of a group can be forced to exist, a "we" in the form of collective sensemaking (a "K2M-we") cannot. Despite the appointment of a steering group, it is still difficult to establish a speech community and a sense of a professional collectivity, which hinders the successful establishment a self-conscious collectivity. That indicates that *sensemaking* cannot be forced.

The analysis further demonstrates that incarnation (phase 6) is successfully accomplished by non-human actors, such as the K2M chart and the K2M code of conduct, but apart from Sam and Lucy, no human actors are seen to incarnate K2M. Indeed, some employees express the viewpoint that they find it difficult to incarnate K2M convincingly, or that incarnation of K2M is a task for the K2M department. In conclusion, the process about constituting K2M as an "it" proceeds successfully when it comes to the engagement of non-human actors, but the process is more troublesome when it comes to the engagement of human actors. It becomes evident that while it is possible to produce *surfaces* to the brand (text and materiality), it is much more complicated to produce a *site* where organizational members engage in K2M. A vital difference between the constitution of an organization and the constitution of a brand is thus the difference in environment. A brand is constituted in an already organized environment, which makes it possible to produce a *surface* to the brand, but the *site* still has to be constituted.

Nicotera's seven phases are thus helpful in identifying successful as well as problematic parts of the process of constituting K2M as an entity (a brand).

Suitability of the phasic model

The use of a phasic model is in many respects contrary to the 'communication as constitutive' perspective, but the strength of a phasic model is its ability to concretize abstract processes and ground the analysis. As Nicotera pinpoints herself, stage models have historically been used in communication research to frame questions, and have been abandoned when research has moved beyond the initial underlying studies (Nicotera, 2013).

I find that Nicotera's seven phases serve well to examine the ontology of a brand. The phases present a framework that points out fundamental stages of development and thereby the phases can explicate how we get from initial conversations about the brand to the brand as entitative being, or in other words, how we get from "process" (branding activities) to "product" (brand). However, I also find the sequence of the seven phases not to be linear in time but rather cyclical and iterative, as can be seen in the way the work with K2M goes back and forth between the phases. This finding is in accordance with Vásquez et al. (2017b) who found branding to be a process of organization, disorganization, and reorganization. In the next paragraph, I will present a cyclical model of brand creation based on the findings spurred by Nicotera's phasic model.

4.10 Brand management as practical authorship

Nicotera's stage model frames the question of how a brand is first brought into being. The above analyses demonstrate how K2M was first established in con-versation led by Sam and his business partner, and by Sam and a managing director in Apparella (phase 1). The analysis further demonstrates that the coining of a brand name is essential in order to create a nodal point that the discursive brand space can start to form around. Conversation does not become goal-directed until there is a common signifier to talk about. But, in this case, when conversations were named as branding activities, they served to reconstitute the participants as actors in a narrative (phase 2). Text was produced in the form of a book and a presentation on Globalco's webpage (phase 3); and talk (phase 1) and text (phase 3) formed a self-organizing loop. Nicotera's model is able to explicate how this loop unfolds when conversation is translated into a text in the form of the *Kind2Mind* book, and later texts, such as the K2M chart, a K2M code of conduct, and a MyK2M.com webpage. These texts come to inform later conversations about K2M, and they help to create an account of the *repertoire* about K2M. The K2M chart is particularly central in informing subsequent conversations about K2M; its centrality can be explained by Nicotera's phase 5 "Presentification". *Presentification* is significant in explicating the difference between "ordinary" text and the texts and artifacts that come to function as material frames for the conversations. The

K2M chart will be analyzed in greater detail in Chapter 5 but let me just point out that it *structures* the conversations about K2M, due to its subdivision into three pillars that each explicate a part, and it *informs* conversation based on the language about K2M that is represented in the model. Accordingly, production of a text-world is simultaneously the production of a discourse-world (Taylor & Van Every, 1999).

The constitution of a self-conscious collectivity (phase 4) does not happen spontaneously, but given the pre-existence of organizational structure, the K2M department is able to appoint a steering group with the task of discussing and further developing K2M. Even so, it turns out to be difficult to establish a self-conscious collectivity among the *human actors* due to a lack of naturalization of K2M. But the K2M chart and the K2M code of conduct become important *non-human actors* in the production of a self-conscious collectivity, as a self-conscious collectivity is understood to be a nexus of practices used to construct the identities of actors. The K2M chart *pinpoints* the content of K2M, and the K2M code of conduct *establishes* a number of procedures for ongoing work with K2M. Therefore, in the case of K2M, it is *presentification* (phase 5) that spurs the construction of a *self-conscious collectivity* (phase 4), as it is the K2M chart and the K2M code of conduct that establishes a nexus of practices which serves to spur the sense of a professional collectivity among the participants in the steering group. Even so, it turns out to be difficult for human actors to incarnate K2M (phase 6), except for Sam and Lucy, but K2M is successfully incarnated by non-human actors, such as the K2M model and the K2M code of conduct, who are able to speak in its name. Reification (phase 7) is primarily spurred by the K2M code of conduct and the CSR report.

The above analysis thus demonstrates that the ontology of a brand does indeed share some similarities with the ontology of an organization, and Nicotera's phases provide a useful framework to analyze the *process* by which a brand is constituted as an entitative being. Like an organization, a brand emerges in communication, and it is made present through different kinds of materialities (i.e. conversation, text, materiality).

However, the analysis also illustrates the circularity of the phases because, as explained previously, the phases are not completed successively, instead there is a going back and forth. It can be argued that K2M is *born* (phase 6) in the minute that Sam incarnates the concept in his public speeches, which precedes the production of *text* (phase 3). The first production of *text* (phase 3), the *Kind2Mind* book, is immediately broadcasted to an external audience, which, according to Nicotera's model, would be part of the *reification* (phase 7). *Presentification* (phase 5) in the form of the K2M chart and the K2M code of conduct precedes phase 4 – a *sense of a self-conscious collectivity* among the human actors.

Naming and *distanciation* turned out to be important additions to Nicotera's phases, and another important finding is the difference between constitution of organization and constitution of brand. The constitution of a brand takes place in an already organized environment, but even so, sensemaking cannot be forced. Based on these findings, I make two suggestions. Firstly, I suggest talking about 'elements' in the branding process instead of 'phases'; secondly, I suggest abandoning the linear organization of phases used by Nicotera's model in favor of a circular process (Figure 4.1).

Figure 4.1 provides a conceptualization of the elements in how a brand comes to exist as an entity. Naming and distanciation are added to the number of elements as I find both naming and distanciation to be of central importance in the creation of the brand as an entity that was able to transcend and eclipse the human beings. There is no temporal sequence to the brand elements. Although naming will normally occur very early in the branding process, a brand may be re-named as part of a re-branding process; accordingly, all the elements may occur at any moment in the ongoing process of brand (re-) creation. A brand manager must thus pay attention to all nine elements, but as the following chapters will demonstrate, it is not possible to control the development of the brand. I therefore re-conceptualize the brand manager as a practical author, in line with Golant (2012). The notion of the brand manager as a practical author will be further elaborated in Chapter 8.

In the next chapter, I will focus on the *site* of doing branding. From the above analysis, it became evident that K2M is talked into in existence in different *conversational spaces*. In this regard, the steering group meeting is seen to constitute a central *site* since it is a conversational space deliberately set-up to spur the further development of K2M and the establishment of a self-conscious collectivity. Accordingly, I will turn my attention to the set-up of this *conversational space* to examine which actors participate in the conversations.

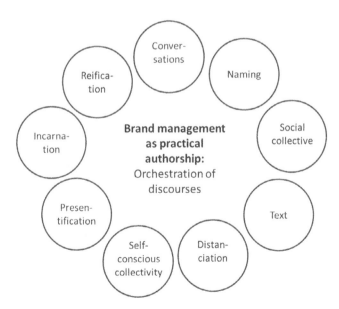

Figure 4.1 Brand management as practical authorship

5 Conversational space, ventriloquism, and hybrid agency

To understand a brand as a *discursive brand space* is to understand the brand as conversationally co-created. The *discursive brand space* is a bricolage of discourses, and brand meaning emerges as some discourses become dominating, or put in other words, they succeed in achieving hegemony. But hegemony is only provisional, since there is a constant discursive struggle going on. As stipulated by Hatch and Schultz (2008), a multitude of stakeholders can participate in the conversations about the brand and accordingly, the *discursive brand space* is produced by everybody who participates in conversations about the brand. Conversations take place in a *conversational space* (Iglesias et al., 2013; Ind, 2014; Ind et al., 2013). The purpose of this chapter is to analyze the notion of a conversational space in more detail since this is where a brand is conversationally co-produced.

A conversational space is the settings of space that allows for conversation and interaction, in other words, it is *the sites* of *doing branding*. In Chapter 2, it was explained that a conversational space is the space where interlocutors can come together. A conversational space can be corporeal (e.g. a meeting room, a shop, a brand event) or virtual (e.g. social media, like Facebook, Instagram and Twitter; review forums, like Trustpilot or Tripadvisor). Every conversational space offers its own set of affordances. For instance, Facebook offers reactions, commenting, sharing and tagging; and a meeting room offers a certain kind of seating, arrangement, facilities for presenting and recap, and space dimensions. The set-up of a formal conversational space thus ought to be a point of attention for the brand manager as the affordances of the conversational space will affect which kind of interaction is stimulated or hampered. The material or digital settings of a conversational space provide the resources available for interaction (or the infrastructure for conversations) about the brand. The set-up of a conversational space is thus a way to work with sensegiving in relation to brand meaning.

However, informal conversational spaces will be formed as well. Employees may form a conversational space in the canteen, by the coffee machine, or at the Christmas party. Employees may also talk about the brand in private settings, such as dinner parties or family gatherings. Customers can discuss the brand face to face or online, and other stakeholders can interact in many different ways. It will not be possible for brand management to discover all these informal conversational spaces, but brand management ought to look out for

DOI: 10.4324/9781003050100-5

more organized conversational spaces such as, for instance, brand communities that might emerge. As already mentioned, all discourses produced about the brand add to the discursive brand space, and brand management can learn a lot about how the brand is being discussed by listening to conversations about the brand. In some instances, it might be possible to participate in the conversations and thus practice sensegiving in relation to the production of brand meaning.

The focus of this chapter will be on a corporeal conversational space, namely the meetings in the steering group where the brand K2M was further developed, as well as some local meetings in the subsidiary GoNuGa. The purpose of the analyses is to shed light on the construction of a conversational space and to see who participates in the conversations. I will demonstrate that both human and non-human actors are present and actively participating in the production of the discursive brand space. An important concept in this respect is the notion of *ventriloquism* since absent actors can be seen to *speak through* other participants. The use of ventriloquism affects agency as *hybrid agency* is produced and, as the analysis will demonstrate, a non-human actor is able to display agency even though it does not have any physical existence.

5.1 The creation of a conversational space

In 2018, the decision is made to launch K2M as a corporate brand in Globalco. A steering group is put together to further develop the brand as well as to disseminate the brand in all subsidiaries. Though K2M had been discussed earlier, the establishment of a steering group marks a shift, in that it signals a strategic decision to further develop K2M. The establishment of a series of meetings with carefully selected organizational members is the set-up of a formal *conversational space*. In this case, the conversational space is constituted by material settings, namely the physical facilities provided by conference rooms. The subsidiaries take turn in hosting the meetings. The affordances of the conference rooms vary as do the power relations seeing as the participants are sometimes visitors and sometimes hosts on their home ground. As mentioned in Chapter 2, the material affordances of conference rooms, such as the setting of furniture, can be of significance in relation to the interaction enabled in the conversational space. However, the psychical setting of the conversational space will not be the focus of my analysis. I will focus on the efforts to set-up boundaries to the conversational space, and the participation of non-human actors in the conversations.

The set-up of boundaries to the conversational space

Occasional talks about K2M had been going on in Globalco for some years, but in 2018 a strategic decision is made to develop K2M as a corporate brand that is to be implemented in all subsidiaries. On October 6, 2018, a first meeting is held, and thus a conversational space is created. A key concern to the design of a conversational space is how boundaries are enacted. A conversational space can be open to anyone (e.g. a mass meeting or a Facebook page) but if boundaries are enacted, it is immensely interesting to see who is invited and who is denied access. In Globalco, the conversational space is set up by the CEO and the K2M department. They invite four middle managers from different subsidiaries, which means that each branch of the conglomerate is represented.

When the first steering group meeting is summoned, it has been decided that managing directors of the individual subsidiaries would not be invited despite an earlier decision about getting them involved. This fact is articulated in the opening of the meeting when Dave explains the background:

Excerpt 5.1

> We had a meeting in June [...] and the group, that is present here today, decided on the next step, which was to involve the managing directors and organize a K2M-Camp [...]. But then you and I [pointing at Lucy] had a talk and we agreed that it was important to meet, and to have you present [referring to the CEO] in order to reach a common understanding of what we believe K2M is.

Based on these opening lines, it is evident that it was a conscious decision not to invite the managing directors to participate in this meeting. That means that the steering group meetings are not open to everyone, which signifies that a *boundary* to the conversational space is enacted. The creation of a boundary is reinforced when the CEO adds:

Excerpt 5.2

> Well, I will add ... one of the things we discussed, and which was initi-ally the idea, was that we should get together with the managing direc-tors at this workshop, but we concluded that we might end up having too many chiefs with all the managing directors sitting around the table at the same time. We agree that they need to be involved, that they must take ownership, but we would like to ask you today whether you think it is a good idea to have them all come together or whether we should talk with them individually ... .

It appears from these excerpts that a joint decision to involve the managing directors by arranging a K2M-Camp has been overruled by the CEO, Dave, and Lucy. The overruling of this decision is a clear enactment of boundaries to the conversational space, and the enactment of boundaries is repeated on sev-eral occasions. At both the second and the third steering group meetings, one of the middle managers asks if it is possible to summon a meeting that includes the managing directors, but the CEO declines. It is thus made clear that the CEO controls who can participate. The conversational space, where K2M is to be further developed, is thus presented as a closed or at least a delimited space to which some have access and others do not. At the fifth steering group meeting, the CEO, and the Chief K2M Officer initiate a roundtable where everybody has to argue whether they see themselves as the right person to represent their company in the steering group, and they also discuss the number of participants. This issue is taken up again at SGM8. It is thus clearly demonstrated that there is a limited number of seats in the conversational space, which reinforces the enactment of boundaries. It also makes participation in the conversational space an exclusive privilege, and it produces the unfortunate affordance that participants are reluctant to air concerns or questions. Seeing that all participants fight for their right to participate, nobody wants to ask critical questions. They do not want to position themselves as someone who does not understand the brand. There is also a discourse about 'resistance' that the participants clearly dissociate themselves from. For instance, they refer to the managing directors as someone who do not completely grasp the brand:

Excerpt 5.3

How do we … we have some managing directors that have to be able to sell this to the employees and to defend it in relation to the questions that may appear, right? I think we have been fighting shy of this in the last couple of meetings in relation to how we make sure that there is support in each sub-sidiary. Because it is the managing directors that must vouch for this, right? It's one thing to involve the employees, but the managing directors also have to grasp this, right? […] They have to be able to defend it by themselves … .

I think the gap … and I say this with the utmost respect, and I would even say love, because I have known these people for 10–20 years … but this is a conceptual sphere that they are not used to navigating

If I am to be a bit rude, I would say, if you don't understand it by now, it's because you don't want to understand

[laughing] Do I sense a bit of resistance? [laughing again]

The managing directors are clearly positioned as those *outside* the conversational space and even outside the conceptual sphere of understanding. By excluding the managing directors – both physically and in relation to whether they understand the brand or not – the members of the conversational space are positioned as an ingroup that share a privileged understanding of the brand. But as stated earlier, this positioning produces the unfortunate consequence that members of the conversational space are reluctant to air any doubt or hesitation. It discourages members' from asking questions as they do not want to risk positioning themselves as outsiders who do not completely grasp the brand. When they do not ask questions, they miss out on the opportunity to develop their repertoire about K2M.

It is thus evident that boundaries to the conversational space are enacted seeing as access is restricted and guarded by the CEO. The set-up of boundaries produces the affordance that participants are reluctant to air concerns. The question is, however, whether it is actually possible to enact boundaries to the conversational space? The attempt to create a delimited conversational space for the co-creation of K2M to take place within is clearly influenced by a transmission-based understanding of brand management, one where communication is understood in line with the *container metaphor*. In such an understanding the steering group meeting is a container for communication to take place *within* and access to the "container" can be controlled and regulated. Decisions and agreements reached in the "container" can later be transmitted to other, relevant organizational members. Such an understanding of brand management is in line with Edlinger's (2015) findings. In her study of employer brand managers, Edlinger (2015) found that the managers understood brand creation as a step-by-step process that took place in a sheltered environment, where the brand managers controlled involvement in the process.

However, the purpose of the present analysis is to break with this container-metaphor understanding of brand management in order to broaden the understanding of which voices participate in the co-creation of brand meaning. In the next paragraph, I will illustrate that there are more participants in the conversational space than just the people who have been invited.

5.2 Participation of non-human actors

In Chapter 2, I argued that texts and/or materiality may function as non-human actors as they have a voice of their own, and they are able to display agency. D-discourses can also display agency as they speak on behalf of a collectivity and can be conceptualized as macro-actors. Non-human actors do not have a certain agency per se. Their agency is dependent on how it is being appropriated and by whom. The agency is thus an instance of *hybrid agency*. An important concept in this relation is that of *ventriloquism*. As described in Chapter 2, a ventriloqual approach is based on "noticing that a variety of forms of agency are always in play in *any* interaction" (Cooren, 2012, p. 4). The concept of ventriloquism thus introduces the idea that human actors participating in a conversational space are never alone on the site of construction of meaning. Ventriloquism can be used to make someone or something *speak through* you, and it is a way of inviting absent actors to participate in the conversational space. Ventriloquism may also be used to *tele-act*. By producing a dummy, for instance a text, the original author is able to *speak through* that text, thus to *tele-act* (Cooren, 2006, 2016). A text is always produced by someone. It can be said to speak in the name of its author, but when a text leaves its site of construction, it is no longer controlled by the original author. Hence, even though a text is produced with a certain objective in mind, it does not have a certain agency per se. The agency of a text will depend on who reads it, and how (or whether) it is being appropriated. Ventriloquism is also a strategy that can be used to bolster (or question) authority. As Cooren and Sandler (2014) explain, a way to back one's argument is to position oneself "as *not the only one who says what he or she says*" (p. 234, italics in original).

In my analysis of Nicotera's sixth phase of her phasic model (Chapter 4), I briefly mentioned that the CEO is a ventriloquist who animates Lucy. In my data, I found that Lucy is not the only one to be animated by the CEO, and the CEO is not the only ventriloquist. Rather there exists a plethora of ventriloquists and dummies, and a ventriloquist needs not be human. A non-human actor can function as a ventriloquist as it can animate a human actor to speak on its behalf. I therefore argue that the people, things, institutions, and D-discourses that are being ventriloquized participate as nonhuman actors or macro-actors in the conversational space. The agency of these actors will depend on how their voices are orchestrated by the actors who invoke them, since it is a matter of hybrid agency constituted by the ventriloquist and the dummy, and as will be seen, the different agencies are entangled.

K2M chart as non-human actor

An important aim of the first steering group meeting is to reach a common understanding of K2M (cf. excerpt 5.1), and as explained in Chapter 4, the CEO, Dave, and Lucy have drawn up a chart to graphically represent K2M (hereafter the K2M model), which is distributed at the beginning of the meeting. As explained in Chapter 4 (4.6. Phase 5), the K2M model is a *pre-sentification* that has been produced in order to define and map K2M. This model (Figure 5.1) visualizes a number of tools that are deemed central to the communication of K2M.

The production of a model is a re-semiotization of earlier conversations into a permanent medium; it presents K2M as "a fact" because meanings presented

Figure 5.1 Data material – The K2M model

in printed written text are harder to challenge than talk (Iedema, 2003). Talk and text form a self-organizing loop since talk is re-semiotized into text (as seen in the K2M model), and text is the raw material of talk as it informs and guides future conversations. The K2M model is a *surface* (a set of done discourse) to the brand, and accordingly, the K2M model makes the brand present (*presentification*). But the production of the K2M model is also the production of a *non-human actor*.

The K2M model is a non-human actor because it is able to *speak for* the K2M philosophy (see for instance, Cooren, 2012). The model *divides* K2M into three pillars, which the CEO refers to as the "trinity of K2M", and each pillar *identifies* an area of key concern. The model *delegates* the power of authoring K2M to the people who engage with the model (see Iedema, 2003), and it *incites* the participants in the steering group to make sure they consider all three areas in their work with K2M, given that the labelling of the model as a trinity signals the importance of each pillar. The three pillars thus become *structuring* for every steering group meeting as the participants continually orient towards the model to check their progress and consider what their next step ought to be. Metaphorically speaking, the model gains a seat at the table on an equal footing with the human actors as it participates in the discussions about K2M.

The drawing up of a non-human actor thus serves to distanciate K2M from the original authors because they vanish from view. As discussed in Chapter 4, the CEO has been the primary author of K2M, and it has been difficult for other authors to participate in the authoring process. But with the model, K2M is no longer an idea that solely exists in the head of the CEO; it is an idea that is materialized and represented by a non-human actor. Therefore, a naturalization of K2M takes place, and that makes it possible for other actors to participate in the authoring of K2M.

Agency of the K2M model

The significance of the K2M model's attendance in the conversational space is brought to the fore when a middle manager asks how a coupling might be created between the branding-pillar and the CSR-pillar, and the CEO states that he does not think everything can be integrated. However, the participants go on discussing the possible correlation between branding and CSR, and based on the examples discussed, the CEO acknowledges that there might be a closer coalition between the three pillars than he had originally thought. In this instance, the CEO is ready to revise his own understanding of K2M even though he is the original author of the concept. It is thus seen how the model becomes vested with authority and is able to distribute agency to the people present. Due to its modality as printed text (that represents a fact already agreed upon) it is able to specify an aspect of K2M and thus affect the conversation. This supports the point that text and conversation form a self-organizing loop. The CEO has been the sole author for a long time but the creation of the K2M model is the creation of a powerful non-human actor that specifies K2M, and it is an actor that can act in its own name.

It is, however, noteworthy that this is a question of *hybrid agency*. Since the K2M-model (Agent$_1$) is a non-human actor, it cannot make itself heard unless it is being appropriated by a human actor. In the example above, the middle manager (Agent$_2$) manages to create a hybrid (Agent$_{1+2}$) that convinces the CEO to adjust his own understanding of K2M. Everybody who engages with the model creates a new hybrid constellation of agency. If the model is Agent$_1$ (A$_1$) and the human participants are A$_2$, A$_3$, A$_4$ and so on, there is the constellation of (A$_{1+2}$), (A$_{1+3}$), (A$_{1+4}$) and so forth (see Taylor, 1999). There are thus many different constellations of hybrid agencies as the hybrid agency is constituted between the model and each of the participants. Because the model only forms one part of the hybrids, the person who appropriates it constitutes the other part. Hence, every hybrid will be different from one another, and thus the agency will be different. A non-human actor does thus not have a certain agency per se; its agency is dependent upon how it is being appropriated and by whom. Whoever appropriates the model exercises his or her agency on it, and the model is thus rephrased (see Taylor & Van Every, 2011).

From a ventriloqual perspective, the K2M model can be understood as a dummy. The K2M department (i.e., the CEO, Lucy, and Dave) has delegated the agency of defining K2M to a nonhuman actor that is supposed to speak on their behalf. In that sense, the K2M model is a dummy animated by the K2M department. The CEO, Lucy, and Dave are *speaking through* the model, thus the model is *tele-acting* on their behalf. But the previous finding illustrates that once a dummy leaves its site of construction, it is no longer controlled by the original ventriloquist as other ventriloquists may appropriate the dummy and speak through it with a different voice. The fact that the K2M model (the dummy) is able to act back on the CEO is in line with the discussion of ventriloquism put forward by Cooren (2016), who states that the relationship between the ventriloquist and the dummy is reciprocal. By this, he means that it is not only the ventriloquist who animates the dummy but that the dummy acts back and animates the ventriloquist. Accordingly, every actor is both a ventriloquist and a dummy, which is also known as passer (i.e. someone or something through which other actors or concerns can express themselves).

This paragraph illustrates that the K2M model becomes an important non-human participant in the conversational space. A non-human actor is, however, dependent on a human actor to activate its agency in a hybrid constellation. It is therefore relevant to consider non-human actors from a ventriloqual perspective given that a non-human actor can be conceptualized both as a dummy and as a ventriloquist. A dummy is always produced by someone and is thus pre-programmed to speak with a certain voice. But once a dummy leaves its site of construction, it is no longer controlled by the original ventriloquist, and other actors can animate the dummy to make it speak with a different voice. The dummy is, however, also able to animate, seeing that it participates in the conversational space on an equal footing with the other participants. As argued by Cooren (2012), there is seen to be a constant oscillation (or vacillation) between the dummy and the ventriloquist. They animate each other and, in the case in point, we see that the K2M model is able to assume the role of ventriloquist and animate or speak through other organizational members when they appropriate the model.

In the next section, I will illustrate how the K2M model is able to invite other non-human actors to participate in the conversational space. The first kind of actor I will focus on is the D-discourse.

D-discourse as macro-actor

In Chapter 2, I argued that D-discourses are macro-actors because they express collective agency. A D-discourse speaks on behalf of a group of people or a profession, and D-discourses can be identified in d-discourses (Cooren et al., 2013). Looking at the K2M model, we see that each pillar features a headline: "CSR and Sustainable Growth", "Branding", and "Corporate Culture". These headlines can be understood as D-discourses, as the signifiers belong to a professional D-discourse. A D-discourse is an account that you recognize in the sense that you are able to recognize the typical content of the D-discourse as well as its typical context (Cooren, 2015). A D-discourse represents a socially accepted truth and thus expresses a universal, historically situated set of vocabulary about a certain phenomenon (Fairhurst & Putnam, 2004). Hence, the signifier 'CSR' is recognized as an account of companies assuming a social responsibility, 'branding' is recognized as an account of emotional selling proposition, and 'corporate culture' is recognized as an account of employees as a central resource. The three D-discourses are what Alvesson and Karreman (2000) term a *Mega-Discourse*. A Mega-Discourse is a discourse of a more or less universal way to perceive a phenomenon. The three headlines of the pillars in the K2M model can thus be understood to reflect a universal understanding of 'CSR', 'branding', and 'corporate culture'. Another way to put it is that the D-discourses function as ventriloquists. Due to their material presentification in the K2M model, they are allowed to *speak through* the model. In this section, I will elaborate how the CSR D-discourse participates in the conversational space.

CSR D-discourse

The first pillar in the K2M model is labelled "CSR & Sustainable Growth", and when the human actors at SGM1 discuss CSR, their ideas about what constitutes CSR do not emerge spontaneously at the meeting, rather they are retrieved from an existing CSR D-discourse. At the first steering group meeting, Lucy introduces CSR as concern for environmental or social aspects, such as employee wellbeing, but otherwise CSR is referred to as "traditional CSR", which implies that a common understanding of CSR is taken for granted. Therefore, I see the CSR D-discourse as a macro-actor that *informs* the discussions in the conversational space and thus participates as a non-human actor. The D-discourse *speaks through* the participants whenever they voice understandings informed by the CSR D-discourse. This might be when they talk about working conditions, accidents at work, slow steaming, fuel consumption, dangerous cargo, animal welfare, battery chickens, waste and wastewater reduction or water consumption. It can also be when the CEO states that water is the new oil, and "there is no planet B", or they discuss the need to prevent the use of child labor in their production. The CSR D-discourse is being ventriloquized by the human actors present at the steering group meetings, and so it becomes a voice in the conversational space.

Yet, as already argued, the CSR D-discourse is a Mega-Discourse that functions at a general and universal level (Alvesson & Karreman, 2000), or as expressed by the CEO:

Excerpt 5.4

> [...] CSR is a lot of things and everybody cannot ... we cannot do it all, ehm ... and I think it is important to realize that, and therefore I think it is important that, the individual subsidiaries work out what kind of KPIs *they* have in that company in relation to CSR [...].

Even though, the CSR D-discourse informs the conversations in the steering group, the macro-actor does little to explicate how CSR is to be comprehended in relation to Globalco and K2M specifically, or how the organizational members are supposed to go about the task of working with CSR. The CEO, Lucy, and Dave have thus incorporated another macro-actor into the K2M model in order to guide the work with CSR, namely the KPI D-discourse.

The KPI D-discourse functions as another ventriloquist that is allowed to *speak through* the K2M model. It is used to *dictate* that the subsidiaries need to formulate a number of company-based KPIs and the managing directors of the subsidiaries are made accountable by the introduction of a new instrument of performance measure. In addition to the company based KPIs, the K2M model stipulates that each managing director ought to be held accountable according to a set of personal KPIs linked to the individual managing director. The KPI D-discourse is thus given a voice in the conversational space, and Lucy substantiates the importance and necessity of the KPIs by ventriloquizing CSR legislation.

CSR legislation as non-human actor

CSR legislation is a new kind of macro-actor that is given a voice in the conversational space. The legislation is invoked to *lend weight* to the CSR pillar in the K2M model. At the fourth steering group meeting in particular, CSR legislation is assigned a central voice. The CEO states that there are new legal requirements that they need to meet:

Excerpt 5.5

> Today Lucy arrives with the law in her hand.

Lucy uses the same figurative language, when she says:

Excerpt 5.6

> I have been looking in the statute book.

The CEO and Lucy speak metaphorically as if the CSR legislation was physically present, thereby creating a phantom existence of an invisible macro-actor that needs to be respected. Hence, what the CSR law *dictates* is not up for discussion, so if it is *required* by the law, it is something, they *need to* do as expressed by the CEO:

Excerpt 5.7

> We have a law – you could say there is a statutory requirement levelled at Globalco – and because of that, we have to make sure that you all meet [the requirements] all the way through the system.

CSR legislation is given a voice in the conversational space that *states* that the subsidiaries as well as Globalco *are required to* work with CSR. CSR legislation is thus an active participant in the conversational space and a powerful one too as it has the authority to *dictate* activities. Since CSR legislation is a non-human actor, it cannot act on its own. Its needs to be appropriated by a human actor and it is made to speak through ventriloquism. Both Lucy and the CEO are seen to ventriloquize the CSR legislation. They position themselves (and the K2M model) as the dummies and make CSR legislation *speak through* them. In this way, it is the law that *states requirements* rather than the CEO or Lucy. Lucy and the CEO use the strategy of ventriloquism to bolster the authority of the CSR pillar in the K2M model as well as their own authority. When Lucy and the CEO appropriate the CSR legislation, a hybrid agency is formed that is able to communicate the necessity of working with CSR in a very authoritative way which underscores that the work with CSR is not up for discussion.

When Lucy introduces the K2M model, she establishes that the main point with the CSR activities is that Globalco is legally required to produce a CSR-report once a year. She explains that the KPIs are part of the K2M model because she needs some dry figures from the subsidiaries that she can use to feed into the CSR report. Lucy thus appropriates the CSR legislation to produce a hybrid agency consisting of Lucy (Agent$_3$) and the legislation (Agent$_4$) to back the legitimacy of KPI being part of the K2M model. Lucy positions herself as a dummy that ventriloquizes a powerful macro-actor – CSR legislation – that Globalco has to comply with. By doing so, she bolsters her own authority, seeing that no one can argue against the legislation. But her use of ventriloquism also serves to bolster the authority of the CSR pillar in the K2M model, the authority of the Globalco CSR report, and the authority of KPIs. These non-human actors are thus seen to become entangled, making it impossible to single out the agency of each actor. It is thus not the sorting out of single agencies that is of interest but rather the authority created by the production of hybrid agencies.

Lucy is backed by the CEO who informs the participants that the requirements for the CSR report will be even more rigorous in 2020, and at the fourth steering group meeting, the CEO states that the work with KPIs is not something they do because they find it fun and enjoyable; it is something they *need to* do, because Globalco is legally required to publicize a CSR report. It is however relevant to pinpoint that the CSR legislation does not specifically state that companies need to identify KPIs. Hence Lucy and the CEO are deceitful dummies because they make it appear that they are simply mouthing the CSR legislation when they are in fact twisting the words of the ventriloquist. When a middle manager directly questions Lucy at the fourth steering group meeting about whether KPIs need to be measurable in percentages, Lucy acts as a loyal dummy in conceding that the company just needs to be able to account for results.

Deceitful dummies or not, CSR legislation becomes a macro-actor that *speaks through* Lucy and the CEO. It is the legislation that has animated the K2M department to incorporate KPIs into the K2M model and accordingly, CSR legislation *guides* the construction of K2M by *requesting* that a number of KPIs are identified. In addition, the CSR legislation has *urged* Lucy to produce another macro-actor, namely a K2M code of conduct. The agency of the K2M code of conduct is inextricably linked with the agency of another macro-actor, namely the UN Global Compact Guiding Principles.

The UN Global Compact guiding principles as macro-actor

The participants at SGM1 find it difficult to narrow down what CSR means in relation to K2M. A middle manager suggests that they take a look at the Ten Principles of the UN Global Compact and choose two or three principles as their area of focus. Accordingly, the Ten Principles of the UN Global Compact becomes a macro-actor participating in the conversational space, and it has agency in the sense that it *guides* the selection of focus areas based on the 10 areas of concern defined by the UN. It is, however, a question of hybrid agency as the ten principles of the UN Global Compact only *identifies* and *describes* ten principles; it is up to the human actors in the steering group to *select* a number of principles they want to concentrate on and *specify* how they will put it into practice.

The ten principles of the UN Global Compact seem to be a helpful macro-actor to the middle managers, and thus it is also invited to participate in the local meetings in the subsidiaries. Based on the K2M model, the middle managers have been asked to have a meeting with their managing directors in order to identify a number of focus areas and to set KPIs. At the first local meeting in GoNuGa, a middle manager pursues the idea of using the ten principles of the UN Global

Compact to select some focus areas. She mentions that hitherto GoNuGa's work with CSR has been informed by UN Global Compact and so introduces its ten principles as a framework. She suggests that they focus on the environment part, which the managing directors agree to. When the steering group meets again for a second meeting, the middle managers are asked to present the focus areas that have been identified at the local meeting. When a middle manager presents the group's chosen focus areas, it is evident that UN Global Compact has been an active agent in the selection process:

Excerpt 5.8

MM: Yes, and then headhunted from Global Compact. That is what is called principle number 7, 8 and 9. They are the ones … those are the areas we wish to work with, right. And say … maybe we will develop something else along the way, right. But for now, this is our focus areas for the next … until 2022, right.

CEO: Yes.

MM: So, we have made … under principle number 7 … it says "In GoNuGa we want to approach our uses and treatment of water resources, here under wastewater treatment, in each company around the world" … I have mailed it to Lucy … and number B "In GoNuGa we want to approach the uses of energy in each company around the world".

CEO: Yes. These things you mention, is that your KPIs or is it some guidelines?

MM: They are guidelines. I simply adhere to Global Compact

CEO: Yes. Fine. That is what I thought. I just wanted to make sure.

The middle manager clearly ventriloquizes the ten principles of the UN Global Compact. It is evident that it is the macro-actor 'UN Global Compact Principles' that has *guided* the choice of focus areas. Another middle manager even expresses it directly when she says:

Excerpt 5.9

So, in our perspective, CSR is UN Global Compact.

The UN Global Compact is clearly a participant in both of the conversational spaces (the steering group and the local meetings in GoNuGa). It turns out that GoTech has chosen the same three principles, which means that the UN Global Compact is also an active participant in the conversational space constituted by the local meetings at GoTech. When Jill realizes that several of the subsidiaries have partnered up with the ten principles of the UN Global Compact, she establishes that CSR *is* UN Global Compact, and she suggests writing it in the K2M model:

Excerpt 5.10

> Maybe we should even write it in the model in order to respect that it applies to all of us. That is what we have decided.

Jill's suggestion illustrates the importance of material presentification. The ten-principled UN Global Compact is present as an immaterial macro-actor in the conversational space, but Jill would like to materialize the partner. As long as the macro-actor has no material existence, its presence is dependent upon presentification through talk (i.e. ventriloquism). A material existence would remind the organizational members about the macro-actor's presence, even when it is not being ventriloquized, and make sure that UN Global Compact is remembered as a matter of concern. It would also affirm that the UN Global Compact is a regular member of the conversational space, since a decision is harder to challenge when it is re-semiotized into text because a text reflects a decision already agreed upon (Iedema, 2003).

Though the UN Global Compact is not given a material presentification in the K2M model at this stage in the process, it is being incorporated into another macro-actor that becomes a regular member of the conversational space, namely the K2M code of conduct.

Code of conduct as macro-actor

At the fourth steering group meeting, Lucy introduces a K2M code of conduct. The code of conduct has been formulated because of the legal requirements in the CSR legislation in order to communicate that Globalco complies with the law. Another purpose is to make it easier for the subsidiaries to follow up on each other and to promote transparency about what Globalco demands of the subsidiaries, and what the subsidiaries can demand of Globalco. The code of conduct is thus a macro-actor that *delegates responsibility* and *establishes* a number of procedures for the ongoing work with K2M as mentioned in Chapter 4 (4.6). The code of conduct is introduced subsequent to the talk about Lucy arriving with the law in her hand (see excerpt 5.5), thus the authority of the code of conduct is inextricably linked with the authority of the CSR legislation. Together the two macro-actors produce a hybrid agency that substantiates the legitimacy of the K2M code of conduct.

The K2M code of conduct *establishes* that K2M is an overarching philosophy of how Globalco defines and conducts its corporate responsibility. It *states* that this code of conduct will elaborate on the definition of K2M and on its policies and principles that all subsidiaries are expected to meet. The first section is titled "What is K2M?" It *explains* K2M as a belief that Globalco's actions will reflect back on the organization, and that Globalco acts up to the mantra of "doing kind business". Globalco does so by considering an "all-win" strategy that benefits its partners, customers and employees, as well as charity.

The code of conduct thus has a voice of its own that produces discourses (a surface) about K2M that become part of the discursive brand space. It *determines* that K2M is about "doing kind business" and pursuing an "all-win". Like the CSR legislation, it is a powerful participant in the conversational space because it is a text that is positioned as a policy. Accordingly, the middle managers must make sure their subsidiaries comply with the code of conduct (cf. the code of conduct establishes that the subsidiaries are *expected to meet* the policies and principles stated).

The second section is titled "K2M Guiding Policies", and it *states* that Globalco has implemented a set of guiding principles emanating from the UN Global Compact Principles, and the code of conduct further *identifies* three key focus areas, namely the "human", the "globe", and the "economy". The K2M code of conduct thus materializes the inclusion of the UN Global Compact principles in the conversational space as it specifically *mentions* how Globalco aligns its principles with those of the UN Global Compact. The UN Global Compact is thus given a voice, since it is its guiding principles that *define* Globalco's guiding principles; accordingly, the discourses produced by UN Global Compact principles is made part of the discursive brand space constituting K2M.

The K2M code of conduct is an important non-human participant in the conversational space because it *establishes a set of guidelines* that all other participants have to adhere to. It is presented by Lucy as a policy that has been formulated due to CSR legislation (i.e. something that must be respected). The authority of the K2M code of conduct is thus strengthened due to the *hybrid agency* that is formed between the K2M code of conduct and the CSR legislation. Legislation must be obeyed without discussion or exception and accordingly, CSR legislation *lends authority* to the K2M code of conduct. In the opening of the subsequent steering group meeting, the CEO repeats that compliance with the code of conduct is mandatory, thereby enforcing its authority once again.

The presence of Buddha

At the second steering group meeting, Buddha is made present. The participants talk about Globalco awards, and a middle manager mentions that a Buddha is bought for the winner. The CEO mentions that Lucy has become an expert in ordering Buddhas which indicates that Buddha is a commonly used artifact at Globalco. Buddha is not otherwise made to speak at the meeting, but the figure remains present in the discourse throughout the steering group meetings, and a Buddha figure is physically present at all subsidiaries (i.e. it is a material discourse).

At the fourth steering group meeting, Lucy introduces a Buddha Baton. The Buddha Baton is supposed to work as a delegate for the K2M department. It works in the way that a Buddha figure travels from subsidiary to subsidiary around the world in the suitcase or briefcase of employees. When an employee receives a visit from the Buddha, the employee is supposed to take some photos and write a story that tells what the Buddha has experienced and post it on the My K2M webpage. The employee then passes the Buddha on to a colleague, who continues the baton. Lucy says the Buddha is a symbol of their common value, and the idea behind the Buddha baton is to create some interesting and different content to My K2M that will make it attractive for the organizational members to use the page. The Buddha Baton is supposed to *remind* employees about a common value and *incite* them to use the My K2M page, which is an integral part of the 'Corporate culture' pillar of the K2M model.

As mentioned, Buddha does not directly participate in the conversations of the steering group, but in the next chapter I will return to Buddha and how Buddha is seen to affect the *discursive brand space* after all.

The analyses above serve to demonstrate that a conversational space is not only made up of human actors that have been invited. Non-human actors are also important actants. The Globalco case demonstrates that at least six non-human actors participate as active participants in the conversational space, namely the K2M model; the model *divides* K2M into three pillars and *identifies* a number of areas of key concerns. CSR legislation *lends weight* to the CSR pillar in the K2M model and states that Globalco is *required to* report about its CSR. The K2M code of conduct *establishes procedures* and the UN Global Compact *guides* the selection of focus areas. The CSR D-discourse *informs* the conversations and the KPI D-discourse *demands* specific measuring. All of these non-human actors display a certain agency that affects the conversations going on in the conversational space, and thus they all contribute to the production of the discursive brand space.

The above analyses have mainly been informed by data from the steering group meetings and accordingly, the analyses center around the conversational space constituted by the steering group. However, I briefly mentioned that the middle managers were instructed to conduct a meeting with their managing directors. The next part of the analysis will therefore focus on another conversational space, namely the conversational space constituted by the local meetings in GoNuGa.

5.3 Ventriloquism as a strategy to bolster or question authority

At the first steering group meeting it is decided to leave the identification of focus areas and the determination of KPIs to the managing directors in each subsidiary. Consequently, the middle managers are instructed to arrange a meeting with their managing directors to start the process. By the end of SGM1, Dave has encouraged the CEO to send out a director's email to inform the managing directors about the decision and the middle managers agree that it would be appropriate. In the following, I will focus on the meetings at GoNuGa. I will analyze how the director's email becomes an important non-human actor in this conversational space as well as how ventriloquism is continuously used as a strategy to either question or bolster authority.

The local meetings at GoNuGa constitute another conversational space, where two managing directors and three middle managers are invited. The two conversational spaces – the steering group meetings and the local meetings – exist as two separate conversational spaces. The linkage between the spaces is the two middle managers who participate in both. The fact that the managing directors have not been invited to the steering group meetings means that the traditional organizational hierarchy in Globalco has been circumvented. The circumvention of hierarchy puts the middle managers in the position of having to return to their managing directors and instruct them in what they are supposed to do/what is required of them. As a rule, the middle managers do not have authority to instruct their managing directors. The only one who can grant the middle managers that authority is the CEO, but he does not participate in the local meetings. However, a director's email authored by the CEO would authorize by proxy and grant the middle managers the needed authority, by stipulating that they have been appointed to carry out the process of developing K2M. The director's email is therefore an important non-human actor as it can be seen to function as a delegate for the CEO, able to inform the managing directors about what is expected of them and empower the middle managers to lead the process. A director's email can thus be understood as the CEO tele-acting. However, the director's email is not sent out until much later in the process, and that causes some problems.

Since GoNutri and GoGastro market themselves jointly as the GoNuGa Group, a joint meeting is summoned. As already mentioned, the linkage between the two conversational spaces is the two middle managers, but it will be seen that one of the middle managers invites a number of other actors from the steering group meeting to participate in the GoNuGa meeting, namely some non-human actors.

Presentation of the K2M model

At the first meeting with the managing directors, one of the middle managers chooses to draw the K2M model on a white board. The K2M model is thus the first non-human actor the middle manager introduces in the conversational space constituted by the GoNuGa meeting. The middle manager opens the meeting by saying:

Excerpt 5.11

> Well. We have had this chart handed out, and I have tried to illustrate it on the board so that we can all see it.

It is not clear why the middle manager chooses to draw the model on a whiteboard instead of making a photocopy, but even though the modality is different, the K2M model is physically present as a text in the GoNuGa meeting. The middle manager goes on by saying:

Excerpt 5.12

> This is of course Sam's interpretation … overall interpretation … of K2M.

The middle manager presents the K2M model as a non-human actor created by the CEO. By introducing the K2M model in this way, she makes the CEO *speak through* the model. The middle manager is thus creating a phantom presence of the CEO at the meeting. The invocation of the authority of the CEO is a strategy to bolster her own authority. Seeing that the director's email has not yet been sent, the managing directors have not been informed about the decision made at the first steering group meeting. The middle manager is thus put in a position where she has to instruct her managing directors about the future development of K2M and how the two managing directors are expected to participate in that process, but the middle manager has not been formally authorized to do so. She therefore needs to invoke the voice of someone who outranks the managing directors, as the middle manager herself is not authorized to instruct her superiors. She thus creates two different kinds of hybrid agencies: the CEO (Agent$_5$) and herself (Agent$_6$), which make the hybrid (A$_{5+6}$), and the CEO (Agent$_5$) and the K2M model (Agent$_1$), which make the hybrid (A$_{5+1}$). The authority of the CEO is thus used to bolster both the middle manager's authority and the authority of the K2M model. The middle manager goes on to explain the K2M model but she is soon interrupted by a managing director, who asks:

Excerpt 5.13

What is the scope? I suppose there are some deadlines.

The managing director is apparently animated by a lack of knowledge, which can be ascribed to the missing director's email. The middle manager was relying on the director's email to inform and prepare the managing directors for what was expected of them but it has not been sent. The missing macro-actor creates a concern that animates the managing director to interrupt the middle manager's presentation as he reacts to a lack of knowledge. However, the interruption also marks a power relation; the managing director obviously thinks of himself as authorized to interrupt the middle manager. The middle manager answers the question by stating that the scope of today's meeting is to discuss how they will approach the work with KPIs, but that prompts a question from the second managing director:

Excerpt 5.14

MD1: But KPIs …
MM: We are going to start up the process.
MD1: But KPI's … just in order to define KPI's in this context … because, I thought we were going to find a new branding project?
MM: There is more to it …
MD1: Or what are KPI's in this context? I don't really understand …
MM: Well, if we start with pillar number one, CSR, that is what he [the CEO] calls business strategies. That means that is how we support sustainable growth in the companies.

We see from these two excerpts that the middle manager is challenged by both of the managing directors. One interrupts in order to inquire about the scope of today's meeting, and the other managing director interrupts to inquire about the meaning of KPIs. Both managing directors thus seem to be animated by a lack of knowledge. The middle manager does not explicitly answer the question about what KPI's are. Instead, she starts explaining the model, clearly ventriloquizing the CEO, when she says, "that is what *he* calls business strategies" (emphasis added). By making the CEO *speak through* her, she invokes his authority and creates a hybrid agency that can bolster her own authority. As already mentioned, the middle manager faces the challenge of communicating against the traditional hierarchy granted by Globalco, and by acting as a dummy animated by the CEO, the middle manager positions herself as the messenger (or passer). She makes it very clear that the K2M model is not a proposal coming from her; it is coming from the CEO. Hence, if the managing directors are questioning the tasks she puts forward, it corresponds to questioning tasks put forward by the CEO. The middle manager continues her explanation, but she is soon interrupted by the first managing director once again:

Excerpt 5.15

MM: Well, if we start with pillar 1 here, that is what he calls business strategies.
    That is, what is it that we do in the factories that spurs sustainable growth?
MD1: Yes.
MM: How can we do it better? And how can we measure it so that we are able
    to see that we have become better at it. And that is—
MD2: [interrupts] Better at what? Really …

It is clear that the two managing directors are not afraid of interrupting and asking clarifying questions. As stated earlier, there is a reluctance to ask questions at the steering group meetings and accordingly, middle managers do not develop their repertoire about K2M. That makes it very difficult for the middle manager to answer the questions from her managing directors and, as it is seen, she does not answer the question about how KPIs are to be understood in the context of the K2M model.

The interruptions from the managing directors disturb the middle manager's start-up of the meeting and undermines her authority. Due to the traditional hierarchy in Globalco, the managing director is in a position where he can interrupt the middle manager, given his position as her superior. Hence, not only does the missing director's email fail to inform the managing directors about important decisions, it also fails to empower the middle manager. She has not been constituted as the "K2M-executive" and she has thus not been granted a position that authorizes her to do the talking at the meeting. The managing directors' behavior underscores the importance of the director's email. An email from the CEO corresponds to a dummy tele-acting on behalf of the CEO, and a director's email would thus have created a phantom presence of the CEO in the conversational space. But since the director's email has not been produced yet, the CEO is not present. The middle manager thus uses a strategy of ventriloquism, where she evokes the CEO's authority by positioning herself as a dummy and making the CEO speak through her. Multiplying the sources of authorship amounts to multiplying the sources of authority (Cooren et al., 2012). Consequently, ventriloquism is used as a strategy to strengthen authority and a way to do so is to demonstrate that your claims are backed by other actors. However, the question is whether the middle manager actually succeeds in bolstering her authority? By ventriloquizing the CEO, she is giving him a voice at the expense of her own voice. As a delegate from the steering group, the middle manager ought to be authorized to speak, but when she positions herself as a dummy, she erodes the impact of her own voice.

Due to the interruptions and the challenges from the managing directors, it is clear that the non-human actor 'the K2M model' is not able to display the same authority in the GoNuGa meetings as it did at the steering group meeting. As mentioned, a non-human agent does not have a certain agency per se; its agency depends on how it is being appropriated and by whom. At the steering group meeting, the K2M model was introduced by the K2M department; it was clearly backed by the CEO and the K2M department. The hybrid agencies formed thus enjoyed the authority granted by the traditional hierarchy at Globalco, where the CEO and the K2M department enjoy a higher level of authority (when it comes to K2M) than the middle managers present. However, at the local meeting in GoNuGa the situation is reversed. The K2M model is now being presented by a middle manager, who holds a position that is inferior to the managing directors, when it comes to formal authority. The hybrid agency formed by the middle manager and the K2M model ($Agent_{6+1}$) is thus not as powerful as the hybrid agency created by the CEO and the K2M model ($Agent_{5+1}$), thus it becomes challenging for the middle manager to go against the traditional hierarchy in GoNuGa. By using the strategy of ventriloquism, the middle manager seeks to create another hybrid agency that includes the authority of the CEO ($Agent_{6+1+5}$). However, the middle manager still lacks authority, and at the second steering group meeting, she asks about the director's email.

Director's email as non-human actor

The middle manager clearly misses the director's email as an actant to empower her. At SGM2, she specifically asks Lucy if the director's email will be sent out, which Lucy promises it will. But when they get together at the second meeting in GoNuGa, it turns out that the director's email has still not been sent, and the managing directors request more information. The middle manager explains that she does not think she should be the one to inform them:

Excerpt 5.16

> It is going to be … and it is very wrong that the director's email has not
> been sent to you … because I have said that I think it is wrong that I am
> the one to tell you this, but I can say that it is a request from Sam that the
> managing directors are going to have these KPI's as a part of their con-
> tracts … and he [the CEO] will bring it up at the board meeting.

The middle manager explicitly mentions the director's email and states that the
information ought to have been conveyed by this actant instead of her. The
director's email would have had more authority since it would have been a
delegate communicating on behalf of the CEO. The director's email is thus an
authoritative non-human actor, and the fact that it is absent from the conversational space affects the middle manager's agency because she misses a
partner that can help her form a more authoritative hybrid agency. She is thus
invoking the director's email even though it does not exist yet by stating that *it*
ought to be the one to communicate this.

By the end of the second meeting in GoNuGa, they have agreed to write a
letter to GoNuGa's subsidiaries to involve them in the process, but another
middle manager interjects that he hopes they will receive a director's email
before they send out the letter because it is important that things are done in
the right order. They end up concluding that they will not do anything before
they have received a director's email, which prompts one of the managing
directors to ask:

Excerpt 5.17

> So, I am just gonna ask one question … why have we had a meeting today?

The middle manager replies that it is because they should have received the
director's email today. The (missing) director's email thus keeps being an active
non-human actor despite its lack of physical existence. The mere fact that a
director's email was suggested by Dave at SGM1 has created certain expectations, and those expectations have created the email as a nonhuman actor. As
Cooren and Sandler (2014, p. 233) explain, "Expectations are interesting in
terms of ventriloquism, because they *dictate* that some specific actions be taken
at specific moments". The fact that the managing directors have been promised
a director's email, creates an expectation about the appearance of this non-
human actor. As already discussed, the email is an important actant because it is
a delegate for the CEO. Hence, when the email is not produced, it might
signal a lack of interest or commitment from the CEO, thus the managing
directors are not being urged to prioritize the work with K2M.

In relation to the middle managers, the email is an important non-human
actor because it is supposed to be a central partner/ally in the conversational

space. The email is a seal of approval of their work from the CEO, and when the middle manager's expectation about the assistance of a non-human actor in the form of a director's email is not met, it makes her job harder to perform. Since she lacks obvious approval from the CEO, and even though she can make the email present in talk (discourse), it is more difficult to invoke its authority as long as it only exists as an intention. Accordingly, as long as the director's email is missing, its authority is missing. However, that does not mean that the (missing) director's email does not act. The middle managers have promised their managing directors that they will receive the director's email, and its lack of existence hinders the organizational members in GoNuGa from taking action. When it is agreed to postpone a decision in GoNuGa because of the missing director's email, it becomes evident that the email has agency, it does in fact act despite its (physical) non-existence. The email thus clearly affects the interaction going on in the conversational space, and the email is actually present as a non-human actor despite its non-existence. It is made present through presentification in talk, and the mere talk about a (future) director's email is enough to attribute agency to the email. Or it could be argued that the (missing) email fails to empower the managing directors to take action just like it fails to empower the middle manager as an authorized voice.

This analysis has mainly focused on ventriloquism as a strategy to bolster the authority of arguments put forward. In the next section, I will address how the loaded nature of macro-actors may complicate the communication in the conversational space.

The complexity of loaded macro-actors

The focus of this chapter is to demonstrate that a conversational space is not just made up of human actors. Rather a plethora of non-human actors participate through ventriloquism, and they become part of different hybrids of agencies. In the examples provided, I have focused on the participation of non-human actors who are invoked to support an argument by speaking with a voice that backs the dummy. For instance, the examples of the middle manager ventriloquizing the CEO and the example of Lucy ventriloquizing CSR legislation are both examples of this strategy. However, when a macro-actor is invited to participate, it can be seen to complicate the communication due to the complexity of loaded macro-actors. In the following, I will illustrate how different macro-actors prompt the managing directors to question the proposals put forward by the middle manager.

In excerpt 5.15, it was seen that one of the managing directors questioned the meaning of KPIs in the context of the K2M model. When the middle manager sets out to explain the notion of KPIs, it becomes evident that it is not so much the meaning of the concept of KPIs that the managing director is questioning as it is the legitimacy of the concept in the K2M model. This becomes evident when the middle manager starts explaining:

Excerpt 5.18

> [...] Are we going to reduce CO_2, are we going to save electricity or what
> is it that we do? Maybe we can identify some low-hanging fruit, where we
> can say, well we can actually measure this and become better at it [...].

The middle manager enumerates ideas or suggestions as to what could constitute a KPI, and she also mentions that the KPIs should feed into the K2M
report. Interestingly the concern that animated the managing director to ask the
question about what KPI is supposed to mean in the context of the K2M
model was not a need for an explanation of what the concept of KPI entails.
When he responds to the middle manager's explanation, it becomes clear that
what he is questioning is the authority of the K2M model:

Excerpt 5.19

MD1: Yes, I see. What I don't understand is ... if we look at business strategies,
sustainable growth and value based blah blah blah ... ehm ... actually that
is what is discussed in the boardroom ... ehm ... what are our strategies,
but is that disconnected from... is it only towards the employees?
MM: No.
MD1: I just need to understand ...
MM: The assignment from Sam is that you – as managing directors – are going
to be measured according to how you run the business ...

In the K2M model, the concept of KPI is placed under the heading "Key
factor in managing directors 2019–2022 strategy plans". A 'strategy plan' can be
conceptualized as a macro-actor in that it is a text that *states* objectives and
initiatives on behalf of the organization/management. Most importantly in this
situation, it is a macro-actor that is produced or modified in a specific conversational space, namely the board meeting. By incorporating a 'strategy plan'
into the K2M model, the macro-actor 'strategy plan' is made an actor in the
conversational space where K2M is discussed (i.e. the steering group meetings
and the local meetings). However, we see in the excerpt that the managing
director is questioning the legitimacy of the K2M model to invoke the macro-
actor 'strategy plan', since he states that business strategies are something that is
decided at board meetings. Hence, the identity of 'strategy plan' is not neutral,
rather is has a loaded character.

It is made apparent that the managing director attributes a certain managerial
right to the board meeting, but he does not attribute that same managerial right
to the steering group meetings or the local meetings in GoNuGa. Therefore,
he resists making decisions about KPIs and business strategy at a local meeting
like the one that the middle manager has summoned. He does not see the local
meeting in GoNuGa as the right forum for deciding on aspects that are part

of a business strategy because he does not recognize the middle manager/the steering group as authorized to making that request. He asks if the strategies only concern the employees. Hence, we see that the managing director is animated by a reluctance to accept a 'strategy plan' as a legitimate actor in the conversational space constituted by the local meeting. He reinforces this position at GoNuGa2 when he states:

Excerpt 5.20

> [...] if the board asks me to spend 80% of my time on reducing water waste, well then that is what I am supposed to do.

His statement indicates that only the board can order him to set new KPIs or change his business strategy. The macro-actors 'KPI' and 'business strategy' thus trigger a power struggle between the managing director and the K2M model as the director challenges the legitimacy of the K2M model to invoke those macro-actors. The power struggles at GoNuGa illustrate that labelling (i.e. choice of words) is not innocent, because labelling can invoke a macro-actor, and macro-actors are not neutral. Macro-actors like 'KPI' and 'business strategy' indicate at what levels decisions are to be made, and therefore the managing director challenges the legitimacy of invoking these macro-actors in the present conversational space. The middle manager's job is thus being complicated[1] by these macro-actors as her task is no longer just to explain the K2M model, but also to argue for the legitimacy of certain macro-actors.

ROI as macro-actor

The other managing director does not explicitly question the legitimacy of the 'business strategy' or the authority of the K2M model, but he invokes a new macro-actor to challenge the idea about KPI:

Excerpt 5.21

> And then you can say ... launch initiatives, yes, but it does not make sense to launch initiatives, if we do not get a reasonable ROI [return on investment], because you do not want to spend a million if you only receive 10 euro a month in return. There is no point in that.

The managing director ventriloquizes a new D-discourse and thus invites yet another macro-actor to participate in the conversational space, namely the D-discourse about ROI. ROI is a D-discourse about the profitability of different investments/initiatives (return on investment), and the ROI D-discourse is a macro-actor that is generally acknowledged as a voice to be reckoned with in the business community. By contrasting the CSR D-discourse/KPI D-discourse with the ROI D-discourse, the managing director expresses his skepticism towards launching CSR-based initiatives, and he questions the legitimacy of CSR-based KPIs. The ROI D-discourse is thus invoked to bolster the authority of a counterargument. Hence, by introducing the ROI D-discourse to the conversational space, the managing director backs his skepticism towards the CSR-based KPIs by introducing an accepted macro-actor that possibly contradicts the idea about launching CSR-based initiatives. According to the managing director and the ROI D-discourse, such initiatives should only be launched in cases where they are able to generate a satisfactory ROI.

At the second steering group meeting, 'ROI' is invoked by another middle manager; Anna supports her point of view by stating that 'ROI' was also part of the discussions in GoNuGa. The fact that a company first and foremost needs to make a profit to survive is questioned neither by the CSR D-discourse[2] nor by the CEO, who refers to the company as one of the winners in his all-win mantra, in the sense that K2M ought to provide a profit to Globalco. He expresses this in the following way:

Excerpt 5.22

You got to be in the blacks to go green.

He states that the K2M philosophy is tough business, and the CEO also invokes the ROI D-discourse. The ROI D-discourse is thus accepted as a legitimate macro-actor in the conversational spaces, even though it is invoked in order to question the reasonability of CSR-based KPIs, which is a central aspect of the K2M model.

Based on the examples above, it is evident that macro-actors have a loaded character. Their identity is not neutral, and one of the managing directors challenges the authority of the K2M model to invoke macro-actors such as 'KPI' and 'business strategy'. He believes those macro-actors belong to a different conversational space with a different managerial right. The other managing director challenges the legitimacy of the demand to launch CSR-based initiatives, and in order to back his resistance, he invites a new participant into the conversational space, namely the ROI D-discourse. Accordingly, we see how some macro-actors complicate the communication and how they can also be invoked in order to bolster a counterargument. As stated previously, multiplying the sources of authorship amounts to multiplying the sources of authority. Ultimately, the discursive struggles going on in the GoNuGa meetings illustrate how different actors are being ventriloquized to either question an idea or to back a claim.

5.4 Discussion of the conversational space

With this chapter, I set out to explicate the notion of a *conversational space* and to discuss the set-up of such. I have identified the set-up of two formal conversational spaces: the steering group meetings as one and the local meetings in GoNuGa as another. The purpose of both of these conversational spaces is to discuss the understanding and further development of K2M. The conversations in these conversational spaces are thus important contributions to the *discursive brand space* since a discursive brand space is the bricolage of all discourses produced about K2M.

In both instances, it is seen that boundaries are enacted. Since both of the conversational spaces are instances of organizational activity, there is an organizational hierarchy that enables the practice of inclusion and exclusion of human participants. The managing directors are excluded from the steering group meetings and the participating middle managers can be said to be included, as other middle managers could have been chosen. This fact is made present at the fifth steering group meeting, where Lucy and the CEO initiate a roundtable in order to question (or ask) whether the present middle managers are the right ones to participate in the conversational space; this happens again at SGM8. Due to the power positions granted by Globalco, it is possible to control access to the conversational space when it comes to participation of human actors. Yet, even though the managing directors are excluded from the steering group meetings, they are made present through ventriloquism on a number of occasions. A comment from a middle manager illustrates this:

Excerpt 5.23

> Right now, I can hear a managing director saying, "Easy now, they are also going to work".

The remark is uttered as a comment during a brainstorming process about the development of different hashtags in order to engage the employees in conversations about K2M on social media. Even though the managing director is not present, he is allowed to utter his concern as a middle manager lets him speak through her. The middle manager is thus voicing a concern on behalf of the managing director about allocation of time, that is, whether the employees are going to spend their time on communicating K2M or in performing their traditional tasks. This use of ventriloquism proves that the idea of being able to control access to the conversational space is only an illusion. The boundaries of the conversational space are fluid and impossible to control. This is a fact that is only underscored when we turn our attention to the participation of non-human actors.

These analyses have demonstrated that several non-human actors are invited to participate. The emergence of the K2M model, CSR legislation, the UN Global Compact, the K2M code of conduct, and a number of D-discourses in the conversational space, demonstrate that K2M is not just being authored by the human actors present. It further demonstrates that Globalco's members are not the only ones to participate in the authoring process. Macro-actors outside of the organization, such as CSR legislation, the UN Global Compact, and the KPI D-discourse, are invited to participate in the conversations and thus co-produce discourses that become part of the discursive brand space. Hence, it may be possible to control which of the organizational members can physically participate in the conversational spaces but it is impossible to control which actors are allowed to participate through ventriloquism. A plethora of macro-actors are invoked and used to create hybrids of agencies, and the analyses above allow us to see that a conversational space is characterized by polyphony. It is possible to identify an additional number of voices apart from the human actors present. Accordingly, the distinction between internal and external members of the organization is therefore meaningless since external partners can become important co-authors in the conversational space, and the production of branding discourses is essentially multivocal as many actors (human and non-human) are entangled.

However, the legitimacy of actors can be questioned as was the case in GoNuGa, when a managing director questioned the presence of 'business strategy'. A conversational space is formed at a certain hierarchical level in the organization, and that hierarchical level can, according to the managing director, dictate whether the participation of a certain actor is legitimate or not. He expresses an understanding that the conversational space constituted by the board meetings outranks the conversational space constituted by the steering group, which is a valid interpretation according to the power positions granted by Globalco. Since 'business strategy' is a macro-actor that is created by the board of directors at board meetings, he does not see the steering group as authorized to invite that macro-actor to participate as a practitioner of power in the conversational space constituted by the steering group meetings. In other words, he presents a point of view that a conversational space, constituted at a lower hierarchical level, cannot appropriate an actor residing at an upper hierarchical level in the organization. The participation of macro-actors is thus not unproblematic; it is an issue that is open to discussion. At the second meeting in GoNuGa, a suggestion is made to invite the macro-actor 'environmental report' into the conversational space by one of the managing directors, but the invitation is rejected by the other human actors due to the complexity of that macro-actor. The attempt to enact boundaries to the conversational space is thus not restricted to the participation of human actors; it also applies to the participation of non-human actors.

Polophony and hybrid agency in the conversational space

Besides the finding that the boundaries of conversational spaces are fluid and impossible to control, another important finding is the use of hybrid agency. In Chapter 2, I argued that organizations are *polyphonic,* and I will extend that argument to apply to the notion of a conversational space as well. It has been demonstrated that a plethora of human and non-human actors participate in the conversations and accordingly, it can be argued that multiple and heterogeneous voices "engage in a contest for audibility and power" (Belova et al., 2008, p. 493). However, the different voices are not of equal status[3] and the agency they are able to display is different. An often-used strategy to create a more authoritative voice is to *ventriloquize* another actor. By positioning oneself as a dummy that ventriloquizes another actor, a hybrid agency is produced that can be used to create a more authoritative voice. However, there is the risk of eroding the impact of one's own voice when ventriloquism is used. While Lucy succeeded in empowering her own voice by ventriloquizing CSR legislation, Anna eroded the impact of her voice when she ventriloquized the CEO. The use of ventriloquism should therefore be carefully considered.

When non-human actors are invoked, they do not have a certain agency per se. It has been demonstrated that it depends on the way they are being appropriated by a human actor and by whom. For instance, it was seen that a middle manager was able to appropriate the K2M model in a way that made the CEO revise his own understanding of K2M, but when another middle manager appropriated the K2M model in the local meeting in GoNuGa, the model was questioned by the managing directors. This finding suggests that hybrid agency is not only dependent on the human actors that appropriate a non-human actor, but also on the context (see also Taylor et al., 1996).

In the first example, a middle manager appropriates the K2M model and manages to change the CEO's perception. The context is the steering group, where everybody accepts the K2M model as a powerful non-human actor since it has been worked out by the CEO and the K2M department, thus the model tele-acts on their behalf. The agency of the K2M model ($Agent_1$) is not questioned in this conversational space at all, hence the middle manager ($Agent_2$) appropriates a powerful non-human actor ($Agent_{2+1}$). In the second example, the context is the local meeting in GoNuGa. The K2M model ($Agent_1$) has not been introduced in this conversational space (due to the missing director's email) and accordingly, it is being presented by a middle manager ($Agent_6$). Even though the middle manager makes use of ventriloquism in order to make the CEO ($Agent_5$) present the model, the hybrid agency produced by this middle manager and the K2M model ($Agent_{6+1}$) is not nearly as powerful as the hybrid agency produced by the other middle manager and the K2M model ($Agent_{2+1}$). This finding is in accordance with the proposition put forward in Chapter 2 that meaning is re-found in a text in each reading and that readings are affected by situational context (see also Taylor et al., 1996). The hybrid produced at GoNuGa can be said to be constituted by three agents in that the middle manager ventriloquizes the CEO ($Agent_{6+5+1}$), but it is evident that the agency of the CEO is not nearly as powerful when he is ventriloquized as when he is physically present. Another contextual factor that probably affects the agency is the distribution of power at Globalco. The hybrid agency produced by the K2M model and the second middle manager ($Agent_{1+6}$) is affected by the fact that the middle manager's formal position in Globalco is inferior to that of the managing directors to whom she is presenting the model. The managing directors are thus in a position where they can question and challenge the middle manager since she is their subordinate and they do not answer to her. Even though she ventriloquizes the CEO, the managing directors can challenge the authority of the K2M model without risk because the CEO is not physically present and accordingly, he cannot pick up on their resistance.

When ventriloquism works counterproductive to the creation of entitative being

As evident from the analyses above, a commonly used strategy to bolster authority is to ventriloquize the CEO. There is however a downside to this strategy. In Chapter 4, I established that K2M is very much seen as the CEO's personal philosophy and a lack of distanciation makes it difficult for other organizational members to incarnate K2M. The production of text is generally acknowledged to create distanciation from the original author. The main purpose of the production of the K2M model is to create a common understanding of K2M and to distanciate it from the CEO in order to make it possible for other organizational members to participate in K2M development. But when the CEO is being ventriloquized, it sustains the idea that he is the only one who can author K2M, the use of ventriloquism thus works counterproductive to the creation of distanciation. When the middle manager introduces the K2M model by saying, "This is of course Sam's interpretation … overall interpretation… of K2M" (excerpt 5.13), K2M is not being distanciated from the CEO, rather the coupling between the CEO and K2M is just being reaffirmed. The K2M model has been developed by the K2M department (i.e. the CEO, Lucy, and Dave), but the middle manager only attributes the model to the CEO and thus emphasizes the interdependence between K2M and the CEO. From this analysis, it became clear that the middle manager used the strategy of ventriloquism because she lacked authority in the conversational space. The finding thus pinpoints the importance of empowering the people who are supposed to lead the development of the discursive brand space. It is important that they are given a voice that is strong enough to speak authoritatively in the conversational space.

Conversational spaces are stages in a Tamara play

In my analysis, I have focused on two conversational spaces, namely the steering group meetings and the local meetings in GoNuGa. I argue that the conversational spaces (e.g. the steering group meeting, the local meetings, and the board meetings) correspond to different stages in a Tamara play. None of the organizational members have access to all stages, which means that their overall comprehension of the process is limited by their insight into what goes on at the stages to which they have access. It also means that the members listen to fragments of stories and never get the full picture.

The four middle managers have the important job of translating between the steering group meetings and the local meetings. Their job is to communicate to the other participants what goes on at the other stage, which requires the delivering of messages back and forth. For instance, at the first meeting in GoNuGa, participants ask about talk that has taken place at SGM1 or they express a desire to ask about something, and they agree to let the middle manager carry a question about clarification of the KPIs back to the steering group. At the next steering group meeting, the middle manager asks about the KPIs. The answer from the CEO is that each subsidiary ought to define three KPIs per parent company and that he wants some KPIs written into the managing directors' contracts. When the middle manager brings this message back to her managing directors at the second meeting at GoNuGa, they respond by stating that this would imply a renegotiation of their contracts, but the other middle manager believes that the KPIs will be incorporated as a bonus incentive. At the third steering group meeting, the middle managers from GoNuGa report that the managing directors are not opposed to having KPIs incorporated into their contracts even though they might "wriggle a bit". It is thus seen that the middle managers make a translation that softens the outright opposition expressed by the managing directors, who stated that only the board of directors could ask them to set new KPIs.

The complications about carrying messages back and forth is in line with Kornberger et al.'s (2006) thinking that the management of a polyphonic space corresponds to deconstructing and translating between different language games. The CEO clearly applies a different language game to the managing directors' contracts than the managing directors themselves. The task for the middle managers is thus to translate between these two different language games to help the participants understand what kind of discussions go on at the other stage. But in a Tamara play, insight will always only be partial as nobody is able to participate at all stages and accordingly, interpretation is affected by the story fragments that appear within their angle of view. It is, for instance, not clear why Sam, Lucy, and Dave overruled a joint decision to host a kindness camp for the managing directors as no one but these three people were present at the stage where the decision was made. One of the managing directors is reluctant to make decisions about business strategy and KPIs outside the board meetings, which is yet another stage, and one that the middle managers do not have access to. Hence, as no actors have access to all stages, understanding of organizational reality is based on the glimpses that each member is offered at the stages they have access to.

5.5 Summary

In the present chapter, I have analyzed the constitution of conversational spaces at Globalco, where K2M is discussed and brand meaning is constructed and negotiated. Some members try to enact boundaries to the conversational spaces by deciding who is invited and who is not, but I have demonstrated that conversational spaces are not just comprised by human actors; a number of nun-human actors participate as well. Some of these non-human actors have a physical presence in the form of texts (e.g. the K2M model and the K2M code of conduct), whereas others are made present through ventriloquism (discourse) (e.g. CSR legislation, UN Global Compact, and D-discourses). Ventriloquism is also used to invoke absent human actors. All actors – both human and non-human – are seen to participate in the production of discourses that feed into the discursive brand space which constitutes K2M.

Some of the non-human actors have deliberately been invited by brand management. For instance, the K2M model is invited to explicate how K2M is to be understood, CSR legislation is invited to lend weight to the importance of CSR, and the K2M code of conduct is invited to establish procedures. But other non-human actors are invited by other participants. For instance, the UN Global Compact is first invited by a middle manager at the first steering group meeting but is taken up by the K2M department and incorporated into the K2M code of conduct. The ROI D-discourse is invited by a managing director, and the 'environmental report' is being proposed as an appropriate participant but is being rejected by other members. It is thus not possible for brand management to control which actors participate in the conversations; all brand management can do is accept or challenge the legitimacy of the actors.

An interesting finding was the fact that the mere anticipation of a possible non-human actor is enough to make it present. The expectation of a director's email is created at SGM 1, October 6, but the email is not sent out until November 27, just the day before the third meeting of the steering group. Nevertheless, the (missing) email displays agency because it has been constituted as a non-human actor by Dave. The missing director's email has interfered with the process in that its non-existence hinders the organizational members from taking action. The director's email thus stands out as a non-human actor that affects the process because while it has been made present in talk and this presentification ascribes it agency, due to its lack of materiality it cannot deliver the input it is supposed to.

Accordingly, we see how the interaction between the human actors present is affected by the non-human actors, and all actors (human or not) are participants in the conversational space. Hence, to examine the constitution of a brand it does not suffice to look at the human actors participating in the conversational space. It is necessary also to recognize the agency of other actors that are invoked and participate in the negotiation and co-creation of meaning by the production of discourses. The findings demonstrate that the boundaries of the conversational space are not corporeal but discursive, meaning they are open and fluid and impossible to control. Accordingly, a conversational space is polyphonic. An organization will never be able to control who participates in the conversations about the brand, since (absent) actors can be made present through ventriloquism. It is also important to notice that the agency of the different actors is entangled. Anna's agency is entangled with the CEO when she ventriloquizes him and with the K2M model when she presents it. The K2M model's agency is entangled with the agency of the KPI D-discourse and CSR legislation and so forth. It is thus not possible to single out the individual participants as a plethora of human and non-human actors are inextricably linked in constellations of hybrid agencies.

As argued in Chapter 2, the understanding of a brand as a discursive brand space requires a new understanding of brand management. The findings in the present chapter demonstrate that management of the conversational space is not about controlling access since the brand manager cannot control which actors enter the different conversational spaces, and he cannot even control the number or set-up of conversational spaces as informal spaces may emerge. Rather, management of the conversational space becomes a question about management of talk and interaction, as conversational spaces are sites of struggles over meaning (see also Mumby, 2016). In the next chapter I will examine how meaning is negotiated and how the different human and non-human actors participate in circuits of sensegiving and sensemaking.

Notes

1 Once more, the middle manager's response is to ventriloquize the CEO, when she says, "the assignment from Sam is…".
2 For instance, Carroll (2016) ascertains that the economic responsibility is a primary concern for all businesses.
3 I do not refer to the formal organizational rank but rather the ability to make oneself heard.

6   Sensegiving by non–human actors

In the previous chapter, I examined the establishment of conversational spaces since this is where the discourses that feed into the discursive brand space are produced. It was demonstrated that human and non-human actors alike participate in the conversational spaces. It was also established that boundaries to the conversational space are not corporeal but discursive and thus fluid and permeable, seeing as actors who are not physically present can participate through ventriloquism. Accordingly, management of the conversational space is not about controlling access, but rather about managing talk and interaction. Another important question is therefore *how different actors affect the production of discourses* that feed into the *discursive brand space*. Therefore, in this chapter, I will address how non-human actors participate in sensegiving.

As established by Hatch and Schultz (2008) a brand is shaped and informed by all the voices that participate in the production of discourses (see also Kornberger, 2015; Mumby, 2016; Vásquez et al., 2017b). Brand meaning thus emerges as a result of circuits of sensegiving and sensemaking (Golant, 2012), therefore it is relevant to examine how human and non-human actors participate in sensegiving activities and how brand meaning is negotiated in subsequent circuits of negotiation of meaning.

6.1 Sensemaking, sensegiving, and hybrid agency

In order to navigate the world, we must interpret all the sense impressions we encounter throughout the day, that is, we must make sense of our circumstances and environment. *Sensemaking* is, therefore, a never-ending everyday activity as we are constantly making sense of what is happening around us (Mills, Thurlow, & Mills, 2010). Sensemaking is the process of constructing answers to the question "what is going on here?" or "what is the story?" (Weick, Sutcliffe, & Obstfeld, 2005), and as such, sensemaking is the discursive construction of reality (Maitlis, 2005) which is illustrated in the meaning making model (Figure 6.1).

The meaning-making model represents how people create narratives (as illustrated by the line) or, as suggested by Weick et al. (2005), produces an answer to the question "what is the story" or "what is going on here" by

DOI: 10.4324/9781003050100-6

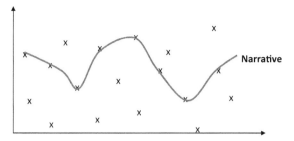

Figure 6.1 The meaning-making model
Morgan (2000, p. 7)

connecting some sense impressions in a story with a plot. The world is always much richer in detail (as illustrated by the X's) than what can be incorporated into a single story. To create a story is thus a question of selection and deselection – a process called punctuation. Punctuation is guided by retrospective sensemaking that allows us to structure our story according to a plot – what White (1973) would call *emplotment*.

Weick (2001) explains sensemaking by comparing it to the activity of cartography. A cartographer has to make sense of a vast territory with no established boundaries. The map that is produced will depend on what the mapmaker deems pivotal and decides to represent. It is a crucial point that there is no 'One True Map' of a particular terrain. For any terrain there will be multiple ways to represent it, depending on the purpose of the map as well as what the mapmaker pays attention to. The terrain itself does not display any build-in mapping; the mapping is a construction created by the mapmaker. Looking at the meaning-making model, the X'es are all the sense impressions that one encounters in a never-ending flux of experience. It is, in other words, the terrain that has to be mapped or made sense of. The sensemaker has to orientate him- or herself in a messy and chaotic flux of experience. Like the mapmaker has to seek out certain points of orientation, the sensemaker has to convert the undifferentiated flux of fleeting sense impressions into an intelligible world by carving out cues and connecting these cues by creating a narrative about what is going on or what the meaning might be. The narrative is, in other words, the map. Sensemaking is the discursive construction of reality, seeing as "[s]ituations, organizations, and environments are talked into existence" (Weick et al., 2005, p. 409). "Reality" is an ongoing accomplishment that emerges from the sensemaker's efforts to create order in the flux of experience by the production of accounts (Maitlis, 2005). No account is able to embrace all aspects of experience – just like no map is able to display all details of a terrain – therefore, the sensemaker focuses on particular elements and punctuates the story by extracting some cues and ignoring others (Mills et al., 2010). There is no one true story; the story emerges based on past experiences, outlook, labelling, categorizing, and frames. Accordingly, different people can make different sense of the same circumstances.

Weick (1995) originally established seven properties of sensemaking but the more recent research by Weick et al. (2005), which inspires my thinking, sums up sensemaking as:

- Noticing and bracketing (salient cues)
- Labelling
- Retrospective
- About presumption (plausibility)
- Social and systemic (social context)
- Personal identity (construction)
- Enactment
- About action
- Organizing through communication

I have developed an adjusted version of the meaning making model that incorporates the concepts of Weick to explain meaning making in further detail (Figure 6.2).

Sensemaking starts with *noticing and bracketing* (Weick et al., 2005). In the undifferentiated flux of raw experience, past experience and mental models will guide the sensemaker to *notice* some sense impressions above others. Social objects and phenomena do not have an independent existence, rather they are forcibly carved out of the flux of fleeting sense impressions and conceptually fixed (Chia, 2000). Once *bracketing* occurs, the world is simplified, because bracketing determines what to pay attention to and what to ignore. *Labelling* or naming the bracketed sense impressions is a crucial step in interpreting the events. When a sense impression is labelled, it is identified or categorized as something specific; labelling makes a sense impression nounable. Labelling is a strategy of differentiation that suggests plausible ways of managing or acting. Sensemaking happens *retrospectively*, seeing as we "rely on past experiences to

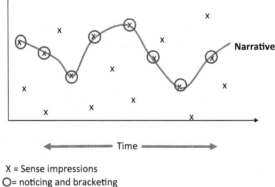

X = Sense impressions
O = noticing and bracketing

Figure 6.2 The meaning-making model and sensemaking

interpret current events" (Mills et al., 2010, p. 184). In order to make sense of the present, we search our memory for similar experiences from the past in anticipation that prior training or experience can guide current action. Accordingly, sensemaking is also based on *presumption* and driven by *plausibility*. People presume how events are connected or hang together, and sensemaking is very much about creating a coherent story. To make sense is to test a hunch; it connects the abstract with the concrete (Weick et al., 2005). Sensemaking does not happen in a void, it is influenced by our interactions with others, whether these others are physically present or not (Mills et al., 2010), human or non-human. A sensemaker is never alone in their attempt to create meaning; rather sensemaking is a social process that is "influenced by the actual, implied, or imagined presence of others" (Weick, 2001, p. 461) and is, therefore, *social and systemic*. The sensemaker is influenced either by direct interaction with other actors or by the imagined expectations of others (concerns) as well as, for example, routines, scripts, the institutions of language and mental models (Degn, 2015). Sensemaking happens in a social context, where the personal identity construction also influences the sensemaker. Personal identity is continually being co-constructed and redefined based on interaction with others, therefore there is always something at stake for the sensemaker. A person's sense of who he or she is in a setting, what role he or she plays, how the self is threatened or enhanced, all provide a base from which judgements of relevance and importance emanate (Weick, 2001). In the previous chapter, it was evident that the role of *managing director* and *middle manager* affected interaction and sensemaking in the conversational space.

Sensemaking is ultimately about *action*. As Weick et al. (2005, p. 412) explain, "If the first question of sensemaking is, "What's going on here?" the second, equally important question is, "What do I do next?". We make sense in order to determine how we are going to behave or respond to sense impressions. It is, however, important to point out, that we respond to a social world that we have enacted ourselves.

A central term in Weick's conceptual framework is *enactment* or *enacted environment*. Enactment is an act of invention rather than one of discovery (Weick, 2001). To explain how an environment is enacted, Taylor and Van Every (1999) use a flashlight analogy in the following narrative visualization. Imagine that you find yourself in a dark field at night. Most of your surroundings are unidentifiable to you with your unaided sight. You can vaguely pick out some of the objects closest to you, but they are ambiguous and obscure. "Is that just a bush or is it a dangerous animal, crouching to attack?" (p. 145), you ask. You have a flashlight and, by turning it on, you create a circle within which you can shed light and make things clear. Within this circle of light, your surroundings stand out clearly to you, meaning that you can act with some assurance. But no flashlight is powerful enough to light up everything. You only have a limited circle of light, and everything outside the circle remains ambiguous and mysterious. You can alter the direction of your flashlight and make something else stand out, but the totality of your environment remains forever obscure and equivocal. The key point is, however, that by turning on the flashlight and directing the circle of light, you *enact* your environment. When it comes to sensemaking, the flashlight is mental. In the process of noticing and bracketing, you point your flashlight at selected cues. These cues come to stand out clearly to you, and you label the cues according to what you see and how you interpret the cues. This punctuation guides you to take the appropriate action, but you have, in fact, enacted the environment – to which you respond – yourself. You have produced a cause map that allows you to interpret what goes on in a situation and to produce an appropriate response. An enacted environment is the output of organizing sense impressions. Meaning is not a built-in property of activities, it is socially constructed by the sensemaker (Gioia & Chittipeddi, 1991).

Accordingly, action and talk should be viewed in a flatland perspective with no precedence for one over another. Action is merely part of the undifferentiated flux until it is bracketed by talk, and thus *named* or *labelled* and assigned some meaning; action and cognition are recursively linked. Such "action-meaning cycles occur repeatedly as people construct provisional understandings" (Maitlis & Christianson, 2014, p. 67). Action is, therefore, not more significant than talk or the other way around (Weick et al., 2005).

Sensemaking is an activity that takes place as much in private as in professional life as it is basically a question of *organizing through communication*; in the context of organizational life, sensemaking is framed as an alternative way of looking at the process of organizing (Mills et al., 2010). When we look at sensemaking as organization, the adjacent term *sensegiving* becomes of special interest.

Sensegiving

Whereas sensemaking is about how people construct their own reality (Nijhof & Jeurissen, 2006); *sensegiving* "is concerned with the process of attempting to influence the sensemaking and meaning construction of others toward a preferred redefinition of organizational reality" (Gioia & Chittipeddi, 1991, p. 442). Sensegiving is about making sense for others by supplying a viable interpretation of what is going on and what is at stake. In other words, sensegiving is a fundamental leadership activity (Maitlis, 2005) and it ought to be strategic. Sensegiving activities, where the sensegiver is clearly engaged in behaviours that attempt to influence others' sensemaking, can be referred to as *high sensegiving* (Maitlis, 2005). An example of the use of high sensegiving would be the K2M model (see section 6.3).

Sensegiving is carried out by carefully selecting salient cues then labelling and categorizing the cues strategically, which will frame the cues in a certain way. The sensegiver may seek to activate existing accounts by connecting the new cues to well-known narratives (i.e. part of the organizational memory), or the sensegiver may seek to develop new stories, and thus enact a new context from which employees can extract meaning in their future sensemaking. Stories foster recollection by repeating and highlighting salient cues and plots over and over again and, as such, stories can produce organizational learning. Although, attempts at sensegiving can never control the outcome of sensemaking "the use of language in the describing of an event enacts the construction of sensemaking about the event" (Mills et al., 2010, p. 189). Attempts at sensegiving play a part in shutting down alternative interpretations of sense impressions and may limit who can participate in organizational processes (Giuliani, 2016).

Sensegiving can be said to happen every time we articulate sense impressions into words. That means that sensegiving is not necessarily as deliberate, intentional, and strategic as assumed by most literature. Sensegiving activities where the sensegiver exhibits few sensegiving behaviours can be referred to as *low sensegiving* (Maitlis, 2005). The fact that (low) sensegiving happens incessantly means that sensegiving and sensemaking takes place iteratively and sometimes concurrent, which will be evident in the subsequent analysis.

Sense and hybrid agency

The literature on sensemaking does acknowledge the existence of non-human actors (e.g. scripts, the institutions of language, mental models) (Degn, 2015) as well as the ability to teleact (e.g. the imagined presence of others) (Weick, 2001). However, the term 'hybrid agency' is not much explored in the sensemaking literature. As noticed by Cooren (2012), human actors are never alone on the site of construction of meaning, rather a plethora of agencies are entangled. The entanglement of agencies highlights the inseparability of sensemaking and sensegiving. As recently explained, sensemaking is a never-ending daily activity with no starting point. Weick (1995, 2001) points to the breakdown of routines (or organizational shock) as that which initiates sensemaking processes, but one cannot act in the world without making sense of it. Accordingly, sensemaking is a ubiquitous part of human life. Even though much sensemaking may be characterized by routine and recurrence, at other times (e.g. in new or unknown situations), it may be more apparent that an individual struggles to make sense. Likewise, sensegiving is normally treated as intentional and strategic in the literature. But one could argue that sensegiving takes place each time bracketing and labelling takes place, that is, every time experience is put into words. In order for strategic sensegiving to take place, the sensegiver must first have made his or her own sense of the situation but, as will be seen in the analysis, sensemaking sometimes happens in the midst of discussions and talk about events, and accordingly sensegiving becomes much more accidental and casual. Ultimately successful sensegiving is a question of the discursive power of an actor.

When we introduce the notion of hybrid agency, it becomes clear that it is impossible to state a beginning or an end to sensemaking and sensegiving. Language will draw upon capital D-discourses and thus *D-discourse* functions as a macro-actor in sensegiving and sensemaking. The production of *text* is an attempt at *sensegiving*. Human actors are seeking to create a preferred definition of organizational reality by producing a non-human agent that can *state a truth*. In other words, *sensegiving is delegated* to a non-human actor. But the non-human actor cannot act on its own as it is dependent upon appropriation by a human-actor and the creation of a hybrid agency. Appropriation of a non-human actor implies that the human actor who appropriates the non-human actor makes sense of it. *Sensegiving* performed by a non-human actor is thus inextricably linked with *sensemaking* by a human actor, meaning that when hybrid agency is at play, sensegiving cannot be separated from sensemaking. We therefore see that although the literature treats *sensegiving* and *sensemaking* as separate concepts, the separation is merely a theoretical one given that the two are closely interlinked, and the interrelatedness of sensegiving and sensemaking is key when hybrid agency is discussed. Sensegiving and sensemaking is a circuit; it is not possible to state exactly where one stops and the other begins.

The focus of the succeeding analyses is to demonstrate the agency of non-human actors in circuits of sensegiving and sensemaking.

6.2 How materiality participates in sensegiving

Previous writings have discussed how human actors are involved in sensegiving and sensemaking (see for instance, Cunliffe, 2001; Gioia & Chittipeddi, 1991; Holman & Thorpe, 2003; Nijhof & Jeurissen, 2006; Weick, 2001), but little attention has been given to the participation of non-human actors. Sensegiving need not be acted out in spoken or written language. The material turn establishes that discourse is no longer seen to be found in just conversation and text, but in all forms of materialities or modalities (Ashcraft et al., 2009). Sensegiving and sensemaking activities are therefore always situated in sociomaterial environments (Fayard & Weeks, 2014). Materiality is an integral part of discourse, actively participating in constructing it (Cooren et al., 2012). Accordingly, text and talk ought to be considered side by side with other forms of social and material activity (Nicolini, 2012). Therefore, the use of non-human actors plays an important role in giving sense to the discursive brand space.

There are several uses of materiality related to K2M that are deliberately introduced by brand management, such as the Globalco logo, the use of orange, and the presence of Buddha. Hence, the Globalco logo, the use of Buddha and the color orange are examples of how the K2M department works in *giving sense* to K2M. The use of these is a different modality than text. Written text is governed by rules and syntactic conventions (Iedema, 2003) which communicates very explicitly, whereas "the figural communicates through icons which are not systematically structured in the same way as language" (Salzer-Mörling & Strannegård, 2004, p. 229). Therefore, the use of materiality communicates K2M in a different way than talk and text. The communication is more implicit and thus more open to different interpretations.

In the subsequent paragraphs, I will analyze how the logo, the color orange, and Buddha are involved in circuits of sensegiving and sensemaking.

The Globalco logo

The Globalco logo was designed in the late 1990s. It resembles a network inspired by the imagery of a spider's web and Indra's Net. Indra's Net is a Buddhist symbol that communicates the interpenetration of everything (Loy, 1993) and is intended to symbolize the interconnectedness of all subsidiaries. In the Globalco corporate movie, the imagery is explained as a dew drop in which you see the reflection of all the other dew drops and so on, ad infinitum. The voiceover in the corporate movie explicitly states that the imagery of the spider's web is inspired by Indra's Net. The explanation contains a reference to Alan Watts, who was a British philosopher famous for being one of the first to interpret Eastern philosophy for a Western audience. The logo is thus a symbol that has been carefully crafted to represent a *high sensegiving* of interconnectedness by the explicit references to Indra's Net and Alan Watts who connote Eastern philosophy.

The design and presentation of the logo and the corporate movie can be seen as *restricted organizational sensemaking*. Restricted organizational sensemaking is characterized by a one-time action that is controlled by leader sensegiving and communicated top-down without the involvement of other actors (Maitlis, 2005). The Globalco corporate movie that explains the symbolic value of the logo was presented at a Globalco event. The movie had been worked on by the K2M department and is clearly an example of top-down communication. Though it is possible for organizational members to re-watch the corporate movie, it is questionable whether they would choose to do so in their spare time.

Restricted organizational sensegiving produces a narrow account, which stakeholders typically tend to accept. A narrow account may reflect a limited repertoire, which can make it difficult for actors to engage in conversations. Maitlis (2005) found that restricted sensemaking often produced unitary accounts, but the unitary accounts resulted from a lack of alternatives to the management sensegiving constructions rather than from an integrated perspective. A narrow account does not provide actors with the discursive resources they need in order to engage intelligibly in conversations about the brand. It may instead hamper the development of a self-conscious collectivity as well as the actors' ability to incarnate the brand (see Chapter 4 for clarification).

When employees talk about the logo, they do not talk about "interconnectedness", instead they talk about the color orange or Buddhism:

Excerpt 6.1

> Our new logo has gotten an orange Buddha-profile.

The first edition of the logo was blue on a white background but in 2018 the logo was redesigned to incorporate the color orange, which is what the previous comment by a middle manager refers to. It is thus clear that the middle manager's sensemaking is more affected by the material discourse of the color orange than the oral discourse about interconnectedness and Indra's Net. It is thus interesting to examine how the color orange participates in sensegiving.

The color orange

The color orange has gradually been incorporated into the visual design to a greater and greater extent. In the Globalco CSR reports for 2016 and 2017, orange font is used for the word K2M and orange is used to highlight certain information in the report. However, in 2018 the front page, previously a traditional white background with a blue logo, is now different shades of orange, a color also used significantly throughout the whole report. Orange is often used at CSR events in orange decorations or the wearing of orange clothes or accessories, or in the incorporating of some kind of orange artifact. There is no explicit sensegiving in the use of orange, that is, the sensegiving is low as orange is not articulated as a symbol of Buddhism or interconnectedness, but employees notice the use of the color, and they *make sense of* it as a symbol of Buddhism:

Excerpt 6.2

EMPLOYEE C: It is his color ...
EMPLOYEE D: It is the ...
EMPLOYEE C: Color of Buddhism ...
EMPLOYEE D: Buddhism, yes ...

Excerpt 6.3

EMPLOYEE E: I remember we made that thing with orange. It was something world-wide.
INTERVIEWER: Yes.
EMPLOYEE F: It is something Buddhist ...

Other employees indicate that orange makes them think of a monk's robe, and an Apparella employee indicates that it makes her think of her company's big Buddha figurine in the foyer.

The use of orange can be seen as *fragmented organizational sensemaking*. Fragmented sensemaking is characterized by a low sensegiving from management (i.e. sensegiving that is not controlled) but high sensegiving from employees (Maitlis, 2005). Maitlis (2005) found that fragmented sensemaking resulted in multiple individualistic accounts that were not integrated and tended to accumulate over time. That was not the case in my data material. If actors made sense of the use of orange, they agreed that the color connoted Buddhism. This may signal that orange is a very strong cue. However, it is more likely that orange was not made sense of on its own but in interplay with other forms of materiality, such as the logo, the use of Buddha and perhaps the brand name itself, Kind2Mind. Taken together this materiality produces a discourse about Buddhism.

Buddha

Buddha is omnipresent in Globalco. Buddha is used on posters, in newsletters and as a physical artifact in the form of figurines of different sizes. For example, Apparella has a giant Buddha to welcome people in its foyer, GoGastro has a Buddha sitting at the desk in its reception, and GoTech has a large Buddha sitting in front of its new headquarters; GoDeliver has a meeting room decorated with Buddhas and GoNutri has a large Buddha sitting in the staircase of its headquarters. Organizational members also report how they use the Buddha as artifact. For instance, a middle manager explains that she bought a Buddha figurine for everybody who had been nominated for a Globalco award in GoTech, and the CEO regularly promotes Buddha as a well-chosen artifact. At the Globalco event 2017, all employees received a goodie bag with a wooden pearl bracelet and two charms: the Globalco logo and a Buddha charm. Plus, a Buddha baton was initiated during spring 2018. Globalco uses several different versions of Buddha and the organization even had a Buddha designed specially.

The employees are generally very much aware of the presence of Buddha but there is no explicit sensegiving related to the use of Buddha as artifact, hence the sensegiving is low. Not surprisingly, employees differ in their sensemaking about the use of Buddha. A middle manager comments that the Buddha is there to remind the employees about what kind of company they are, while others see it as a mascot. In Chapter 7, I will demonstrate how there is a frame game going on between *K2M is a Buddhist philosophy* versus *K2M is not Buddhist*. It is evident that the material discourse of the color orange does play an important part in sensegiving and sensemaking about the brand.

6.3 How macro-actors participate in sensegiving

A macro-actor is an actor that speaks on behalf of a collectivity. It therefore speaks with an enhanced authority, seeing as it does not represent the voice of one actor but rather the voice of a 'we' or a group (Taylor & Van Every, 1999). When dealing with a macro-actor, the original author has vanished from view, and a 'naturalization' of the discourses that the macro-actor represents has taken place. A macro-actor is often non-human and such a macro-actor must be appropriated by a human actor or activated via ventriloquism in order to participate in sensegiving.

In the following, I will analyze how a material (ie. the K2M model) and a somewhat immaterial (D-discourse) macro-actor participate in circuits of sensegiving and sensemaking.

How the K2M model participates in sensegiving

The K2M model is a graphic presentation (a text) of the main elements of the brand, and in the previous chapter, it was demonstrated how the K2M model functions as a non-human actor that participates in the conversational space. In this section, I will explicate how the K2M model participates in sensegiving activities. When Dave opens SGM1, he acknowledges that it is difficult to make sense of K2M:

Excerpt 6.4

> We have had some ... I won't say problems ... but challenges as to how we are to understand the concept of K2M. In many ways it has been a pioneer project and branding projects that have served to differentiate the separate companies and Globalco through some projects, such as Africa or green architecture in Bogotá, that all buy into some kind of marketing idea ... ehm ... And here we have tried to broaden the definition and show the purpose with each pillar as well as which tools we have in each. So I think, we would like to present ... [the K2M model] [Dave makes a gesture toward Lucy]

The way Dave introduces the K2M model illustrates that the model is an attempt to *give sense* to the concept of K2M. The model has been worked out by brand management, and the materiality of the K2M model adds *restance* to the brand. The K2M model *gives sense* to K2M by *identifying* three areas of key concern; it *points out* three pillars of K2M and *divides* K2M activities into this *grouping*. Further sensegiving is applied by the use of D-discourses to *label* the pillars. The K2M model is thus an example of high sensegiving.

Through materiality K2M goes from being an immaterial 'idea' or 'understanding' to a model. Achievement of *sensegiving* is thus attempted by creation of a map (a visual metaphor) that makes it possible to grasp K2M in its (constructed) totality. As explained above, Weick compares sense-making to map-making and, as stated by Taylor and Van Every (1999), a map is for going places. The K2M model provides a direction for K2M. It *gives sense* by adding content (i.e. in the three pillars); by adding specific content, the model enacts a set of boundaries that delimits K2M. It is important for a brand to claim its territory (Hatch & Schultz, 2008), which is what the K2M model does in stipulating that K2M is a trinity of 'CSR and sustainable growth', 'Branding', and 'Corporate Culture'. Via the three pillars, the model produces an account of K2M, and by claiming these three areas as the territory of K2M, everything else is constructed as an 'outside'. Sensegiving thus happens by simultaneously stipulating what K2M is and what it is not. The K2M model is an attempt to create a hegemonic discourse about K2M by translating 'CSR and sustainable growth', 'Branding', and 'Corporate Culture' into a coherent whole (see Selg & Ventsel, 2010).

The K2M model is thus developed in order to help employees make sense of an otherwise chaotic welter of impressions and ideas. The material pre-sentification punctuates certain elements that are included in the model, and this punctuation seeks to create a coherent narrative about K2M. By producing the model, the CEO, Lucy, and Dave, delegate the responsibility of explaining K2M to a macro-actor. As a macro-actor, the K2M model invites a number of other non-human actors to participate in the conversation. In the next section, I will analyze how D-discourses participate in sensegiving activities by focusing on first the CSR D-discourse and next the KPI D-discourse. I will further demonstrate how insufficient sensegiving prompts other actors to look for someone or something that can fill the void.

How the CSR D-discourse participates in sensegiving

In the previous chapter, I identified a number of D-discourses that participate in the conversational space, namely the KPI D-discourse, the ROI D-discourse, and the three headlines in the K2M model: 'CSR and sustainable growth', 'Branding', and 'Corporate Culture'. All these D-discourses relate to a profes-sional D-discourse and participate in *sensegiving* because they activate an exist-ing account. By activating an existing account, they give sense to K2M by incorporating existing and acknowledged understandings into the account of K2M. Accordingly, D-discourses reflect a frame for discussion (Alvesson & Karreman, 2000). In Chapter 5 I analyzed how the CSR D-discourse informed talk about K2M. The CSR D-discourse is thus *giving sense* to K2M by invoking a certain frame of CSR that stipulates that CSR is about working conditions, animal welfare, reduction of water and energy consumption, and the preven-tion of child labor in their production.

However, as noted in Chapter 5, the CSR D-discourse is a mega-Discourse and since a mega-Discourse operates at an overall level, the macro-actor only stipulates what CSR is about on a very general plane. It puts forward a historically devel-oped body of knowledge, also known as a 'regime of truth' (Alvesson & Kärre-man, 2011), but the D-discourse is not able to explicate how the overall topics can be translated to fit the everyday of the subsidiaries. From the perspective of the brand manager as a practical author, it is the responsibility of the brand manager to manage such a translation by providing a language that makes CSR intelligible for the middle managers. At the first steering group meeting, Lucy seeks to explicate CSR by relating it to 'high impact areas'. She explains that the companies need to figure out where they risk negative publicity:

Excerpt 6.5

LUCY: And then you need to figure out what your high impact areas are. That is, where is your greatest risk of negative publicity? Where is it that you may encounter problems …?

MM: Or you could turn it around and ask yourself, "Where can we identify some low hanging fruit?"

LUCY: Yes, that is possible too.

In this excerpt we see that Lucy *gives sense* to CSR by stating that it is about identifying the companies' 'high impact areas' and to take care of these areas in order to
avoid negative publicity. But a middle manager offers another sensegiving, namely
that instead of identifying 'high impact areas', the companies could go about CSR
by identifying 'low hanging fruit'. The sensegiving originally offered by Lucy, *CSR
as high impact areas*, would be in accordance with the CSR D-discourse. But
apparently Lucy is unable to appropriate the D-discourse in that precise moment,
and therefore she gives in to the alternative sensegiving offered by a middle manager. The alternative sensegiving, *CSR as low hanging fruit*, is apparently easier for
the middle managers to make sense of, and the sensegiving of *CSR as low hanging
fruit* is seen to outperform the sensegiving of *CSR as high impact areas*, given that the
frame of *CSR as low hanging fruit* is the frame most frequently invoked. The participants use the frame of *CSR as low hanging fruit* to back their decisions about how
they go about developing K2M.

Unfortunately, a sensegiving of *CSR as low hanging fruit* is devoid of specific
meaning and this sensegiving does not guide middle managers in selecting their areas
of focus. But the notion of 'high impact areas' is not the only way that Lucy (on
behalf of the K2M department) seeks to give sense to CSR. In the K2M model, the
KPI D-discourse is used to specify how the companies should go about CSR.

How the KPI D-discourse participates in sensegiving

In the K2M model, CSR is *given sense* by being translated into 'KPI'. The KPI D-
discourse is thus another macro-actor that participates in *sensegiving* by invoking an
existing account. For a D-discourse to succeed in sensegiving, it has to be recognized
by all members of the conversational space. The K2M department could have offered
additional sensegiving by explicating that account at the first steering group meeting,
but neither the CEO, Lucy, nor Dave elaborate on what they mean by KPI. The
concept of KPI is never formally elaborated or explained. The *organizational sensemaking* is thus *minimal* (Maitlis, 2005) since there is low sensegiving from brand
management and no interaction (questions) from the middle managers. Instead, the
concept of KPI is used rather broadly, and it is difficult for the participants to get
concrete about possible KPIs. The CEO tries to *give sense* by naming some examples:
animal welfare, battery chickens, use of water, accidents at work, slow steaming, and
CO_2; a middle manager mentions energy, water, and residual products. The concept
of KPI is thus not discussed as part of a professional D-discourse, it is merely used to
brainstorm about possible focus areas at a very broad and general level. In that sense,
the notion of KPI does not assist the middle managers in *making sense* of CSR. Lucy
offers the sensegiving that KPIs ought to feed into the Globalco CSR report:

Excerpt 6.6

> Well, you can say, all of this is supposed to lead to the Globalco CSR
> report that we need to publish once a year. It is legally required that we

report what we have done. At the moment it is difficult to keep track. We sense that a lot of things are going on, that you focus on various aspects, but there is no uniform way of communicating about it. Ehh … so we need that reporting-part and that is where the KPIs come in, because then we have numbers, ehh … which we can say … It would be really good to have one or two common figures that we measure … .

By making this statement, Lucy gives sense to the notion of KPI as a measureable input to be used in the Globalco CSR report. However, the sensegiving offered about KPIs does not state *what* the subsidiaries are supposed to measure or *how*. Thus the notion of KPIs turns out to be a complicated macro-actor, as will be seen from the discussions in GoNuGa and later steering group meetings.

In Chapter 5 I explained how a middle manager's authority was challenged by her managing directors when she introduced the K2M model and asked the managing directors to identify a number of KPIs. I will now return to excerpts 5.15 and 5.16 and excerpt 5.20 in order to analyze the role of KPIs in the light of sensegiving. To briefly recapitulate, a managing director has asked about the scope of the day's meeting, and the middle manager has informed him that it is to formulate a framework for the KPI's and that she is to give feedback to the CEO about their choice of KPIs right after the meeting. That prompts the other managing director to ask what KPI's are in this context:

Excerpt 6.7 (Reproduction of excerpt 5.15)

MD1: But KPIs …

MM: We are going to start up the process.

MD1: But KPI's … just in order to define KPI's in this context … because I thought we were going to find a new branding project?

MM: There is more to it …

MD1: Or what are KPI's in this context? I don't really understand …

MM: Well, if we start with leg number one, CSR, that is what he [the CEO] calls business strategies. That means that is how we support sustainable growth in the companies.

At the steering group meeting the notion of KPIs was not questioned, but at the local meeting in GoNuGa the meaning of KPI is questioned by a managing director. He wants to know how he is supposed to understand (*make sense of*) KPIs in this particular context, in other words, he is asking for a more detailed *sensegiving*. However, the K2M department did not *give sense* to the notion of KPI in any further detail at the first steering group meeting, and the middle managers did not ask. Therefore, the middle manager does not have a repertoire about KPIs, so she is unable to explain how KPI is supposed to be made sense of in this context. Instead, she starts to explain the model:

Excerpt 6.8 (Reproduction of excerpt 5.15)

MM: Well, if we start with pillar 1 here, that is what he calls business strategies.
   That is, what is it that we do in the factories that spurs sustainable growth?
MD1: Yes.
MM: How can we do it better? And how can we measure it so that we are able
   to see that we have become better at it? And that is ...
MD2: [interrupts] Better at what? Really ...

Since most of the talk about CSR and KPIs at the steering group meetings takes place at an abstract and general level, it is difficult for the middle manager to explain what is meant by KPIs in the context of the K2M model since that *sensegiving* has not been offered to her. She is therefore having a hard time informing the managing directors and, due to the lack of specificity in her explanation, she is challenged by the other managing director, who asks the obvious question, "better at what?" However, as mentioned in Chapter 5, it is clear that the sensemaking struggle is not primarily about understanding the concepts, it is really a question of *making sense* of power relations. A managing director expresses apparent confusion about what a middle manager is telling him:

Excerpt 6.9 (Reproduction of part of excerpt 5.19)

Yes, I see. What I don't understand is ... if we look at business strategies, sustainable growth and value based blah blah blah ... ehm ... actually, that is what is discussed in the boardroom ... ehm ... What are our strategies? But is that disconnected from ... is it only towards the employees?

The managing director makes sense of 'business strategy' as a macro-actor that belongs to a different conversational space. It is therefore not possible for him to make sense of that macro-actor in this context. We therefore see that sensemaking is not only affected by the accounts that are produced but also by the context in line with the premise suggested in the introduction to sensemaking. The managing director does not see the context of an informal meeting to be the right context for deciding on business strategies and KPIs. This prompts him to ask if KPIs are to be made sense of in a different way in the context of the model. Hence, the use of the concept KPI activates an existing account (a D-discourse) with the managing director, but he cannot get that account to make sense in this context so he needs to ask if he is to produce a new account of KPIs. When the middle manager repeats that KPIs are related to how they run the business, the managing directors comment that it is going to be an arduous process to state KPIs since it seems to involve their business strategy and board meetings reports:

Excerpt 6.10

MD2: Well, that is … if that is the case, it is going to be a very arduous process to go through.

MM: Yes, that is what I am saying. I do not think that we will be able to complete it today.

MD1: Well, this … this includes everything … If we are to take everything at face value, as I hear it, then it involves our entire business strategy and … well, that is everything we are engaged in, right?

MM: Yes.

MD1: And a lot of it … is in our board meeting reports, right. When we have [our meetings] … we have produced a plan, a three-year plan that states our objectives etc. Well, you can say …

'KPI' and 'business strategy' are part of professional D-discourses, and when one chooses to use technical terms like 'KPI' and 'business strategy', one must expect actors, who are familiar with these concepts to draw on that macro discourse in order to make sense of what KPI means in the model. As is evident from these excerpts, the managing directors make sense of the KPIs as something that must be decided at a board meeting since that is the forum for deciding or making changes to the business strategy. The macro-actors thus trigger a sensemaking that is more concerned about power relations than the specific meaning of 'KPI'.

From the discussions at GoNuGa1, it becomes clear that the participation of the macro-actors 'KPI Discourse' and the 'business strategy' D-discourse is not straightforward. It is obvious that the managing directors appropriate the two D-discourses in a more literal and specific sense than the participants at SGM1, who did not question the meaning of the Discourses, and since the managing directors appropriate the macro-actors according to the usual use of the D-discourses in Globalco, it triggers a sensemaking-struggle that is related to power relations.

In Chapter 7, there will be an elaboration of how the use of the KPI D-discourse triggers a frame game between a *frame of measurability* and a *frame of stating objectives*. In the following, we will see how a middle manager invites another macro-actor (i.e. the UN Global Compact) to aid her sensemaking, seeing as the sensegiving by the CSR D-discourse and the KPI D-discourse is not sufficient.

6.4 Appropriation of macro-actors to make sense

Neither the CSR D-discourse, the notion of 'high impact areas' or the KPI D-discourse offer sufficient sensegiving as to how the middle managers are supposed to identify a number of focus areas. To overcome the abstractness of KPI as a CSR tool, one of the middle managers invites a macro-actor to help guide her sensemaking of CSR, when she introduces the UN Global Compact:

Excerpt 6.11

JILL: But ... but ... but ... would it ... would it be possible to narrow it down a bit? Because I am asking myself, what could be meaningful? And then there are a thousand things that could be meaningful and suddenly, I cannot think of a single one. Therefore ... I wonder if ... if ... well, we use those global impact in our CSR-work ... those ten guidelines. Maybe we could ... ehh ... in this framework too say, well we choose two or three to be our focus area. It could be ... ehh ... environment or what-ever ... ehh ... employer-something ... ehh ... protection ... ehh ... child labor ... What do I know? But some of those [areas]. And then choose a few and say, This is it. This is our focus area. And within this field...what could be an idea? ... Because I would be worried to spread ...

ANNA: [interjects] Yes, it is too broad.

JILL: ... it too much, because that leads to paralysis ... in case we are supposed to go all the way ... ehh ... at that plane and say ... ehh ... Pick this! This is our focus area. And then start something.

Jill expresses very clearly that she needs someone (or something) to assist her in the forthcoming work by pointing out where she is supposed to look or what she is supposed to concentrate on, when she says that suddenly, she "cannot think of a single one". Given that the sensegiving at hand is seen as insufficient by Jill, she turns to a macro-actor, namely the UN Global Compact, to aid her sensemaking. In Chapter 5, I argued for the UN Global compact as a macro-actor that comes to participate in the conversational space through ventriloquism. Here we see that the reason why the macro-actor is invited to participate is to help make sense of the CSR pillar in the K2M model. The sensegiving provided by the CEO, Dave, Lucy, and the K2M model is not sufficient for the middle manager to make sense of the CSR pillar or to guide her in how she is supposed to work with it (i.e. how she can take action), therefore she invites another actor to contribute with sense-giving of that pillar.

The UN Global Compact is a macro-actor that supports the interpretation of *CSR as high impact areas,* as suggested by Lucy. But interestingly, Lucy actually invokes the alternative sensegiving of *CSR as low hanging fruit* to argue against the Un-Global Compact. She says that the 10 Principles may not be a good partner because the companies work in such different areas and it would be undesirable to force somebody to work with an area short on low hanging fruit. It illustrates that the sensegiving offered by the middle manager, of *CSR as low hanging fruit,* is quite pervasive. In view of that, Lucy now abandons her own sensegiving (in line with the CSR D-discourse) of *CSR as high impact areas* in favor of the sensegiving of *CSR as low hanging fruit.* It is however seen later that Lucy returns to the sensegiving of *CSR as high impact areas* when she has worked out a K2M code of conduct which states that each subsidiary must "work with their individual challenges and impact areas" (SGM4). This sug-gests that Lucy herself is struggling to make sense of the CSR pillar in the K2M model as the conversation goes on. In her preparation for the meeting, she has chosen the notion of 'high impact areas' to give sense to the pillar, which is in accordance with the CSR D-discourse. But in the midst of conversation, she seems to forget that 'high impact areas' stem from the CSR D-discourse and she goes along with the alternative sensemaking offered by a middle manager about understanding focus areas as 'low-hanging fruit'. This incident demonstrates the challenges of a brand manager in functioning as a practical author and participating in circuits of sensegiving and sensemaking. To work successfully with sensegiving, it is important to be aware of which discourses to promote and which to discard. Lucy seems to lose perspective as the conversation unfolds and she thus fails to act successfully as a practical author in that moment. It is seen that when Lucy has had time to prepare herself, she returns to the sensegiving of focus areas as 'high impact areas', since this notion is incorporated in the K2M code of conduct.

6.5 Discussion of sensegiving in the conversational space

The present chapter has focused on demonstrating how non-human actors participate in sensegiving and sensemaking activities. Some of the non-human actors were introduced in the conversational space by brand management in explicit attempts at sensegiving, others were invoked (perhaps by accident) by non-human actors and finally some were invited by organizational members to aid them in their sensemaking.

The non-human actors produced by brand management – for instance, the K2M model, a corporate movie, the Globalco logo, and the use of orange and Buddha – are non-human actors that have been produced as a sensegiving tool. The sensegiving offered differs in its explicitness (i.e. high or low sensegiving), but the present data material is generally characterized by low sensegiving from brand management, which challenges the middle managers in their efforts to make sense and give sense to their managing directors. It also leaves ambiguous non-human actors (i.e. the logo, the color, and Buddha) in an open field of sensemaking. The extent to which the non-human actors that are present in the two conversational spaces (i.e. the steering group meetings and the meetings at GoNuGa) are seen to participate in the conversations is very different. For instance, the K2M model is seen to play a central role in the sensegiving activities, whereas Buddha is hardly seen to have a voice at all.

However, the degree of participation changes significantly when the focus is flipped from the steering group meetings and the meetings in GoNuGa to the interviews I performed with managers and employees across Globalco and thus, the degree to which the non-human actors participate in sensegiving changes accordingly. When organizational members make sense of K2M, they find their cues in the use of Buddha and orange (which are related to the CEO) rather than in the texts mentioned. A possible explanation could be sought in the difference of modality, and thus the sensegiving potential of different materialities, but a more plausible explanation in this case is the degree to which the non-human actors are made present. As mentioned, Buddha is omnipresent whereas the K2M model is known by few employees outside the steering group. Another part of the explanation is to be found in the fact that the use of Buddha as organizational artifact is inextricably linked with the CEO. As stated earlier, the CEO is a very authentic author of K2M, and since Buddha and the CEO are seen to be more or less synonymous, they can be seen as animating each other. Buddha is understood to be an organizational artifact introduced by the CEO so, as an organizational artifact, the Buddha figure is a dummy that ventriloquizes the CEO because it makes the CEO's personal values omnipresent in Globalco. Buddha thus reminds the employees that K2M emanates from the CEO and is something he prioritizes. At the same time, the Buddha figure is also made sense of as a Buddhist symbol by many employees. In that sense, Buddha can be understood as the ventriloquist that animates the CEO and speaks through him, as the CEO is inspired by Eastern philosophy. The Buddha figure is thus also a symbol that makes the Buddhist philosophy materially present in Globalco. Buddha is thus *giving sense* to K2M as something that is prioritized by the CEO and as a Buddhist philosophy. The CEO states that K2M is not a Buddhist philosophy, but the use of materiality (i.e. Buddha, orange, the logo) works contrary to this sensegiving and states that K2M is indeed a Buddhist philosophy.

These analyses demonstrate that sensegiving is not the preserve of brand management. This is in line with the findings of Maitlis and Christianson (2014, p. 78) who suggest that "when organizational leaders engage in sensegiving, organizational members are not simply passive recipients of meaning but instead engage in their own sensemaking and adopt, alter, resist, or reject the sense they have been given". I found that when organizational members perceive the sensegiving offered by brand management to be insufficient, they invoke other macro-actors to assist their sensemaking, as seen in the example with the middle manager who invoked the UN Global Compact. The CEO does not comment directly on the suggestion to turn to the UN Global Compact. Hence, he neither accepts nor rejects the idea. Lucy is a little skeptical since she believes it should be a task for the managing directors to decide. She believes that the most relevant focal areas to work with will vary significantly from subsidiary to subsidiary due to their different industries, and she believes the managing directors will be best suited to point out such areas. Hence, like the CEO she does not directly support the idea of turning to the UN Global Compact, but she does not reject the idea either. Sensegiving from brand management in relation to the UN Global Compact is low and thus not controlled, which leaves it up to middle managers to make sense of whether the UN Global Compact is a relevant source of inspiration or not. From the successive meetings in the subsidiaries, it is demonstrated how GoTech and GoNuGa chose to find inspiration in the UN Global Compact and that it is eventually incorporated into the K2M model. Accordingly, texts produced by the UN become part of the texts that constitute K2M. It is a useful illustration of how authorship happens in living response to circumstances (Cunliffe, 2001). One middle manager suggests turning to the UN

Global Compact for inspiration and, since the suggestion is not rejected, the idea is picked up by another middle manager, and eventually the K2M model is modified to incorporate a text from UN. It also illustrates how brand meaning emerges in circular processes of sensegiving and sensemaking. The UN Global Compact is not part of the original sensegiving about K2M, but because the sensegiving, provided by the CEO, Dave, Lucy, and the K2M model, is seen to be insufficient for the middle managers to make sense, one of the middle managers takes part in the sensegiving activities by ventriloquizing a macro-actor. UN Global Compact thus comes to be an important macro-actor that participates in sensegiving activities. As a practical author, the brand manager needs to consider how co-creation happens in the ongoing conversations about the brand. If the UN Global Compact had been seen to be inappropriate to give sense to K2M, it would have been the responsibility of the brand manager to reject the suggestion and to counter the D-discourses offered by UN. In this instance, the UN Global Compact is accepted as a useful partner in the authoring of K2M, and the macro-actor is thus accepted as a non-human participant in the conversational space.

It becomes evident that human and non-human actors alike participate in sensegiving activities, but non-human actors do not act on their own. They are being appropriated by human actors, due to their sensegiving affordances, in order to sustain other actors' legitimacy or support them in their sensemaking. As pinpointed by Taylor and Van Every (2011, p. 75), an account does not so much picture reality as it isolates aspects of it that we want to highlight for each other. The non-human actors are thus used to isolate certain aspects of an undifferentiated flux of impressions in order to bracket and label these aspects. In other words, the non-human actors are actants intended to tele-act on behalf of their authors by drawing attention to aspects that the authors want to highlight. The agency of actors is thus interrelated and entangled.

The analyses in the present chapter have focused on explicating how human and non-human actors alike participate in authoring the discursive brand space. It has been found that even though non-human actors are produced as a sensegiving tool, their agency escapes the control of their authors. It has also been found that sensegiving is often equivocal because actors engage in circuits of sensegiving and sensemaking where meaning is negotiated. In Chapter 7, I will introduce the notion of *frame games* in order to further explicate the circularity of sensegiving and sensemaking. I will expose how sensegiving by brand management might be rejected for the benefit of another sensegiving offered by other actors. It serves to demonstrate the importance of mastering the brand language if one is to succeed as a practical author.

7 Frame games and negotiation of meaning

Theories of sensegiving and sensemaking, as introduced in Chapter 6, serve well to explicate the performative nature of brand meaning. Meaning is not found inherently in words or actions themselves but are enacted by actors who participate in conversations about the brand and thus take part in producing the discursive brand space.

However, most theories about sensemaking are vague when it comes to the negotiated character of sensemaking. Even though it is an established ontological perspective that sensemaking should be understood as intersubjective and characterized by plurivocality (Maitlis & Christianson, 2014), there is little research that actually studies the co-construction of sensemaking. In this chapter, I introduce the notion of *frame games* in order to shed light on the discursive battles, where sensegiving is attempted and either accepted, rejected, or reframed in actors' efforts to make sense. Chapter 6 sought to explicate how not only human actors, but also macro-actors and non-human actors, participated in circuits of sensegiving and sensemaking. This chapter seeks to explicate the negotiated character of sensemaking and thus of brand meaning.

7.1 Frame games

Taylor and Van Every (2011) use the notion of a *frame game* to describe the ongoing negotiation of meaning. To participate in a frame game is to participate in circuits of sensegiving and sensemaking, where "people do their best to have their perspective accepted, not merely as *a* perspective, but as *the* perspective" (Taylor & Van Every, 2011, p. 35, italics in original). The notion of a frame game thus builds on Foucault's premise that "[t]ruth is a discursive construction and different regimes of knowledge determine what is true and false" (Jørgensen & Phillips, 2002, p. 13). A frame game is about constitution of authority, since the one who settles the frame game gets to determine the "truth" (at least momentarily), and "[o]rganizational discourse is thus always potentially game-oriented" (Taylor & Van Every, 2011, p. 45). At the micro-level, frames emerge in the daily talk and interaction. If a frame is accepted as the "truth", it can succeed in establishing itself at the meso-level, where it becomes a "truth" in the organization. Other frames exist at the macro-level as relatively stable modes of representation that are

DOI: 10.4324/9781003050100-7

grounded in broader cultural-belief systems; such frames can be invoked by actors in order to convince interlocutors about the rightness or appropriateness of something (Cornelissen & Werner, 2014). The use of a D-discourse is an example of a frame that exists at the macro-level. The analysis of sensegiving and sense-making as frame games is thus in line with the *flatland view* as proposed by Taylor and Van Every (1999), where the text-world and the discourse-world are seen as complementary. It is thus appropriate to analyze the authoring of the discursive brand space according to what goes on in the conversational spaces and to examine how the different actors participate in sensegiving and sensemaking, that is, in frame games.

7.2 The K2M model: a frame game of coupling versus subdivision

At SGM1, a graphic presentation of the brand is introduced that divides the brand K2M into three pillars: CSR, Branding, and Corporate Culture. The model of K2M is an attempt of sensegiving by brand management. Taylor and Van Every (1999, p. 40) state that: "If the finality of conversation is to sustain interaction, the finality of text is to produce a collectively negotiated interpretation of the world: to turn circumstances into a situation that is comprehensible and that serves as a springboard for action". The purpose of the K2M model is thus to enable the middle managers to further develop the work with K2M. The sensegiving offered by brand management vacillate between high and low, and the organizational sensemaking can thus be said to be a mixture of *guided sensemaking* (i.e. when sensegiving by brand management is high) and *fragmented sensemaking* (i.e. when sensegiving by brand management is low) (see Maitlis & Christianson, 2014).

The introduction of a graphic representation of the brand (a map) is highly welcomed by the middle managers, but a map only works through being read and interpreted and it never quite corresponds to "reality". As pinpointed in Chapter 6 sensegiving cannot be considered in isolation from sensemaking when hybrid agency is at play. Brand management is able to control the layout of the model (a non-human actor), but it cannot control how other actors *make sense* of it and thus how they appropriate it in hybrid agencies. The model needs to be interpreted, that is, the users of the model need to make sense of it: "One person's expressions are now read and translated into someone else's impressions: something to be reconstructed in the meaning system of the hearer, who in turn must project his or her own vision" (Taylor & Van Every, 2011, p. 43). According to Weick's enactment theory, "sensemaking involves invention rather than discovery" (Weick, 2001, p. 194), hence enactment is an active and creative process. Taylor and Van Every (2011) describe the way that the disparity between map and reality invites a *frame game*. Playing a frame game is to invoke a frame that justifies a particular interpretation, and the understanding of the K2M model is thus a negotiation between different frames of interpretation taking place in processes of sensemaking and sensegiving.

In the following, I will analyze how different actors appropriate the K2M model in different ways, and how they play a frame game of coupling versus subdivision. At the initial presentation of the model, brand management invokes a *frame of subdivision*.

Sensegiving as subdivision

When Lucy first presents the K2M model, she uses a *frame of subdivision* to explain (or give sense to) the model:

Excerpt 7.1

> Well, as Dave said, we are working with three subdivisions of K2M. Until now, we have focused a lot on the K2M projects, which we all know, and that is what we have spent time communicating. Then we have an internal part or a corporate culture part in K2M, which we communicate through our different channels, and it will become an even bigger element when we get My K2M up and running. The subdivision we are lacking, or where Globalco has not been focusing, is the CSR part, the sustainability part, in order to make that part of our companies.

The *frame of subdivision* is used to *break* K2M *down* into smaller units in order to be able to identify different components of K2M. So even though, the K2M model is a map that provides an overview of K2M, the model is given sense by Lucy through a *frame of subdivision*. Here the ability of the K2M model to *break* the work with K2M *down* into smaller units is emphasized. However, the CEO invokes a *frame of coupling* when he presents the K2M model.

Sensegiving as coupling

The K2M model is initially presented by Lucy at SGM1 but the CEO gradually takes the floor and ends up giving a lengthy talk about the model. He promotes a *frame of coupling*, as he labels the three pillars as a trinity, and he emphasizes that it is important that all companies work with all three pillars. This sensegiving offered by the CEO supports the interplay and interconnectedness of the pillars, and the coupling frame is supported by Lucy when she states that K2M branding projects could be inspired by the companies' high impact areas (the CSR pillar). The CEO goes with Lucy's input and states that high impact area is an important concept. 'High impact areas' is thus a concept that is bracketed and singled out in order to give sense, and in order to couple 'CSR' and 'Branding'. However, even though the *frame of coupling* is promoted by the CEO, the predominant frame used to *make* and *give sense* of the tripartition is a *frame of subdivision*.

A frame game of coupling versus subdivision

The two different readings of the K2M model produce a frame game where the K2M model is made sense of as either a *coupling* or a *subdivision*. But it is evident that it is the *frame of subdivision* that mostly appeals to the organizational members, and also the one mainly used in sensegiving.

Lucy continuously invokes the *frame of subdivision* to *give sense* to K2M, she even *labels* the pillars silos. Lucy's sensegiving, via this *frame of subdivision*, is taken up by the rest of the participants. One middle manager comments that it is useful to have the three pillars visualized, and she states that the CSR pillar is the one that will make most sense at GoTech. Excerpts 7.2 and 7.3 illustrate how another middle manager also believes the tripartition of K2M into three pillars enhances the understanding of the concept, a viewpoint that she repeats at SGM2:

Excerpt 7.2

> I want to add that the division [of K2M] that has been made communicates it [K2M] very well.

Excerpt 7.3

> Well, we have this schema now, it … it set some things straight, and it was an aha experience. Well, okay, that is it and that is the way we do it … And then we had these ideas that we could fit under each pillar, right.

The participants use the K2M model to categorize their thoughts and ideas according to one of the pillars, and the categorization makes K2M easier to grasp. Consequently, it becomes important for participants to be able to distinguish between the three pillars. For instance, a flow of talk about different ideas when Apparella's KPIs are discussed leads a middle manager to comment:

Excerpt 7.4

> But that would be some of the other silos, I would say offhand. Then we are talking about branding and My K2M projects that must be converted into KPIs.

It is clear that the *frame of subdivision* helps the participants *make sense* of K2M since the concept can be broken down into units, such as 'a KPI', 'a branding project', or 'a newsletter'. It also demonstrates that even though a non-human actor is produced with a certain sensegiving in mind, those efforts may not produce the desired sensemaking. The graphic layout of the K2M model is supposed to illustrate K2M as a trinity. The built-in sensegiving is thus a *frame of coupling* in line with the CEO's sensegiving. But, from the way the participants make sense of the model, it becomes clear that the model implicitly *encourages* the categorization of ideas according to the three pillars of the model. Hence, in their sensemaking the organizational members invoke a *frame of subdivision*. It demonstrates that even though a non-human actor (i.e. the model) is constructed with a certain sensegiving in mind, it gains an agency of its own that escapes the control of its creators (Leonardi & Barley, 2011; Nakassis, 2013; Robichaud & Cooren, 2013). In the hybrid agency that is created, based on appropriation of the model by human actors, a *frame of subdivision* is favored in the sensemaking activities. An activity is thus *either* branding *or* CSR *or* corporate culture, and it becomes important for the participants to be able to categorize their ideas according to the model. The abstractness of the floating signifier K2M is thus being ascribed meaning by relating more or less concrete ideas to K2M. The *frame of subdivision* is thus the frame that is most frequently invoked and used to spur sensemaking. Even though, the CEO originally *gave sense* to K2M by advocating the *frame of coupling*, he also invokes the *frame of subdivision* as he continuously talks about the difference between the three pillars. At another point, a discussion about K2M projects (pillar no. 2) leads to a discussion about positioning more clearly the ways in which GoDeliver already conforms to a number of requirements. However, this input leads the CEO to comment:

Excerpt 7.5

Well, that would be pillar one, wouldn't it?

So, although, the CEO seeks to *give sense* to K2M by invoking *the frame of coupling*, it becomes clear that he himself *makes sense* of K2M according to the *frame of subdivision*. This observation is in line with Weick's (2005) proposition that sensemaking is social and ongoing, which suggests that a brand manager makes sense as the conversation unfolds. It also demonstrates that the ability to author a hegemonic discourse is not dependent upon a formal position in the organization; it is a question of successful sensegiving. In this instance, Lucy's sensegiving as a *frame of subdivision* is easier for the organizational members to work with than the CEO's sensegiving as a *frame of coupling*, and he even adopts the *frame of subdivision* himself. A brand manager's sensegiving responsibilities are thus challenged by the fact that the manager's own sensemaking is an endless ongoing process.

The task of being a practical author requires that the brand manager masters the brand language so that they can consciously decide which discourses to promote and which to counteract. The brand manager must listen carefully to the conversation going on (i.e. the doing of branding) to be able to decipher discourses so that they can actively promote the desired ones and seek to counteract or even contradict the ones that conflict with the desired brand meaning. The tripartition of the K2M model invites a frame game about whether it is a *coupling* or a *subdivision*. The brand manager must be able to identify the frames and consciously choose which one to support in order to influence the frame game. The brand manager must also think carefully about their own phrasing because a naming can be picked up easily, as was the case of a middle manager's naming of focus areas as low-hanging fruit.

The K2M model is a non-human actor that invites a number of other actors to the conversational space. One of these actors is the KPI D-discourse. The KPI D-discourse turns out to be a complicated macro-actor. In Chapter 6, it was demonstrated how the KPI D-discourse challenged sensemaking about power relations, and in the next section it will be demonstrated how the KPI D-discourse invites a frame game of measurability versus setting objectives.

7.3 The KPI discourse: a frame game of measurability versus stating objectives

The concept of KPIs is an important cue in the sensegiving of CSR (pillar one). At SGM1, Lucy voices a frame of *CSR as high impact areas.* KPIs are given sense within a *frame of measurability* when she states that the KPIs ought to produce some concrete numbers that she can use to feed into Globalco's CSR report. The steering group decided to leave the identification of KPIs to the managing directors of each subsidiary. At GoNuGa1, Anna goes with Lucy's sensegiving and introduces the KPIs as something that should feed into the CSR report, thus the participants seek to make sense of KPI:

Excerpt 7.6

MM5: A KPI ought to be measurable, right?

MD1: But it matters, whether we state that we want to improve by 20% or if we say that we want to continually improve the performance without stating any figures.

MM2: It is a stated objective that you want to reduce …

MM5: No, it is something measurable … something you can measure in relation to something else.

MM1: It is a goal that you set for yourself.

MM5: Performance in relation to something.

It becomes clear that there is no common understanding of the notion of KPI, hence the *sensemaking* is diverse. This spurs a frame game between a *frame of measurability* and a *frame of stating objectives.* A middle manager invokes a *frame of measurability* when he refers to the professional D-discourse about KPIs that states how a KPI ought to be measurable. The specificity of measurability is discussed by one of the managing directors. He is supported by the other managing director who is reluctant to provide specifics in case they are, in future, unable to meet their own requirements. The managing directors thus invoke a *frame of stating objectives.* The KPI D-discourse is a non-human macro-actor that performs a sensegiving role, buts its agency is dependent on the hybrid agency that is formed, and the KPI D-

Table 7.1 KPIs at SGM2

Apparella	Supplier management
GoNuGa	UN Global Compact no. 7, 8, 9
	1) Treatment of water resources here under wastewater treatment
	2) Uses of energy in each company
GoTech	UN Global Compact no. 7, 8, 9
GoDeliver	1) A mapping process to identify existing initiatives
	2) Work environment

discourse invites a frame game, since different actors make it say different things. When the two managing directors appropriate the KPI D-discourse, they make sense of it in a way that means that the measurability of the KPI does not need to be established specifically. Hence, in their interpretation, the KPI can be used to bring certain areas into focus, but it is not necessary to make a specific commitment.

At SGM2, a middle manager from each subsidiary presents their preliminary discussions. GoTech and GoNuGa have both turned to the UN Global Compact for further sensegiving, selecting principles 7, 8, and 9 as their focus areas. Apparella has chosen supplier management and GoDeliver has chosen to focus on a mapping process of ongoing initiatives, work environment and environment (Table 7.1).

None of the subsidiaries have set specific KPIs. GoNuGa and GoTech present UN Global Compact principle 7, 8, and 9 as their focus areas but they do not present anything specific in relation to GoNuGa or GoTech. GoDeliver wants to start a mapping process to gain an overview of ongoing initiatives as well as to examine its internal work environment as it has too many resignations. Lucy states that the focus area of Apparella is supplier management. A middle manager asks the CEO how specific the KPIs need to be; he replies that they need to be very specific about euros and cents and liters, but another middle manager says:

Excerpt 7.7

No, it needs to be per unit. That is the only thing you can control.

The CEO agrees and says that units are nice and tangible. This sensemaking about the KPIs is in line with the *frame of measurability* but, at the same time, the CEO voices the *frame of stating objectives* (see excerpt 7.8). The sensegiving related to the KPIs is thus equivocal, and there is uncertainty about how KPI is to be understood (i.e. made sense of). However, when they discuss the procedure of authorization of the KPIs, a middle manager seizes the chance to elaborate on the sensegiving:

Excerpt 7.8

MM3: I'm thinking, offhand, do we have qualifications to approve the KPIs?

CEO: Yes, because you define the KPIs yourself.

MM3: Yes, that's what I mean. I am trying to imagine, how am I supposed to evaluate whether the KPIs coming from you are …?

CEO: Yes?

LUCY: Whether it is realistic.

MM3: Whether it is realistic, ambitious enough, too ambitious … ehm …

CEO: Well, I think … when all comes to all, only you can evaluate it, because as I said before, only you know what is relevant. So I suggest you line up three KPIs – and we need to evaluate if three is a good number. That's what I think … offhand …

MM2: And speaking of clarification of concepts. Well, we talked about KPIs – that is a performance measure.

MM3: Mmm.

MM2: It is the stated objective of how much we are going to improve. That is two different things. Or …

CEO: Yes, connected units, right? Uhm …

MM2: Yes, but you need to have a point of reference in order to figure out how much you want to improv.

CEO: Yes, that's plain to see. How much are you going to improve? How much have you improved etc.? Uhm … yes, according to whether you do it based on numbers, or if it is more like, you know, we have made those and those initiatives since the last time, right?

MM2: Well, yes, but if it is related to … if it is energy then it needs to be …

CEO: Then it needs to be based on numbers. That's right. Yes, that's a good point …

MM3: And that's what I mean. That's difficult for me. It will be difficult for me to relate to, so maybe it does not make sense that I am going to approve something that I cannot relate to …

In the exchange above, the CEO voices the *frame of stating objectives*. He uses the concept of KPI rather loosely; he sees it as a measurement or an initiative, but a middle manager voices the *frame of measurability* and states that a KPI is a performance measure. The middle manager's interpretation of KPI is thus in line with Lucy's sensegiving; she stated that the objective of the KPIs was to produce some numbers that can feed into the CSR report. When the CEO and the managing directors voice the KPI-discourse, it is mainly about stating an objective, but when the middle managers are giving the KPI-discourse voice, it is a specific performance measure. A middle manager appropriates the KPI D-discourse (i.e. an existing account) in order to produce a hybrid agency that is powerful enough to settle the frame game by giving sense in a specific way. He ventriloquizes the macro discourse in order to challenge the very broad understanding of KPI introduced by the K2M model and employed by the CEO. By positioning himself as a dummy, he makes the KPI D-discourse speak through him. Since the macro discourse is an established D-discourse, the middle manager can be rather assertive in stating that a KPI is a performance measure regardless of the fact that he is a middle manager speaking to the CEO.

The literature about sensemaking and sensegiving establishes that top managers are involved in sensemaking activities, such as environmental scanning and issue interpretation (Gioia & Chittipeddi, 1991; Maitlis, 2005). However, excerpt 7.8 suggests that top managers are also involved in sensemaking activities in the course of an interaction. The CEO is making sense of the KPI concept as the conversation unfolds. This observation is in line with an earlier observation, where it became evident that the CEO goes back and forth between a *frame of coupling* and a *frame of subdivision* when he is to give sense to K2M. His sensegiving is informed by ongoing sensemaking as the conversations unfold. In the CEO's response to a middle manager's question about the specificity of KPIs, he mentions the number of accidents at work as an example of a specific KPI, but accidents at work is a very unsophisticated example compared to the middle manager's challenges about calculating fuel consumption related to the business of operating vessels. Hence, when the brand manager makes sense as the conversation goes along, it can be difficult to engage in intelligible sensegiving at the same time.

An aspect that complicates the matter about setting specific KPIs is the fact that the subsidiaries are production companies. Consumption of, for instance, water and energy is thus related to the orders they receive (i.e. how many and what kind of production). When a middle manager invokes the *frame of measurability*, it allows him to draw attention to the fact that GoNuGa needs to establish a point of reference in order to be able to set a measurable KPI. The *frame of measurability* thus makes KPI a much more complicated macro-actor than the *frame of stating objectives*. When the CEO realizes that the process of setting KPIs may be a laborious and time-consuming process, he is willing to dispose of the KPI concept and suggests they work with objectives instead. But the middle manager says that it is easier to relate to KPIs and Lucy wants to stick with the KPIs with a view to the CSR report. The CEO's willingness to substitute 'KPI' with 'objectives' demonstrates his lack of commitment to the KPI D-discourse, and it seems coincidental that KPI was the concept chosen for the K2M model. It demonstrates the importance of careful wording (i.e. labelling) when talk is re-semiotized into text. It is important to realize which macro-actors are invited to participate in the conversational space. Though KPI is a complicated macro-actor, the middle manager and Lucy do not want to change the wording of the K2M model. This underscores the point made by Iedema and Scheeres (2003) that it is harder to challenge ideas and understandings that have been put on paper because re-semiotization from talk to text constitutes the ideas as facts.

The frame game about the *frame of measurability* versus the *frame of stating objectives* is more or less settled in favor of the *frame of measurability* at SGM2. However, the question of *how* to measure remains an open one, and the complexity of the KPIs differs greatly from subsidiary to subsidiary, which spurs a new frame game.

7.4 The KPI D-discourse: a frame game of complexity versus action

The KPI D-discourse turns out to be a much more complicated macro-actor than first anticipated at SGM1, where the participants set a time frame of two months for the subsidiaries to work out a set of KPIs. At SGM3, the subsidiaries present their progress in setting KPIs (Table 7.2).

All subsidiaries have now stated three KPIs but the measurability is a point of discussion. GoNuGa has selected three quite complicated KPIs that all require a point of reference and need to be adjusted according to production. At SGM2, a middle manager tried to draw attention to the fact that the subsidiaries need to establish a point of reference, but he did not succeed in communicating the complexity of measuring energy consumption against line of production. At SGM3, the CEO questions why GoNuGa has yet to state any specific KPIs. When another middle manager tries to explain the complexity however, the CEO responds that measuring is simply a question of looking at the bills from the energy company to see how many kilowatts they have used. The *frame of measurability* now dominates the meetings, but a new frame game emerges between a *frame of complexity* versus a *frame of action*. The CEO voices the *frame of action,* requests a status report from everybody, and asks if it is possible to get the exact KPIs before Christmas:

Table 7.2 KPIs at SGM3

Apparella	1	*Look into code of conduct and use external audits to ensure A-suppliers comply*
	2	*Perform 50–60 tests of chemicals per year*
	3	*Increase communication to ensure transparency*
GoNuGa		UN Global Compact no. 7, 8, 9
	1	Look at water consumption
	2	Look at wastewater
	3	Look at energy consumption in general
GoTech	1	Seek a 20% reduction in waste from production
	2	Seek a 20% reduction in water, electricity, and heath in production units
	3	Employ an apprentice in units with more than 50 employees
GoDeliver	1	Seek a 10% reduction in CO_2 emission from vessels
	2	Complete an employee satisfaction survey and identify focus areas
	3	Manage risk: develop "The GoDeliver Way"

Excerpt 7.9

CEO: Can you do it before Christmas or is it unrealistic?

MM1: I think that is unrealistic.

CEO: That is unrealistic?

MM1: Yes, I think so. This ... well, we need to distil all this in relation to figures from 2016 and 2017 ...

CEO: Yes.

MM1: ... And then compare it to the 2018 budgets in the individual subsidiaries. That is a substantial task of calculation ... that takes time.

CEO: Yes.

MM2: I do not see what we will lose by giving it some extra time before we rush into it. If we are to ... massage it into the organization, then preferably they should be able to see that it is realistic ...

CEO: Yes.

MM2: ... instead of getting 20% smacked in the forehead.

MM1: It is also a question about selling it to the production managers around the factories. And the managing directors out ...

CEO: Yes. I just wonder, how much wiser do we get? Because I know it, right! You need to talk to Bob for instance, right! And ... and maybe Jim and so on and ask them. And so, I just wonder, how much wiser do we get in three months?

The CEO advocates a *frame of action* and is quite skeptical to give the process more time because he fears that the examination of numbers will become a pretext for inaction. In fact, he suggests a "fake it till you make it" approach. But the middle managers clearly voice the *frame of complexity* and question what good will come from the *frame of action*. The *frame of action* has, however, been voiced by the CEO from SGM1. At that meeting, he leaves the KPIs completely to the managing directors and envisages that they will present their KPIs at the December meeting. At SGM2, he states that the KPIs must be brought up at the individual board meetings, but a little later he revises his decision because he realizes that not all board meetings will have been executed before the December meeting. Instead, he suggests that they have a third steering group meeting before the December meeting when they will approve the KPIs. Jill questions whether the participants at the steering group meetings are qualified to approve the KPIs (see excerpt 7.8), but the CEO sticks to the *frame of action* and is ready to revise the authorization procedure of the KPIs in order to keep to his timeline. It makes quite a difference whether it is a board of directors that approves the KPIs or the participants at the steering group. As Jill points out, the members of the steering group do not have qualifications to evaluate the appropriateness of the KPIs, which makes the authorization procedure trivial. In addition, one of the managing directors at GoNuGa has already stated that he only answers to the board of directors (see excerpt

5.21). As it turns out, the KPIs are not ready for approval at SGM3, since KPI is a much more complicated macro-actor than had been foreseen when it was incorporated into the K2M model.

Though KPI is part of a D-discourse and thus represents an established frame, it is seen that other frames are invoked in the sensemaking by the organizational members. Thus, an emerging *frame of stating objectives* challenges the established *frame of measurability*. Although the established *frame of measurability* outperforms the emerging *frame of stating objectives*, the *frame of measurability* spurs a new frame game between *frame of action* and *frame of complexity*. KPI is thus seen to be an ambiguous macro-actor and a poor partner when it comes to giving sense to CSR.

The previous analyses have examined frame games that were related to different parts of the branding process. In the following, I will examine a frame game of how to make sense of the brand K2M itself.

7.5 K2M: a frame game of "business as usual" versus "a new way of doing business"

In Chapter 4 (section 4.2), I argued that the constitution of a brand lies not in the activities as such but in how the activities are interpreted (Taylor et al., 1996). K2M does not exist because of certain activities but because those activities are framed as branding activities under the common signifier, K2M. According to Saussure, the relationship between signifier and signified is arbitrary (Culler, 1986). Mumby (2016) builds on this understanding, when he writes "any signifier has the potential to be linked to any signified, and hence any meaning or quality can be connected to any branded product or service" (p. 894). A brand name is arbitrary, but it makes the brand exist because we learn to connect the name/signifier to discourses and activities promoted under the brand's name (a discursive brand space). As mentioned in Chapter 4, K2M is a floating signifier. Since the discursive brand space is just evolving, different discourses struggle to invest K2M with meaning in their own particular way, thus a new brand name will always be open to interpretation. The name Kind2Mind thus spurs a *frame game* that becomes evident when two different discourses struggle to invest K2M with meaning. Kind2Mind is the invention of a new signifier. That is, according to the CEO nothing would come up, if one googled "kind2mind", when he and his business partner coined the name. But it is a signifier that is made up by the combination of two familiar words, namely 'kind' and 'mind', that are connected via a code that spurs the reader to understand "2" as "to". The signifier K2M thus implicitly tells the reader that it is "kind to mind". But what does that mean? Even though the words "kind" and "mind" are familiar, it is not necessarily evident what they are supposed to mean in this specific constellation and, as pointed out by Maitlis & Christianson (2014), ambiguous identity triggers sensemaking.

The endeavor to invest K2M with meaning is thus an ongoing process of sensegiving and sensemaking as different organizational members use different discourses to invest K2M with meaning. Two discourses stand out as the dominant perspectives on how to make sense of K2M. One is a discourse about K2M being a *new way of doing business* (see also Chapter 4), and the other is a discourse about K2M being *business as usual*.

Giving sense to K2M as a "new way of doing business"

The *new way of doing business* discourse is put forward by the CEO and receives promotion in the "Kind2Mind" book as well as in a video on Globalco's webpage. The video displays the CEO sitting on a couch, where he explains K2M as a "core philosophy" and labels K2M as "a kind of CSR on ecstasy". The video is supplemented with a text seemingly written by the CEO, as it is signed by him at the bottom of the page, explaining K2M as "a kind of CSR version 3.0", as an "an all-win strategy that considers our partners, customers, employees and charity", and a "philosophy of doing kind business". K2M is thus being given sense by these discourses that explicate K2M as "CSR on ecstasy", "CSR 3.0", "all-win", "combining doing business with being kind", and "doing kind business". The explanation about "doing kind business" and "all-win" is repeated in the K2M code of conduct. The explanations promoted in these central sensegiving texts[1] constitute a discourse about K2M being a *new way of doing business*.

However, the discourses in the book that seek to explicate K2M are broad and superficial and, as such, they offer little specific sensegiving. The discourses in the video and the K2M code of conduct operate on the same abstract level. Expressions such as "CSR on ecstasy", "CSR 3.0", and "all-win" are devoid of specific content and that challenges the organizational members in their sensemaking processes. It is thus possible to identify a different discourse about K2M that offers a sensemaking of *business as usual*.

Making sense of K2M as "business as usual"

The competing discourse about K2M being *business as usual* promotes a narrative about K2M being just a new way of naming "what we have always done". Quite early in the GoNuGa1 meeting, a middle manager voices the discourse that K2M is just *business as usual*:

Excerpt 7.10

MM2: I don't think it has to be very difficult compared to what we do today.
MM1: No.
MM2: We already have a lot of KPIs. We measure, how many resources we use, how the employees … it could be sickness absence, work-related injuries … so we already measure a lot of things that we can incorporate into this.
MD1: Yes.

And later at the same meeting, the middle manager suggests that K2M is just new labelling of what they have always done:

Excerpt 7.11

MM2: But isn't it just a new labelling of how, we act in the everyday? That's how I have regarded it all the time.

MM1: Yes, that's it.

MM2: We behave … we try to behave well in all contexts, towards customers, towards employees, so in that sense, I don't think …

MM5: Yes, but I think it's more about getting it out there … so to say … make it more transparent, and tell this is how, we work in this conglomerate and so on. This is what we do in GoNuGa. This is what we do elsewhere. And then connect it somehow so that we get this sense of community or … a sense of belonging, right? I think that is important, because that is Sam's goal with Globalco, at least as to how I have understood it … It is about saying, we used to be a large group of individual companies, now we want to try to connect it all, right?

In GoNuGa, they use the discourse about K2M being just a new naming of *business as usual* as a way to make K2M comprehensible: "It does not have to be very difficult" and "it is just a new labelling". When the signifier K2M is invested with the meaning that it is just a new name for "how we act in the everyday", it becomes difficult to develop the understanding of K2M, since it is difficult to see what its newness is or which activities would be appropriate in order to make the brand stand out in the right way. The problems of making sense of K2M can thus be identified as a discursive struggle to invest K2M with a particular meaning that is evident in the *frame game* between the *business as usual* and the *new way of doing business* discourses.

The middle manager's explanation of K2M raises a concern with another middle manager. Right from the beginning, the CEO has sought to position K2M as a *new way of doing business* and especially as a new form of CSR. At first the CEO labelled K2M 'CSR 2.0' to make it stand out from known CSR, and later he reframed K2M as 'CSR 3.0'. In the following excerpt, we see how the discourse about CSR 2.0 makes a middle manager question that K2M can just be *business as usual*:

Excerpt 7.12

MM5: K2M started as … well, Sam used it as marketing by saying that it is CSR 2.0. In my mind 2.0 must mean that it is better than what is.

MD1: Yes.

MM5: So, what is it that K2M brings to the table?

MM1: Yes.

MM5: Compared to ordinary CSR. I think it has been a challenge to define that.

MM1: Yes.

MM5: What is K2M other than ordinary CSR?

MD2: Yes, but I think Ben … it has been more of a … excuse me, but … but maybe it has been more of a clever pronouncement.

MM5: Sure, it has a nice ring to it.

MD1: Well, it all started with the book that he made with his business partner. Where the concept … where he created the concept of K2M and things like that … then it became more … gradually … it develops … it sets buds, right?

MM1: Mmm.

MD1: So, well … I think that is how it came about. And then you can say … well, it has a nice ring to it … and it is definitely different to call it K2M than CSR and so on. And moreover, I think there is also an element of the way that Sam likes to express himself … how he gives lectures and uses some different metaphors and different expressions that are a bit offbeat, right? And that's fine.

It is clear that the middle manager tries to make sense of the signifier 'CSR 2.0', but he cannot do so through the *business as usual* discourse, and that leads him to question what is different about K2M, hence he asks for an elaboration of the *new way of doing business* discourse. But the managing director dismisses that discourse and claims that K2M is just "a clever pronouncement", that "it has a nice ring to it", that it is a "different metaphor". So, the managing director reaffirms the *business as usual* discourse by constructing a narrative that explicates K2M as an offbeat expression that merely functions as a clever marketing trick. K2M is an example of the CEO's tendency to use some "offbeat expressions".

Sensemaking is a process of social construction and it happens through the production of accounts or through the activation of existing accounts (Maitlis, 2005). In order for organizational members to be able to make sense, they must be able to either fit new ideas or information into an existing system of meaning (Gioia & Chittipeddi, 1991) or produce a new account that is able to embrace the perspective in question. The middle manager struggles to make sense of 'CSR 2.0' in the frame of K2M being *business as usual* (the activation of an existing account) since he believes that the use of a new signifier (CSR 2.0) must imply that K2M is a *new way of doing business* (the construction of a new account). When he asks what the *new way of doing business* is about (i.e. what K2M brings to the table), the managing directors answer his question about how 'CSR 2.0' is different from CSR by going back to voicing the discourse that K2M is just *business as usual*. The managing directors tell the middle manager that K2M is just CSR as we know it, and the label 'CSR 2.0' is simply a way to try to make K2M stand out. Hence, there is a *frame game* going on as the two discourses struggle to fix the meaning of K2M in different ways: *a new way of doing business* as opposed to *business as usual*.

The problem with the discourse about K2M being *business as usual* is that it becomes difficult for the organizational members to see what the fuss is about. The *business as usual* discourse explicates K2M as just a new signifier. It is a signifier that has been invented to create a corporate brand across Globalco and its many subsidiaries, but it does not correlate to a new signified. The signified is business as it has always been. This sensemaking is in accordance with the understanding put forward by the managing director of Apparella, who stated that K2M was a labelling of what they have always done (see excerpt 4.2, Chapter 4), and a middle manager expresses the same understanding at SGM2 when she says that she believes it is important that K2M is not seen as an extra assignment but just another way to talk about what they have always done. The *business as usual* discourse is thus a sensemaking that reassures the organizational members that they do not need to worry about how to understand K2M or how to put it into practice, because they are already practicing it, and it is just a matter of communicating what they are doing. It is, however, also a discourse that discourages the organizational members from thinking creatively about what K2M may entail, since K2M is dismissed as just a new labelling.

The other frame that is evoked – K2M as a *new way of doing business* – spurs the organizational members to ask themselves what this new way of doing business entails and how it can be put into practice, but it is a frame that is difficult to handle, because the 'newness' of K2M is not sufficiently elaborated. The *new way of doing business* discourse does not help to fix the meaning of K2M because it does not explain in which ways it is new, or what the 'newness' of K2M is. Hence, more sensegiving is needed in order to enable the organizational members to make sense of K2M as a *new way of doing business*. When it comes to investing K2M with meaning, the discourse about *business as usual* stands stronger than the discourse about a *new way of doing business*, because the latter does not invest K2M with a meaning that aids the organizational members in their sensemaking. The resistance to accepting the frame of K2M as a *new way of doing business* can thus possibly be explained as a lack of repertoire to understand K2M as *a new way of doing business*. In order to make sense of K2M, the organizational members have to stick to the discourse that is able to invest it with some kind of meaning.

At the second meeting of the GoNuGa Group the discussion about CSR 2.0 comes up again. The participants have been discussing the values of locally grounded branding projects versus branding projects with a global outlook, when one of the managing directors comments:

Excerpt 7.13

> It is not going to be either/or, it is going to be both/and. We are both going to do something global, which we can use as a group, and we are

going to do something local that makes us unique in relation to CSR so that it is not just CSR 1.0, but it keeps being something different, this K2M, and not just ordinary CSR. That is my understanding of how Sam has meant it. And as we have talked about many times before, it is CSR 2.0 – ergo it has to be different from what was before, since that was 1.0.

We see how the reference to K2M as 'CSR 2.0' incites the participants to think of K2M as a different kind of CSR than what has been known before. Both CSR (1.0) and CSR 2.0 can be said to belong to macro discourses about CSR, but these macro discourses are not explicitly being ventriloquized at the meeting. The 'CSR 2.0' D-discourse states five principles of CSR 2.0, one of these being what Visser (2014) calls "glocality". It could seem as though the managing director implicitly invokes this macro-actor when he states that they are both going to launch some local initiatives as well as some global ones. However, he does not make any specific reference to the D-discourse. Consequently, it is difficult to tell whether he intentionally ventriloquizes the D-discourse to justify their ideas about launching local initiatives, and thus invokes a macro-actor (the CRS 2.0 D-discourse) to help give sense to K2M, or whether he is simply reaffirming that they will do both. It is however clear that neither the CSR 1.0 D-discourse nor the CSR 2.0 D-discourse is given voice anywhere else at the GoNuGa meetings, hence the macro-actors are not invoked to participate in sensegiving activities.

Since the CEO does not use explicit sensegiving (i.e. by explicating what he understands about CSR), it suggests that he relies on the macro discourses about CSR 1.0 and CSR 2.0 to act as puppeteers. The term refers to actors (human or non-human) that animate (i.e. guide) the managing directors in their work with CSR to make them talk about CSR from a certain knowledge base. But the macro-actors are not seen to be mobilized and do not seem to inform the conversations in GoNuGa. The participants know the signifiers 'CSR 1.0' and 'CSR 2.0', but they do not mobilize the D-discourses. They never articulate any differences between the two, except "ergo it has to be different". Hence the macro discourses do not seem to animate the managing directors or other participants in any particular way (i.e. guide their sensemaking). But since the CEO has labelled K2M as 'CSR 2.0', the middle manager is urged to understand K2M as a different kind of CSR, given that it is 2.0 and not 1.0. It underscores the responsibility of a practical author to contribute to the creation of a common language.

The previous analyses have considered frame games at management level. In the last part of my analysis about frame games, I will flip the focus from the two conversational spaces constituted by the steering group meetings and the meetings at GoNuGa in order to address sensemaking among the employees of Globalco. I mentioned, in Chapter 6, that while Buddha is made present on several occasions in steering group meetings, Buddha is not seen to play an important part in that conversational space. However, Buddha is often evoked by other employees. Therefore, in the next section I will turn my attention to materiality and how a frame game of *K2M is inspired by Buddhism* versus *K2M is not Buddhist* is spurred by the use of materiality.

7.6 Frame game of "K2M is a Buddhist philosophy" versus "K2M is not Buddhist"

In Chapter 6, it was established that one of the ways brand management works with sensegiving is by use of a logo, the color orange, and Buddha as artifact. In the following, we will see how this use of materiality challenges sensemaking and makes some employees invoke a frame of "K2M is a Buddhist philosophy", while others claim that "K2M is not Buddhist".

Frame of "K2M is a Buddhist philosophy"

K2M is never explicitly given sense to by brand management as a Buddhist philosophy but, even so, many employees evoke a frame of *K2M is a Buddhist philosophy*. In this paragraph, I will illustrate what cues they use to reach that sensemaking.

In Chapter 4, I argued that the CEO is a strong incarnation of K2M. I based my arguments on statements like, "Clearly, the kindness-concept stems from Sam via his approach to Buddhism and his faith", and "It is a philosophy that Sam practices because of his own religion and way of thinking". These employees clearly express a sensemaking that *K2M is a Buddhist philosophy*. Not all employees use words like religion or faith, but they clearly associate the CEO and Buddha with each other.

Buddha ... or is it the CEO?

Within Globalco, it is well-known that the Buddha figure has been introduced as an organizational artifact by the CEO, and the two are seen as inextricably linked. For instance, a picture of a Buddha figurine spurred the following comments:

Excerpt 7.14

MM: That is the CEO ... no it isn't ...
INTERVIEWER: No, there is a picture, where it faces the camera here.
MM: Oh, it is that little figurine. Oh my God, don't tell him, I said that!

[laughing]

INTERVIEWER: I won't. But there is a slight resemblance from the back. [smiling]
MM: It is a good photo. I can see it now ... that the sun ... Well, yes but every time I look at Sam, I think about K2M.

The middle manager's first impulse, when she sees the photo of the Buddha figurine, is that it is a photo of the CEO. When she realizes that it is a photo of the Buddha figurine, she mentions that every time she sees the CEO, she comes to think about K2M. Her statement thus substantiates that the CEO is seen as an incarnation of K2M, but her reaction also signals a connection between Buddha and the CEO, which is also expressed by other employees:

Excerpt 7.15

EMPLOYEE G: I have seen that picture.
EMPLOYEE B: I nearly said that it is the CEO. We have this fairly big Buddha figurine over there.
INTERVIEWER: Yes?
EMPLOYEE B: Pretty heavy, about 320 kg.
EMPLOYEE A: [laughing] And you have to lift it?

[everybody starts talking and laughing about the big Buddha that nobody cares to remove from its pallet because it is so heavy]

Like the middle manager, the employee thinks it is the CEO in the picture at first sight. The CEO is bald and could in this respect resemble a Buddhist monk or a Buddha figure, which could explain the misconception. However, the employee quickly realizes that it is a Buddha figurine in the picture and the confusion leads to a discussion about the relationship between Buddha and the CEO:

Excerpt 7.16

EMPLOYEE B: I would dare to claim that it has become Sam's brand.
EMPLOYEE G: Oh yes.
EMPLOYEE B: Right! Through the past 15 years.
INTERVIEWER: Do you think about the CEO, when you see these figurines?
EMPLOYEE B: Yes.
EMPLOYEE G: Yes, you do.

The employees agree that the Buddha figurine is part of the CEO's personal brand. The same understanding is expressed by a managing director, who states that the CEO is referred to as the Buddha-guy. The employees thus see a close relationship between Buddha and the CEO. Whether it is because of a physical resemblance between the CEO and the Buddha figurine or it is more of a symbolic resemblance is not completely clear from these excerpts. But coupled with the excerpts in Chapter 4, where employees suggest that K2M is a philosophy the CEO practices because of his inspiration from Buddhism, it signals an entanglement of the CEO, Buddha, and Buddhism, which is also expressed in the following excerpt:

Excerpt 7.17

> When I learned that the employment policy was called K2M, I had a strong association to the CEO. I could almost see him in his monk's robe and the Buddha.

The image of the CEO in a monk's robe is similar to that described by another employee, who says that she comes to think of the CEO sitting like a Buddha. Hence, it suggests that the CEO is not only seen as an incarnation of K2M but also of the Buddhist idea behind K2M. This leads some employees to invoke the frame *K2M is a Buddhist philosophy*, and their sensemaking is supported by the use of materiality:

Excerpt 7.18

MM: I know that when we speak about kindness, it is a Buddhist …
INTERVIEWER: Yes?
MM: … ehm … concept, and I also know what it means. And ehm … that color is a kindness-color, and the bracelet is also [Buddhist], and that one [a public statue] … she is not related to kindness, but the color is [the statue is lit in orange].

The middle manager clearly perceives the "kindness" part of K2M as a Buddhist concept, and he sees the orange color as Buddhist symbolism. Therefore, he makes sense of communication as expressing Buddhism when the color orange is used, as seen with the public statue. The same sensemaking is evident when another middle manager says that orange adds a Buddha profile to the logo, and an employee identifies orange as a Buddhist color. A middle manager describes how the way this color has been incorporated in the logo makes K2M present in the logo; he is signaling a connection between orange and K2M. An employee from Apparella also says that the color makes her think of their big Buddha figurine in the foyer.

The different kinds of materialities are thus seen as interrelated, and the entanglement of the CEO, Buddha, logo, and the use of orange are thus evoking a frame of *K2M is a Buddhist philosophy*, but not all employees share that frame.

Frame of "K2M is not Buddhist"

Though nobody disagrees about the close connection between the CEO and the Buddha figurine, not all employees make sense of the Buddha figurine as a symbol of Buddhism. In fact, a middle manager from Apparella stresses that the "Buddha" in *not* a "Buddha" figure but a "Kindness" figure. According to her, the Buddha is there to spread kindness in the building. Her point of view is supported by other Apparella employees. Its managing director further denies that the figure is a "Buddha". He describes how the figure originates from a campaign where Apparella produced a special edition shirt for a charity campaign:

Excerpt 7.19

> […] then we made this campaign figure that was a Caucasian man, that is, a white man, who was seated in a lotus position and looked like a Buddhist monk, but he was not, because he was white and then he was holding a baseball. I thought that was cool. There were these contradictions. What the hell, isn't, this guy white? Isn't he wearing a coat? He was too. Wasn't that a baseball? Yes, it was. So in that way we tried to make a joke about it. He sat soaring in the air with a baseball in his hand and then he was actually white. So that is where it [the figurine] stems from. In reality it was just an enlargement of a poster, we made back then. There is nothing more to it. It is not the CEO.

The managing director explains that the figurine is not a Buddha and he furthermore stresses that it is not an image of the CEO. The fact that the managing director feels a need to stress this fact signals that he is aware that many employees see a close relationship between Buddha and the CEO, but it is important to him to pinpoint that the figurine is not a Buddha. At GoNutri, an employee expresses the view that she sees the Buddha figurine as a mascot, and other employees say that the CEO is inspired by Buddhism, but he is not a Buddhist. These employees are thus seen to invoke a frame of *K2M is not Buddhist*. The frame that *K2M is not Buddhist* is primarily expressed at Apparella, which is in accordance with the sensegiving offered by the managing director of Apparella.

The CEO explicitly states that K2M is not a Buddhist philosophy, and is thus seen to support the frame of *K2M is not Buddhist*. However, as argued, the use of materiality at Globalco supports a sensemaking that supports the frame of *K2M is a Buddhist philosophy*. In addition, in the "Kind2Mind" book, "kindness" is explained as action with a clear reference to the Buddhist philosophy, and the co-author explains that everything an organization does plants a seed and thus brings about a certain result. As already mentioned, the logo is also given sense by being explained as Indra's Net, and at a steering group meeting, the CEO reports that they are considering inviting a Buddhist lama to participate in the judging panel to elect the winning My K2M project.

These findings suggest that it is important to pay attention to sensegiving at all times. Even though, the CEO explicitly expresses the frame of *K2M is not Buddhist*, there are other cues that lead the employees to invoke the competing frame of *K2M is a Buddhist philosophy*. It is also seen that sense-giving is not unequivocal. For instance, the use of Indra's net in the logo is a specific reference to eastern philosophy, and when the symbols of orange, Buddha, and Indra's net are put together, it connotes Buddhism. Based solely on the data and the previous analyses, it is not possible to determine whether materiality is a stronger communicator than talk and text. But Salzer-Mörling and Strannegård (2004) argue that the language of brands is pictorial to a high degree, which is more open to interpretation because as they explain, whereas "stories are connected with meanings and persuasion, images are more an issue of feelings and immersion" (p. 226). It can thus be argued that the use of orange and Buddha adds an emotional dimension to K2M, and K2M is partly given sense by being associated with Buddhism, without explicitly mentioning that word. Sensegiving can thus happen unintentionally if brand management is not careful in considering talk, text, and materiality alike.

7.7 Sensegiving and frame games

From the previous analyses, it is evident that sensegiving is rarely unequivocal. Rather, sensegiving is seen to spur a number of frame games, such as *frame of coupling* versus *frame of subdivision, high impact areas* versus *low-hanging fruit, frame of measurability* versus *frame of stating objectives, frame of action* versus *frame of complexity, new way of doing business* versus *business as usual*, and *K2M is a Buddhist philosophy* versus *K2M is not a Buddhist philosophy*. These frame games take place as many different actors, human and non-human alike, produce discourses that all struggle to invest K2M with meaning.

Frame games and authority

It was stated in Chapter 5 that the conversational space is polyphonic and that the voices are not of equal status. The analyses in Chapter 7 verify this statement by demonstrating that authority is linked to the act of sensegiving. If one looks at the participants' formal position within Globalco, brand management is comprised of Lucy, Dave, and the CEO and, according to the formal positions, these actors ought to have the most authoritative voices. When Lucy first introduces the K2M model and the concept of KPIs, she gives sense to the KPIs as *high impact areas*. However, her sensegiving is immediately reframed into *low-hanging fruit* by a middle manager (see Chapter 6, excerpt 6.5), and the frame of *low-hanging fruit* is seen to be much more pervasive in the ongoing discussions. This finding demonstrates that authority and sensegiving are interlinked, seeing as the sensegiving that resonates most successfully with the audience produces authority. Authority is produced through the production of a discursive closure (i.e. a hegemonic discourse). When the participants embrace the frame of *low-hanging fruit* as the frame that guides their talk and interaction, this frame becomes the truth about KPIs, and how they are supposed to go about identifying KPIs. However, as pointed out in Chapter 2 (2.3), any discursive closure will only be momentary because the discursive brand space is constantly evolving. In the fourth steering group meeting, Lucy materializes a non-human actor to support her frame of *high impact areas*, namely the K2M code of conduct. In the K2M code of conduct, the frame of *high impact areas* is re-semiotized into text and, as argued earlier, *text* is harder to challenge than *talk*. Lucy is thus challenging the frame of *low-hanging fruit* by the production of a hybrid agency that supports her frame of *high impact areas*. As argued in Chapter 4 (phase 5), the K2M code of conduct is an attempt to re-enact K2M in a standardized form and, in a performative ontology, the mere presence of materiality can trigger specific behavior (Cooren, 2004). The production of a text (i.e. a non-human actor) that incarnates the frame of *high impact areas* is thus supposedly a very persuasive use of sensegiving given that talk that is materialized into text is perceived as a fact already agreed upon. Yet, as argued, the agency of non-human actors is dependent upon *if* and *how* the non-human actors are appropriated by human actors. Consequently, the re-semiotization of the frame of *high impact areas* into text will only affect the conversations about KPIs if the K2M code of conduct is appropriated by the steering group members, and that is apparently not the case. In the following steering group meeting the frame of *low-hanging fruit* is used by Lucy to back the alteration of a KPI suggested by Apparella. At SGM6 two middle managers use the frame of *low-hanging fruit* to substantiate their subsidiaries' choice of KPIs, and at SGM7 the CEO uses the frame of *low-hanging fruit* to suggest a branding project. It is thus seen that even though the frame of *high impact areas* is promoted by a member of brand management and is re-semiotized into text, it is still the frame of *low hanging fruit* that dominates the conversations. Frame games are thus settled according to the sensegiving that resonates most successfully with the audience or, put in other words, it is the frame that most successfully enables sensemaking that comes to dominate, which is why sensegiving and authority are interlinked. The middle manager who introduces the frame of *low-hanging fruit* has no formal authority, yet it is her sensegiving that affects the conversations the most, and the frame is adopted by brand management in the ongoing conversations.

In the present chapter, we see how the CEO seeks to promote a *frame of coupling* in relation to the three pillars in the K2M model, but it is a *frame of subdivision* that is taken up by the organizational members and comes to dominate the discussions. Ultimately, authority is dependent upon successful sensegiving.

Strategic choice of frames

Brand management makes use of D-discourses in their sensegiving activities. D-discourses of 'CSR', 'Branding', and 'Corporate culture' are incorporated into the K2M model. However, these D-discourses are very broad (mega-discourses) and, even though the D-discourses refer to established frames, the sensemaking spurred by the D-discourses are seen to be quite different. This is due to participants evoking different aspects of the D-discourses and thus understanding them in different ways.

In this respect, it is interesting to notice that sensemaking is apparently strategic. When the managing directors of GoNuGa are confronted with the KPI D-discourse, they first choose to make sense of it in accordance with the usual use of that D-discourse at Globalco, namely as a macro-actor that can only be invoked at board meetings. In this sense, they stay true to an established frame. But when it comes to a discussion about how KPIs are to be put into practice, they abandon the established *frame of measurability* in favor of a *frame of stating objectives*. Hence, their sensemaking is not seen to be determined by established frames but rather in accordance with what they find to be most beneficial or manageable in the current situation. They invoke an established frame of KPIs belonging at the board level in order to challenge the authority of the K2M model, but their use of established frames is inconsistent. For example, they do not hesitate to abandon the established *frame of measurability* when another sensemaking seems to be more advantageous. Frames are thus continually being constructed in a bottom-up process.

7.8 Summary

The findings in Chapters 6 and 7 demonstrate the importance of sensegiving by human and non-human actors alike. Brand management can use the production of non-human actors to give sense. However, non-human actors escape the control of their authors once they leave their site of construction, and it is thus a management task to spur conversations that activate the agency of the non-human actors in the desired way. The K2M model is produced as a sensegiving tool but the model is constrained by limited space, which only allows sensegiving to a limited extent. The graphic layout of the model spurs a frame game of *coupling* versus *subdivision*. The D-discourses incorporated in the model need to be explicated through talk. But when the K2M model is introduced by Lucy at SGM1, she goes through it very briefly (as seen in excerpt 7.1), and the D-discourses are not elaborated on in any further detail. Her use of sensegiving is minimal, which spurs a number of frame games, such as, *high impact areas* versus *low-hanging fruit*, and *measurability* versus *stating objectives*. The data material offers no final evidence as to the sensegiving properties of talk and text versus other kinds of materiality. But it is seen that the use of the color orange and of Buddha as organizational artifact leads many employees to understand K2M as a Buddhist philosophy even though there is no explicit sensegiving stating that and the CEO himself denies it. It is thus worth considering the visibility of different sensegiving tools as well as how much organizational members engage in reading documents.

The notion of frame games points to the importance of brand management to function as practical authors, but it also illustrates that the brand manager is not the only one who authors the brand. Everybody who engages in conversations about K2M participate in producing the discursive brand space. Brand management is thus about engaging in those conversations and paying attention to which frames of interpretations that are evoked, not least paying attention to the frames produced by oneself. These findings build on those of Vásquez et al. (2013), who found that "the brand acts as a frame that is mobilized to make sense of a situation, account for it, and decide what to do" (p. 140). We see that Vásquez et al. (2013) make use of 'brand' as an already established entitative being, and the analyses in this chapter seek to explicate how that entitative being is talked into existence. The 'brand' is an *empty signifier* that encapsulates the dominant meaning that emerges as a result of a discursive closure of the discursive brand space. However, the closure is only momentary as the discursive brand space is constantly developing as a result of competing frame games and discourses that struggle for hegemony. Frame games are informed by frames that emerge in a bottom-up process during daily talks and interactions (e.g. the *frame of low-hanging fruit* and the *frame of stating objectives*) and established frames that are invoked in the organizational members' sensegiving and sensemaking activities (e.g. *frame of measurability*) alike. The frames that are made present organize the way the organizational members go about doing their branding activities. A central task of brand management is thus to invoke frames that support the desired brand meaning and to dismantle frames that are undesirable.

Lastly, these analyses demonstrate that sensegiving and sensemaking are very closely interrelated activities. It is demonstrated on several occasions that the CEO's sensemaking is affected by ongoing conversations (e.g. *frame of coupling* versus *frame of subdivision, frame of measurability* versus *frame of stating objectives, frame of high impact areas* versus *frame of low-hanging fruit*) and that challenges the role of the brand manager to function as a practical author.

Note

1 When a middle manager requests further sensegiving from the CEO at SGM2, the CEO reacts dismissively. He responds that K2M has already been explicated in the "Kind2Mind" book, on the website, and in brochures. The book and the webpage are thus highlighted by the CEO as central sensegiving tools.

8 The brand manager as a practical author

When a brand is conceptualized as a *discursive brand space*, then brand management is about talking the discursive brand space into existence by managing discourse and interaction. Many different actors, human and non-human alike, are seen to participate in sensegiving activities, and the analyses in Chapters 6 and 7 demonstrated that the key to having an authoritative voice in the conversational space is related to successful sensegiving and the settlement of frame games, rather than a formal position in the organization. The understanding of a brand as a discursive brand space therefore requires a new understanding of brand management, where the brand manager (or brand management) is not seen to be in control of brand meaning, but rather is understood to be one among many authors of brand meaning.

Chapter 8 will focus on the concept of the brand manager as a *practical author*. By analyzing an episode of public debate about a brand (a potential brand crisis), the polyphony of conversational spaces will be illustrated in further detail. Previous chapters have demonstrated the fluidity of boundaries to conversational spaces by examining how organizational members invite non-human actors and macro-actors to co-author the brand. This chapter will focus on the participation of human actors normally thought of as external to the organization. It will be examined how they participate in conversations about the brand and thus produce discourses that become part of the discursive brand space. It will further be examined, how (or if) the brand manager engages in these conversations, and whether he succeeds in promoting discourses that are favorable to the brand and to counteract discourses that are detrimental to the desired brand meaning.

8.1 Brand management as orchestration of discourses

The concept of a brand manager as a practical author has not yet been examined in the branding literature (an exception is Golant (2012)). The notion of the brand manager as a practical author reflects an understanding of branding as an ever-evolving process with many actors co-authoring the brand beyond the control of brand management. The brand is always in a state of becoming and brand managers become directors of discourses. They can foster, support and guide conversations, but never control them.

DOI: 10.4324/9781003050100-8

Chapter 4 examined the process of brand creation, and nine elements were found to be of central importance in establishing a brand as an entitative being. It was argued that for a brand to gain entitative being status, it must be able to transcend and eclipse any human being. Naming and re-semiotization into permanent or semi-permanent modalities are essential elements in brand creation and so is the ability of human and non-human actors to incarnate the brand. Brand management was conceptualized as the orchestration of discourses (i.e. discourses embrace both social and material activity), and the brand manager was cast as a practical author, but the responsibility of a practical author was not elaborated. I will briefly recap Figure 4.1 (reproduced here as Figure 8.1) to remind the reader of the nine brand elements before we delve into the role of a brand manager as a practical author.

Inspired by Nicotera's phasic model (see Chapter 4), the CCB approach is able to explicate important elements of brand (re-)creation when a brand is understood as a discursive brand space. It was found that a brand is constituted as an entity in a cyclical process of talk, production of texts and materiality, establishment of a self-conscious collectivity, incarnation, and reification of the brand. *Conversations* take place in a conversational space (see Chapter 5), and a central part of brand management is to pay attention to the number and set up of conversational spaces. Conversations are enabled and constrained by the affordances (e.g. the physical settings) of conversational spaces and the interaction that is enabled. An important aspect of conversations is the participants' *repertoire*, and accordingly, another central part of brand management is paying

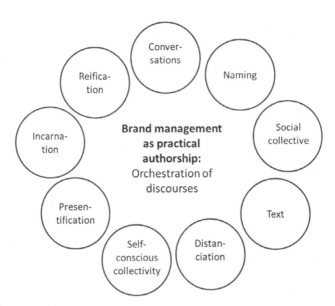

Figure 8.1 Brand management as practical authorship.

attention to developing a fruitful brand language. *Naming* is central, as identity is not in the activities themselves but in how they are given sense and made sense of. Furthermore, it was found that a brand needs a name in order to create a nodal point in the discursive brand space. A brand name is also necessary for the brand to be constituted as an actor in a narrative, and narratives that spur collective sensemaking are the essence of the *Social collective*. When initial talk is re-semiotized into a permanent or semi-permanent modality – *Text* and *Presentification* – these materialities provide a record of past conversations, which can (and often will) feed into future conversations about the brand. Text and Presentification serve to distanciate the brand from its original authors, even though the production of text and materiality in itself is not a guarantee of distanciation. That is why *Distanciation* appears as an independent element in the brand creation process, to emphasize that it is an aspect that the brand manager ought to pay attention to. The production of text and materiality is potentially the foundation of non-human actors. Accordingly, a brand manager ought to pay careful attention to the construction (not least the naming) of these actors, since they become part of hybrid agencies that escape the control of the brand manager. Non-human actors can serve to incarnate the brand, but it was found that *Incarnation* by human actors requires a sense of *Self-conscious collectivity*. If people are not able to establish a speech community and a sense of a professional collectivity, it becomes very difficult to incarnate the brand convincingly. Last but not least, a brand needs to be constantly reproduced through *Reification*. Reification is a representation of the brand in a standardized form that is disseminated to a broader public. Examples of this are a logo, an ad, a video, an artifact, a CSR report, or a human incarnation by a brand representative.

As argued in Chapter 2, a brand is an immaterial abstract construction that does not exist outside its communicational incarnations. Consequently, a brand navigates between concreteness (materiality) and abstractness (idea). Figure 8.1 provides an overall understanding of social and material discourses of central importance and how these interact and affect each other. Combined with insights from the CCB approach, this figure suggests *how a discursive brand space can be influenced*, that is, how it produces a new understanding of brand management, one where the brand manager accepts that they are no longer the sole author of brand meaning and instead seeks to be a leading co-creator. This new role is conceptualized as the *brand manager as a practical author*.

The role of a practical author

Practical authorship builds on an understanding of communication as a relationally responsive dialogical activity, where meaning is negotiated through circuits of sensegiving and sensemaking (Golant, 2012). The traditional concepts of sender and receiver are thus abandoned in favor of an understanding of meaning as co-created. When a brand is conceptualized as a *discursive brand space*, all discourses are fundamentally of equal importance. Discourses produced by brand management do not per se occupy a more privileged position than discourses produced by other actors. Instead, there is an ongoing discursive battle, where different discourses fight for hegemony. It was demonstrated in Chapter 7 that hegemony, or the settlement of frame games, is a question of successful sensegiving. Accordingly, the essence of brand management is engaging in sensegiving activities in a quest to influence how brand meaning is negotiated and created. Management of the discursive brand space can be seen as the task of producing and promoting desired brand discourses and counteracting undesired brand discourses.

Since every instance of discourse about the brand becomes part of the discursive brand space, it is the task of a practical author to promote conversations that spur discourses that are seen as desirable to the brand. Brand meaning emerges as a result of discursive struggles when some discourses succeed in establishing a discursive closure, but discourses are constantly being transformed through contact with other discourses and any discursive closure is always provisional (Jørgensen & Phillips, 2002). Hence, every new articulation has the potential to affect how people make sense of the brand. The discursive brand space is thus a contested and ever-changing arena of human and non-human interaction. In order for a brand manager to engage in sensegiving activities and participate intelligently in conversations about the brand, they must master the brand language or, to put in another way, a brand manager must have a sophisticated brand *repertoire*.

8.2 A practical author must master the brand language

A brand has no intrinsic materiality and thus no obvious limits, hence boundaries are discursively produced and negotiated; this articulating of boundaries is an important aspect of brand management. In order to make decisions about boundaries to the discursive brand space and articulate these boundaries clearly, it is imperative to master the brand language. Taylor (1999) uses the notion of *repertoire* to signify a person's ability to express themselves through words, phrases, metaphors, and anecdotes stored in memory. It is a person's repertoire that functions as a resource for the production of talk. Repertoire can be supplemented by the use of text and materiality, given that talk, text and materiality function as a self-organizing loop (Koschmann, 2013; Kuhn, 2008; Taylor & Van Every, 1999). One of the affordances about text is that it provides a record of past conversations, which allows conversations to move through time and space. Text can thus hold more details than spoken language because it can record and recall details that are lost in the elusiveness of daily interactions and spoken language.

A practical author must master the brand language, because otherwise the brand manager will be caught up in other actors' attempt at sensegiving. It thus becomes impossible to promote the desired brand discourses and counteract the undesired ones if the brand manager does not have a sophisticated repertoire (as demonstrated in previous chapters). It is, however, also the responsibility of the brand manager to stimulate a common language. This makes it possible for other (organizational) actors to co-author the brand in intelligible and desired ways and to participate in sensegiving activities with the objective to influence the conversations according to the desired brand meaning. Brand meaning cannot be forced as it is conversationally co-created in a continuous social process, and the brand is continuously being (re-)produced by participants in the conversational space. Therefore, brand management ought to focus on the construction of a fruitful language that is able to promote desired brand discourses and eventually seek to deconstruct dominating discourses or frames that work counter to achieving the desired brand meaning (Kornberger et al., 2006). Meaning is never fixed but continuously negotiated, and it is by creating intelligible formulations that we are able to make sense of the chaotic welter of impressions. Practical authorship is thus about elaborating and providing a language that enables discussions about the brand by bracketing, singling out, labelling, categorizing, and connecting (see also the meaning-making model in Chapter 6).

Naming

As pointed out by Saussure the relationship between a signifier and its signified is arbitrary. That means that a word does not have certain meaning per se, and any object can be referred to using a number of different words – what we can refer to as naming or labelling. Naming and labelling are, however, not neutral. Words have the ability to evoke powerful poetic images. They are seldom neutral; more often than not they bear either positive or negative connotations (Iglesias & Bonet, 2012). Naming is, therefore, a matter of definition. To name something is to answer the question "What is it?". Naming can be seen as a case of framing (Vigsø, 2010). When you name something, you choose to highlight some qualities at the expense of others. Naming is thus a question of giving value.

As a brand manager, you have to be aware of naming, not only in relation to the product/service brand in itself but also, for instance, in relation to actions, decisions, how you respond to questions or criticism, and how you present new ideas. Naming is challenging because it often happens spontaneously as an instant reaction to a situation. Naming is therefore not necessarily considered and intentional but may be accidental and coincidental. It is the responsibility of a practical author to always pay attention to naming. Accordingly, it is important to recognize that naming is always at play. Words are not innocent or neutral, and language is performative. By having this awareness, a practical author can seek to always be observant of the words he or she chooses and to consider the framing effects that certain words will have. A frame can be constructed intentionally but a frame can also come about unintentionally. An important tool to avoid undesired, unintended frames is to carefully consider naming at all times.

However, naming is not reserved for the brand manager. Other actors can name and thus impose certain values on the brand. In these situations, it is important that the brand manager is sensitive towards this naming and picks up on it in order to consider whether that naming is appropriate or not, and what the consequences might be. If a naming is considered to be undesired or even counterproductive, it is the role of a practical author to try to deconstruct that discourse by, for instance, re-naming the thing or event and/or by offering another frame where other perspectives and values are made salient. In other words, the brand manager must engage in a frame game.

Framing

As explained in Chapter 7, framing is a matter of selecting some aspects of a perceived reality (and thus de-selecting others) and making these aspects more salient in communication in order to promote a certain definition or under-standing of something (Entman, 1993). The essence of framing is thus *selection* and *salience*. As illustrated in the meaning-making model (Figure 6.1, Chapter 6), lived experience is always much richer in detail than what a single story can account for. *Selection* of story elements is thus part of any communication, and a practical author must, therefore, pay close attention to how they single out the details (cues) that are included in an account. The selection of some elements inevitably involves the de-selection of other elements, and this process of selection/de-selection produces framing effects.

In addition to considerations about selection/de-selection, a practical author must also pay attention to the *salience* given to different elements and how elements are connected. Selected elements can be highlighted (or neglected) in different ways based on how they are named, the degree of details given, and how they are being connected. The way elements are ordered in a story spe-cifies the relationship between these elements and thus suggests causal relations as well as motives.

Framing is used to actively construct meaning. When working with framing, a practical author can seek to activate existing frames, that is, frames that are already available to the actors. An existing frame could, for instance, be found in a capital D-discourse. Activation of a familiar frame involves the activation of a particular knowledge and creates certain expectations (Cornelissen & Werner, 2014). It is, however, also possible to seek to construct a new frame in order to talk about the brand or brand elements in a new perspective or from a different angle. One method of creating a new frame is by using a metaphor.

Metaphors

A metaphor is a cognitive frame that allows us to understand and experience one kind of thing in terms of another, and Lakoff and Johnson (1980) argue that "most of our ordinary conceptual system is metaphorical in nature" (p. 4). Our conceptual system guides us in structuring what we perceive, and accord-ingly metaphors play a central role in defining (or giving sense to) our everyday realities. We see in the case of the K2M brand that it is metaphorically described as "CSR on ecstasy", as a "trinity" and as "low-hanging fruit". The use of metaphors is thus a sensegiving tool because metaphors can guide thinking and facilitate the construction of a particular meaning (Cornelissen, Holt, & Zundel, 2011). Metaphors are effective in ascribing salience to some aspects over others because the use of metaphors can keep us from focusing on aspects of the flux of lived experience that are inconsistent with the perspective offered by the metaphor (Lakoff & Johnson, 1980). Accordingly, metaphors play an important role in validating some discourses over others, and thus legitimize certain actions or decisions (Maitlis & Christianson, 2014).

The brand manager faces a complex task in his or her role as a practical author. As already stated, the brand is always in a state of becoming, and brand meaning is never fixed. Rather brand meaning emerges when some discourses come to dominate in the discursive brand space. To manage brand meaning is thus to manage discourses, and therefore a brand manager can be conceptualized as a practical author. The practical author must pay attention to both social and material discourses, as illustrated in Figure 8.1. The paragraphs above have stressed the importance of naming, framing, and metaphors. That list is far from exhaustive seeing that working as a practical author is ultimately a relationally responsive dialogical activity that cannot be listed in a formula. A practical author must be responsive to context and the particular circumstances in which the brand communication occurs. In the next section, I will examine an instance of brand communication that spurred a public debate (and potentially a brand crisis) in order to demonstrate how different actors took part in producing brand discourses.

8.3 Managing the discursive brand space

So far, the analyses in this book have focused on organizational members and how they produce and negotiate brand discourses. In this final chapter, I will turn my attention to an instance of public debate about the K2M brand. The debate was spurred by the layoff of a popular managing director at Apparella. Indeed, the CEO chose to communicate the layoff in a press release. In CCB terms, the CEO produced a text that was made available to the news media, and by involving the news media, a number of conversational spaces were established. An example of a corporeal conversational space is a press briefing that is being TV-transmitted live, and in addition innumerable virtual conversational spaces were established as the brand was discussed on social media in both private and public accounts. It is worth noting that none of these conversational spaces are established by brand management. It is thus impossible for brand management to influence who is invited to speak in these conversational spaces. The only thing brand management can influence is whether they will participate themselves.

Evolution of the discursive brand space

The public debate is initiated by a press release issued by the CEO. It is thus the CEO who informs the media about the layoff and he who initially gives sense to the incident. The CEO applies a sensegiving about a highly disloyal managing director who cannot be trusted. He does this by framing the managing director's actions as "severely disloyal arrangements", involving "serious irregularities", and working "contrary to the company's best interest". The CEO frames himself as "feeling sad", "shocked", and "very aggravated", as, ultimately, "having no choice" about letting this managing director go. When a leading news media outlet invites a business analyst to comment on the incident, the analyst produces discourses about a "cryptic statement", "a risky road", and a "dangerous limbo". The business analyst thus produces a discourse that questions the CEO's handling of the case. The same news media outlet issues a second article the same day that speaks highly of the managing director by highlighting his accomplishments, such as that he "created huge growth". He is named "the growth-maker from Apparella", known as a "strong and popular leader"; he is metaphorically described as "the man who steered the growth-train", a man with the skill of "strong leadership". There is thus a discursive struggle going on with a discourse about 'a highly disloyal managing director' versus 'a managing director who is well-liked and acknowledged for his impressive accomplishments'. These two discourses produce a third, more subtle discourse that indirectly questions the decision made by the CEO about laying off the managing director as he is being portrayed metaphorically as following "a risky road". This discourse is supported by a macro-actor, namely 'the industry' as it is stated that "the industry is shocked".

In a follow-up article, another business analyst is invited to produce discourses. The business analyst is named as "experienced", and he suggests that the CEO would have been better off keeping quiet since he is reluctant to state specific reasons for the layoff. The business analyst implicates the brand K2M as he mentions that the CEO is renowned for his ideas about kindness and a new form of leadership. The business analyst pinpoints that there is a gap between the brand's promises and the current handling of the layoff, and he suggests that the CEO's credibility is severely damaged. This actor thus substantiates the discourse of 'questioning the leadership of the CEO' – a frame that also dominates comments on social media:

Excerpt 8.1 Initial comments on Facebook

> "Unprofessional"
> "He [the CEO] has numerous ugly dismissals in the closet"
> "Professional management is not about what you think, believe, write or say. It is about what you do"
> "It is always a good idea to behave as you preach. This is a clear do-over"

Accordingly, the discourse of 'questioning the leadership of the CEO' is sustained by some actors from among the general public, and it is further supported by another macro-actor, namely, 'legal experts'. 'Legal experts' is a macro-actor because it is a profession rather than a single person who makes a statement. The article (text) refers to 'experts in employment law' and state that this macro-actor finds the case "very peculiar" and, consequently, "raises a warning finger". As explained in Chapter 2, a macro-actor speaks with an enhanced authority, because the macro-actor speaks on behalf of a collectivity and multiplying the sources of authorship amounts to multiplying the sources of authority and hence legitimacy.

What started out as a subtle discourse 'questioning the leadership of the CEO' grows into a hegemonic discourse that is supported by macro-actors, such as business analysts and legal experts as well as the general public, when they engage in discussions on social media. It would be immensely time-con-suming (and probably impossible) to locate all the small conversational spaces on social media. But brand management ought to pay attention to the more established online conversational spaces, such as the social media accounts of established news media and eventual brand communities, where the brand is heavily discussed. The brand itself chooses not to publish anything about the dismissal on its own social media account, but the CEO picks up on the criti-cism of his leadership, and he establishes a corporeal conversational space when he summons a press conference. The CEO is able to control who can (physi-cally) participate in the press conference (i.e. chosen journalists and his own lawyer). The press conference is transmitted live on television, and the CEO is unable to control the establishment of new conversational spaces and the pro-duction of text based on the press conference. At the press conference, the CEO presents (what he believes to be) evidence of the managing director's "severely disloyal arrangements". He ventriloquizes a macro-actor, namely 'some of the best criminal law experts' and cites this macro-actor by stating that this "is the most convincing documentation they have seen in 20 years". The act of ventriloquism is an attempt to back his own ethos. The CEO sharpens the discourse about 'a highly disloyal managing director' as he now introduces a new naming of the managing director as a "criminal" who has committed "fraud" and "breach of trust". Apart from the oral discourses produced at the press conference, the CEO produces several material discourses in the form of body language. The CEO is clearly very affected by the case. He appears angry and frustrated, which is underlined by the material discourse of smacking his hand on the table several times. He also appears emotional as he has to pause a couple of times, seemingly to collect himself, and he struggles to fight back tears. His oral discourse makes it clear that he is not sad because of what the managing director has done but because of the mistrust he has faced from the business community. The press conference is thus clearly a response to the discourse 'questioning the leadership of the CEO'. The CEO is thus seen to act as a practical author as he clearly seeks to counteract this discourse by introdu-cing a more severe naming of the managing director and he works with sen-segiving as he presents further evidence to support his discourse about 'a highly disloyal managing director'. By naming the managing director as "criminal", he introduces a new frame that supports his first statement that he "had no choice".

Based on reactions to the press conference, it is clear that the CEO does not succeed in muting the discourse about 'questioning the leadership of the CEO'. There are strong reactions, especially to the material discourses that are referred to as "smacking the table", his "shaky voice", and "tears in his eyes". The press conference is referred to as "emotional" and "very unusual" with "grave accusations". A communication expert believes that the CEO takes a "great risk", much like "gambling at the casino", and he names the accusations against the managing director as, "slaughtering a completely unknown person" at the time, a discourse that is supported by some of the general public:

Excerpt 8.2 Negative comments on Facebook following a press conference

> "An ungraceful press conference"
> "Shit, he smacked the table"
> "It could be interesting to ask some of his other former employees about how it is working for him. I do not think we know the whole backstory"
> "It is the managing director who built the company. The CEO is just a pretty face in charge of branding and parties"
> "This takes the prize as both disgraceful and unprofessional"
> "He [the CEO] has lost it"
> "No respect for his employees"

The press conference and especially the material discourses produced are thus seen to actually strengthen the discourse of 'questioning the leadership of the CEO', but as we will see later, the press conference also spurs a new discourse about the CEO.

As stated in Chapter 4, the K2M brand is closely linked to the CEO. It is therefore not surprising that the discourse about 'questioning the leadership of the CEO' evolves into a new discourse that questions the trustworthiness of the brand. K2M (Kind2Mind) is branded as a socially responsible brand that preaches kindness, and the CEO is a strong incarnation of the brand. In Chapter 4, it was concluded that the brand and the CEO were inextricably linked, and in response to the press conference, there emerges a discourse about 'kindness being just a marketing trick':

Excerpt 8.3 Comments questioning brand value on Facebook

> "He [the CEO] is motivated by cool cash – not kindness"
> "[ironic] 'Good' kindness leadership"
> "The CEO is just a pretty face. He does not practice kindness leadership"
> "Talk about kindness is just sales techniques, nothing else"
> "Neo-liberal kindness-cowboy in a shitstorm"
> "Capitalism has been coated with a sweet layer of new age kindness"

Yet, it is interesting to see that while the professional business community seems to agree with the discourse of 'questioning the leadership of the CEO', the CEO gains support among the general public, who name him "a CEO with a heart". They sympathize with his emotional reaction because he has been betrayed by a person he trusted and considered a friend. The press conference thus spurs a new discourse about 'a humanistic CEO':

Excerpt 8.4 Supportive comments about the CEO on Facebook

> "He seems like a very sympathetic person"
> "An empathic human being with a Buddhist view of human nature"
> "That is kindness leadership"
> "[The CEO] is an exemplary humanistic leader. He deserves recognition. I hope to see more leaders of his kind"
> "My respect, you are an inspiration"
> "I understand your disappointment"
> "It is terrible to trust someone and then discover they betray you"
> "Your best friend is also your worst enemy"
> "Trust is so important. I understand [the CEO] completely"
> "What a sympathetic and empathic guy!"
> "You are a good man. Best wishes"

The word "respect" is mentioned again and again, and there is thus a hegemonic discourse about 'a humanistic CEO', who has earned "respect" among the general public. This finding supports a proposition put forward by Maitlis and Sonenshein (2010, p. 556) who argue that "public evaluations of a situation can create frames for sensemaking". In Chapter 7, I identified a frame game among the employees between 'K2M is a Buddhist philosophy' versus 'K2M is not Buddhist'. It seems from the public debate about the brand, that the business community and the public in general agree with the discourse 'K2M is a Buddhist philosophy'. They do not explicitly make this argument but they judge the brand according to whether it lives up to its Buddhist philosophy. The general view from the business community and some people in the general public is that the brand fails to live up to its promises in this particular case; the CEO is criticized for not walking the talk. However, the general public produces a new discourse that counteracts the discourse of 'questioning the leadership of the CEO' because they acknowledge that the CEO is just a human being who feels betrayed, and they see his emotional press conference as expressing kindness values. The general public thus produces a new hegemonic discourse about 'a humanistic CEO'. It seems that although the CEO does not succeed in counteracting the discourse of 'questioning the leadership of the CEO' among actors in the business community, he does succeed in doing so among the actors in the general public, as they are seen to produce a new discourse about 'a humanistic CEO'.

The managing director is not very prominent on the public scene, but he produces some discourses to support the discourse of "the managing director being well-liked and acknowledged for his impressive accomplishments". He states that he will "not stoop to that level", that he will file a suit against the company to defend himself against such "defamatory allegations". He believes there has been "foul play" in the handling of the case and he is "sorry about all the fuss".

The above analysis confirms that an organization can be understood as a Tamara play. There is a public debate going on about the CEO and the K2M brand, but the public does not have access to all scenes and all actors. They catch glimpses here and there in the form of statements in a press release and a press conference, but nobody gets the whole story. The discussion of the brand is acted out on many different scenes (i.e. in many different conversational spaces), thus the perception of the brand will be influenced according to which scenes one has gained access to and which actors one has heard giving statements. In relation to this, it is interesting to consider the role of the media.

The media as conversational space

"The media" is made up of many different actors that act in separate conversational spaces. Yet, these conversational spaces are also seen to interact as different news media will cite the same press releases, use the same sources, and refer to one another. "The media" can therefore be seen as a public arena where actors are able to come together and discuss the brand and, as such, "the media" can be seen to resemble a conversational space as it becomes a *site* of 'doing branding'. A true conversational space will, of course, be found in the individual news media's outlets, such as a Facebook page.

When the CEO issues a press release about the layoff, he instigates the establishment of many conversational spaces, where the layoff is being reported and discussed. Common to all of these conversational spaces is the fact that the CEO has no control over how they develop. Numerous news media can participate, journalists can invite an indefinite number of actors (i.e. sources) to participate in the conversations and state their expert opinion. Moreover, press coverage initiates countless new conversational spaces, especially on social media, where new actors participate in the production of brand discourses. Most established news media publish content on social media, which allows their readers to comment and share. They might then start new conversations on their own networks, thus establishing new conversational spaces. All actors that discuss the brand participate in authoring the *discursive brand space* (i.e. they are doing branding), and the polyphony of the discursive brand space is thus clearly demonstrated. There is a plethora of discourses at play in micro meaning negotiations between actors, seeing as "actors at any level of an organization, or outside its boundaries, may engage in sensegiving with others" (Maitlis & Christianson, 2014, p. 69).

Discursive battles

It is possible to identify several discourses that succeed in establishing hegemony, but it is also evident that hegemony is only temporal as new discourses evolve all the time, and the brand is in a constant state of becoming. There is a constant discursive battle going on, where small d-discourses are produced by a multitude of actors. Based on these small d-discourses, I have identified five hegemonic discourses: 1) 'a highly disloyal managing director', 2) 'questioning the leadership of the CEO', 3) 'a managing director who is well-liked and acknowledged for his impressive accomplishments', 4) 'kindness is just a marketing trick', and 5) 'a humanistic CEO'. It is evident that some of these discourses are contradictory and there is thus a discursive battle going on about which discourses come to dominate the discursive brand space. As this is a case that evolves with time, it is seen that the different discourses dominate at different points in time according to media coverage and the establishment of new conversational spaces, such as the press conference. Given the prominence of the media in producing highly visible texts about the brand, the media can be argued to be a very powerful macro-actor. It is also seen that the use of macro-actors, like business analysts or legal and communication experts, is a widely used strategy to produce more authoritative discourses. The CEO clearly ventriloquizes experts in criminal law to back his own authority.

It is interesting to see how powerful material discourses are in authoring the discursive brand space. Following the press conference there is frame game of 'questioning the leadership of the CEO' versus 'a humanistic CEO'. The first discourse is primarily supported by the business community, whereas the latter is promoted by the general public on social media. Accordingly, there is a bricolage of discourses about the CEO's capabilities as a leader. It could be argued that the discourse about 'questioning the leadership of the CEO' stands stronger as it is promoted by experts in the field. But it seems that the sensemaking of the general public is primarily affected by the material discourses produced at the press conference, where the CEO appears very emotional. This finding is in line with my findings in Chapter 7 that actors may not engage very seriously (i. e. only superficially) in the conversations, and therefore material discourses seem to produce some very convincing sensegiving.

Acting as a practical author

Even though it is the CEO who initiates the discussions by issuing a press release, the CEO or the company are not seen to participate actively in the discussions. The CEO does, however, summon a press conference. It appears that the CEO has been animated to do so by a concern about being framed as 'questioning the leadership of the CEO'.

A practical author must acknowledge the different discourses being produced and try to counteract the undesired ones. It could be argued that this is the purpose of the press conference. But some actors respond to the CEO's emotional response with comments like "get over it" and "stop whining"; they state that when you enjoy being in the spotlight, you have to take the bitter with the sweet. These reactions demonstrate that it is impossible to silence all negative discourse. A practical author therefore has to choose wisely in relation to when and how to engage.

This analysis focused on the participation of human actors, normally thought of as external to the organization and their ability to co-author the *discursive brand space*. Participation spanned business analysts, lawyers and legal advisors, anthropologists, communication advisors, branding experts, practitioners of Buddhism, and associate professors, as well as members of the general public. We know from the previous chapters that authority is not linked to a formal position but rather to successful sensegiving. Accordingly, all actors have the ability to create hegemonic discourses about the brand as seen in the case, where the general public constructs the CEO as 'a humanistic CEO'.

8.4 Summing up the CCB approach

I set out to answer a call for the further development of a 'communication as constitutive' approach to branding. It was done by incorporating the language of CCO into the field of branding and by empirically examining branding from a 'communication as constitutive' perspective – an approach I suggest should be labeled CCB (Communication as Constitutive of Brand). An important discussion in this regard is the ontology of a brand, which I have discussed by defining a brand as *a discursive brand space* that is grounded in a performative, relational, and interactional ontology, where humans and the nonhuman are co-constitutive. I have also examined the process of brand creation – how we go from instances of 'doing brand' to the understanding of 'a brand as an entity' (in Chapter 4).

The ontology of brand: a brand is a discursive brand space

When a brand is conceptualized as a *discursive brand space* it follows that every discourse that is produced about the brand becomes part of the discursive brand space. Every discourse is thus competing in the struggle for hegemony in a quest to fix brand meaning (Figure 8.2).

The discursive brand space is produced by everybody who participates in conversations about the brand, accordingly a brand is talked into existence. The production of brand discourses is an ongoing process, thus the discursive brand space is constantly evolving as new discourses appear and others fade into oblivion. The meaning of the brand is negotiated in a continuous discursive struggle for hegemony.

Embracing the ontological premise that a brand emerges in communication, I argued to apply a *flatland perspective* where communication is the *site* and *surface* of the emergence of a brand.

Surface to the brand

Discourses are reflected in different modalities. Some discourses are oral, others are written in text, and some surface in another kind of materiality.

Figure 8.2 The discursive brand space

In a relational and performative ontology, "there is no divide between the world of materiality and the world of discourse and communication" (Cooren et al., 2012, p. 302). Materiality is therefore an integral part of the discursive brand space. All discourses serve to constitute the *discursive brand space* and they are the *surface* to the brand. Brand surface is important because surface is what makes the brand present, but some surfaces are easier to capture than others. Those easiest to capture are the ones that are represented in a permanent or semi-permanent modality, like texts, images, or artifacts (i.e. materiality). When discourses are re-semiotized into a permanent or semi-permanent modality, they gain *restance* and produce a long-lasting *surface*. Though oral discourses do also produce a surface to the discursive brand space, they are transitory and easily forgotten. Discourses that are re-semiotized into a permanent or semi-permanent modality have the advantage that they can transcend the original site of production and become available for appropriation in different contexts (Kuhn, 2012).

The brand surfaces that have been used as data material in the present book are the following: the oral discourses produced at meetings and interviews, written discourses in the K2M model, the K2M code of conduct, CSR reports, the Globalco webpage, MyK2M.com, comments on SoMe, news articles, and materialities, like Buddha, the logo, and orange. These surfaces reflect the discourses (or at least some of the discourses) that constitute the discursive brand space of the K2M brand.

Site of doing branding: a conversational space

The *site* of 'doing branding' refers to the daily interactions of branding activities. I have chosen to apply the term *conversational space* in order to explicate the *sites* of 'doing branding'. The discursive brand space is talked into existence in a multitude of conversational spaces. Some of these conversational spaces are strategically set-up by the organization, some emerge spontaneously, and some are created by stakeholders traditionally thought of as external to the organization. An important implication of this proposition is that a brand is produced as much by stakeholders, traditionally thought of as external to the organization, as much as it is authored by brand management and other organizational members. The distinction between 'internal' and 'external' therefore becomes meaningless.

Some conversational spaces exist independently of each other, while others are seen to overlap, given that the same actors participate in more than one conversational space. This is, for instance, the case with the middle managers who participate in the steering group meetings as well as in the local meetings of their subsidiaries. The individual conversational spaces are all stages in a Tamara play, which means that actors only see story fragments and their sensemaking is based on the fragments they know. No actors are able to participate in all stages, hence no actors know the whole story.

An important finding about the conversational spaces (i.e. the *sites* of doing branding) is that there are more participants than the human actors present; several non-human actors are seen to participate in the production of discourses about K2M. Some of these non-human actors are physically present as texts, such as the K2M model and the K2M code of conduct, while others are made present through ventriloquism, such as the CSR D-discourse and the KPI D-discourse. Some of these non-human actors have been invited to participate by brand management and some are evoked by other participants, but it is seen that even actors that have been invited by brand management escape the control of their masters. For instance, the KPI D-discourse is seen to be a much more complicated macro-actor than was foreseen by brand management.

Ventriloquism

Ventriloquism is used to make absent partners presents, and ventriloquism is often used as a strategy to bolster authority by producing hybrid agency or to guide sensegiving or sensemaking. I find that the ventriloqual approach succeeds in demonstrating how non-human actors are co-creating the brand. Conversational spaces are occupied by multiple forms of agencies, and many different actors can be said to be doing things (Cooren, 2008). No priority should thus be given to human agency over non-human agency (Cooren &

Sandler, 2014). Ventriloquism is found to function in the following four ways: a human actor speaking through another human actor (e.g. the CEO speaking through a middle manager), a human actor speaking through a non-human actor (e.g. Lucy speaking through the K2M model), a non-human actor speaking through a human actor (e.g. the UN Global Compact speaking through a middle manager), and a non-human actor speaking through another non-human actor (e.g. the KPI D-discourse speaking through the K2M model). A non-human actor does not need to exist in a physical form. The mere anticipation of a non-human actor (e.g. a director's email) is enough to make the actor present. It is also seen that a concern (or a lack of knowledge) is able to animate, and so are D-discourses. The voices that are invited to participate through ventriloquism do not always end up saying what the original ventriloquist expected them to say. For instance, KPI turns out to be a much more complicated macro-actor than anticipated by brand management. It illustrates that once a non-human actor has been produced or invoked, it gains an agency of its own and that agency can be made part of different hybrid agencies. Accordingly, a dummy can be made to speak with different voices.

Hybrid agency

A non-human actor cannot act on its own. It needs to be appropriated by a human actor. But even when human actors "simply" talk, it is evident that they invoke other voices than their own, for instance macro-actors. It follows that most agencies are entangled in one way or another, which makes it difficult, if not impossible, to single out the agency of individual actors. For instance, it is seen that the K2M model does not possess agency per se. It is invoked by a middle manager who succeeds in producing a powerful hybrid agency (Agent$_{2+1}$) that makes the CEO adjust his own understanding of K2M. But when the model is being invoked by another middle manager (Agent$_{6+1}$), its authority is constantly being questioned, and it is thus evident that the agency of a non-human actor is dependent upon *how* it is being appropriated by a human actor and maybe also by *whom* and in *what context*. Nicotera (2013) argues that the "I" (i.e. the individual actor) is socially constructed. An individual is to be understood as a text that is a result of previous interactions with others. Each individual who enters the conversational space has been constructed by previous interactions with others and therefore brings a certain "legacy" to the space. An actor's agency is thus constantly being re-produced and accordingly, hybrid agencies are being reproduced every time a human actor appropriates a non-human.

Brand management as the orchestration of discourses

The *discursive brand space* is constituted by oral, textual, and material discourses alike, and they all participate in the discursive struggles to invest the brand with meaning. The boundaries of the discursive brand space are discursive and thus fluid and permeable; it is not possible for brand management to control who gets to participate in the conversations about the brand. Human and non-human actors alike are seen to spur conversations about the brand and thus contribute to the production of discourses. Given the doorway represented by *ventriloquism,* it is impossible to control participation. Taylor et al. (1996) explain the futility of attempting control: "every organization is constructed out of other organizations which, in turn, enfold it. Trying to fix the frontier between them is an unrewarding exercise at best" (p. 30). An important learning is therefore to give up on the prevailing understanding in the existing branding literature that a brand is created by brand management. Brand management does still have a part to play, but the discourses produced by brand management are only seen to constitute part of the discourses that make up the *discursive brand space.* It is by engaging in circuits of sensegiving and sensemaking that a brand manager can seek to influence brand meaning, thus brand management is the *orchestration of discourses.*

Oftentimes discourses will be seen to be conflicting, hence the discursive brand space is characterized by constant discursive struggles for hegemony, which manifest themselves in a number of frame games. In order for the brand manager to be able to function as a practical author, it is of paramount importance that they are able to identify the ongoing frame games, since it is a central management task to support or dismantle frames according to their appropriateness to support desired brand meaning. In order for a brand manager to be able to decide whether a frame is appropriate or not, they need to be well-prepared and well-aware of the purpose of inviting certain macro-actors to participate as well as what frames they bring to the discussion.

It is important that brand management pay attention to the sensemaking spurred by discourses produced by the organization itself. Sensemaking can never be controlled but management (and other stakeholders) can seek to influence it by use of strategic sensegiving. It is therefore important to build a repertoire, a common brand language that is able to promote desired conversations about the brand, as suggested by Golant (2012) and Kornberger (2015). An important task of brand management is thus to develop a more extensive and detailed language to describe the brand to make the brand accessible for actors and to orchestrate the different discourses and elements, as illustrated in Figure 8.1.

When brand management is about talking the discursive brand space into existence, by managing talk and interaction, it is important to pay attention to how interaction in the conversational space is encouraged and managed. As previously stated, the boundaries of the conversational space are fluid, making it is impossible to control access due to ventriloquism. But in an organizational context, it is possible for brand management to decide who is invited to be part of working groups, for example, and it is important to pay attention to the effects produced by purposeful inclusion and exclusion of some members.

There is an inherent understanding in most branding literature that a brand must be managed and controlled by brand management, and as illustrated in the introduction, this understanding is a source of frustration and fruitless attempts at guarding the brand against aberrant decoding (Edlinger, 2015). The CCB approach offers a new understanding of brand management that breaks with the idea that brand management is in control of brand meaning. Instead, the CCB approach stipulates that brand meaning is constantly being co-created and (re-)negotiated by the endless production of brand discourses that compete for hegemony in the discursive brand space, and that sense-making cannot be forced. The brand manager must therefore accept a loss of control and start perceiving themselves as a practical author that seeks to manage brand meaning by constant circuits of sensegiving and sensemaking. The brand is authored by a plethora of voices and authority comes with successful sensegiving. The analyses demonstrated that if the brand language is too abstract, it can be difficult for organizational members (or others) to participate in the conversations about the brand, consequently the discursive brand space will be weak and uninspiring. The analyses also demonstrated that employees do not necessarily listen to (or read) explicit sensegiving but may form their sensemaking about the brand based on sensegiving by materiality and artifacts. Materiality and artifacts are thus just as important as text and spoken words when it comes to managing brand meaning (see also Iedema, 1999).

8.5 How can the CCB approach enrich existing branding literature?

Chapter 1 explains the evolution of the field of branding and in order to continue this evolution it is important to state how the CCB approach contributes to moving the theoretical field forward.

Identification of conversational spaces

Existing research already frames branding as co-creation and negotiation of meaning, and the revised VCI model explicates four flows of communication, but there is very little knowledge of how co-creation takes place. The notion of conversational spaces makes it possible for brand management to become aware of how interaction is enabled by examining the conversational spaces set up by the organization and the affordances (or constraints) they provide. Brand management can also search for conversational spaces set up by others in order to learn where talk about the brand takes place and what discourses are produced, and the notion of a conversational space thus serves to explicate the "myriad forms of communication" (Hatch & Schultz, 2008, p. 206). As argued, it is not possible for brand management to control the number of conversational spaces as some will be set up by stakeholders "external" to the organization, but once brand management has become aware of the existence of a conversational space, it can seek to participate in the conversation and function as a practical author.

Participation of non-human actors

The CCB approach also enriches existing research by bringing attention to the participation of non-human actors in the production of brand discourses. The recognition of non-human actors adds a new understanding to brand creation and brand management seeing that existing research only considers human actors (for an exception, see Vásquez et al., 2017b). The existence and participation of non-human actors points to the importance of hybrid agency and suggests that humans are never alone on the site of construction. Brand management is thus not just about the selection and management of people who participate in brand creation; participation must be understood in a whole new perspective. The recognition of non-human actors is an acknowledgement of actors acting by proxy through ventriloquism. Co-creation is not just a matter of face-to-face situations or online interaction, as suggested by some scholars (Hatch & Schultz, 2010; Iglesias et al., 2013; Ind, 2014; Ind et al., 2013), it is a matter of co-creation in everyday talk and interaction between organizational members and "absent actors". The traditional distinction between internal and external to the organization needs to be abandoned.

When non-human actors are recognized to participate in brand creation on equal terms as human actors, brand management can seek to influence conversations about the brand by producing non-human actors to tele-act on its behalf. Production of non-human actors is thus a way to work with sensegiving. Yet, brand management has to recognize that non-human actors will gain an agency of their own, which means it has to pay close attention to the preparation of those actors. Non-human actors may invite other actors (e.g. the K2M model invited several D-discourses to participate). Text and materiality are not innocent; rather they can become powerful macro-actors.

Role of employees

The present book has demonstrated that a brand is negotiated and created as much among employees (i.e. the steering group) as it is by brand management (i.e. the K2M department). The discussion of brand meaning is an ongoing discursive struggle and (momentary) discursive closures are achieved by successful sensegiving, but the analysis demonstrates that it is not necessarily the frames promoted by brand management that succeeds in creating a discursive closure. Successful sensegiving stems as much from employees as it does from brand management. Hence the concept of *brand ambassadors* ought to be replaced by the notion of *co-authors*, seeing as organizational members will take on different roles as authors and readers when they engage in branding activities (see also Dean et al., 2016; Golant, 2012). The process of authoring involves all kinds of stakeholders, but employees are naturally ascribed a central role as they are members of the organization and thereby the ones to articulate the brand from 'the inside'.

The coining of a CCB approach (Communication as Constitutive of Brands) offers a new language about branding that brings the communicative constitution to the fore. The empirical research in the present book brings an important new insight to brand management on an operational day-to-day level by illustrating the tasks of orchestrating branding discourses and developing a comprehensible brand language.

Bibliography

Aaker, D. A. (2002). *Building Strong Brands*. Simon & Schuster.

Aaker, D. A., & Joachimsthaler, E. (2000). The brand relationship spectrum: The key to the brand architecture challenge. *California Management Review*, 42(4), 8–23.

Alvesson, M., & Kärreman, D. (2000). Varieties of discourse: On the study of organizations through discourse analysis. *Human Relations*, 53(9), 1125–1149.

Alvesson, M., & Kärreman, D. (2011). Decolonializing discourse: Critical reflections on organizational discourse analysis. *Human Relations*, 64(9), 1121–1146.

Ashcraft, K. L., Kuhn, T. R., & Cooren, F. (2009). 1 Constitutional Amendments: "Materializing" Organizational Communication. *The Academy of Management Annals*, 3(1), 1–64.

Ashcraft, K. L., Muhr, S. L., Rennstam, J., & Sullivan, K. (2012). Professionalization as a branding activity: Occupational identity and the dialectic of inclusivity-exclusivity. *Gender, Work & Organization*, 19(5), 467–488.

American Marketing Association (2021) *Branding*. https://www.ama.org/topics/branding/

Balmer, J. M. (2001). Corporate identity, corporate branding and corporate marketing-seeing through the fog. *European Journal of Marketing*, 35(3/4), 248–291.

Balmer, J. M. (2006). *Comprehending Corporate Marketing and the Corporate Marketing Mix* (Working Paper No. 6). Bradford University School of Management.

Balmer, J. M., & Greyser, S. A. (2002). Managing the multiple identities of the corporation. *California Management Review*, 44(3), 72–86.

Balmer, J. M., & Greyser, S. A. (2006). Corporate marketing: Integrating corporate identity, corporate branding, corporate communications, corporate image and corporate reputation. *European Journal of Marketing*, 40(7/8), 730–741.

Balmer, J. M., Powell, S. M., Kernstock, J., Brexendorf, T. O. (2017). *Advances in Corporate Branding*. Palgrave Macmillan.

Balmer, J. M., & Soenen, G. B. (1999). The acid test of corporate identity management[TM]. *Journal of Marketing Management*, 15(1/3), 69–92.

Belova, O. (2010). Polyphony and the sense of self in flexible organizations. *Scandinavian Journal of Management*, 26(1), 67–76.

Belova, O., King, I., & Sliwa, M. (2008). Introduction: Polyphony and organization studies: Mikhail Bakhtin and beyond. *Organization Studies*, 29(4), 493–500.

Benoit-Barné, C., & Cooren, F. (2009). The accomplishment of authority through presentification: How authority is distributed among and negotiated by organizational members. *Management Communication Quarterly*, 23(1), 5–31.

Bisel, R. S. (2010). A communicative ontology of organization? A description, history, and critique of CCO theories for organization science. *Management Communication Quarterly*, 24(1), 124–131.

Boden, D. (1994). *The Business of Talk: Organizations in Action*. Polity Press.

Boje, D. M. (2001). *Narrative Methods for Organizational & Communication Research*. Sage.

Brodie, R. J. (2009). From goods to service branding: An integrative perspective. *Marketing Theory*, 9(1), 107–111.

Brummans, B., Cooren, F., & Chaput, M. (2009). Discourse, communication, and organisational ontology. In *The Handbook of Business Discourse* (pp.53–65). Edinburgh University Press.

Burmann, C., & Zeplin, S. (2005). Building brand commitment: A behavioural approach to internal brand management. *Journal of Brand Management*, 12(4), 279–300.

Carroll, A. B. (2016). Carroll's pyramid of CSR: taking another look. *International Journal of Corporate Social Responsibility*, 1(1), 3.

Chia, R. (2000). Discourse analysis as organizational analysis. *Organization*, 7(3), 513–518.

Christensen, L. T. (1997). Marketing as auto-communication. *Consumption, Markets and Culture*, 1(3), 197–227.

Christensen, L. T., & Cornelissen, J. (2011). Bridging corporate and organizational communication: Review, development and a look to the future. *Management Communication Quarterly*, 25(3), 383–414.

Cnossen, B., & Sergi, V. (2017). *Boundaries on the move: A communication-centered approach to organizational boundaries*. Paper presented at the EGOS, Copenhagen.

Coffey, A. (2014). Analysing documents. In U. Flick (Ed.) *The SAGE Handbook of Qualitative Data Analysis* (pp.367–379). Sage.

Cooren, F. (2004). Textual agency: How texts do things in organizational settings. *Organization*, 11(3), 373–393.

Cooren, F. (2006). The organizational world as a plenum of agencies. In F. Cooren, J. R. Taylor, & E. J. Van Every (Eds.) *Communication as Organizing: Empirical and Theoretical Explorations in the Dynamic of Text and Conversation* (pp.81–100). Routledge.

Cooren, F. (2008). Between semiotics and pragmatics: Opening language studies to textual agency. *Journal of Pragmatics*, 40(1), 1–16.

Cooren, F. (2012). Communication theory at the center: Ventriloquism and the communicative constitution of reality. *Journal of Communication*, 62(1), 1–20.

Cooren, F. (2015). *Organizational Discourse: Communication and Constitution*. John Wiley & Sons.

Cooren, F. (2016). Ethics for dummies: Ventriloquism and responsibility. *Atlantic Journal of Communication*, 24(1), 17–30.

Cooren, F., Brummans, B. H., & Charrieras, D. (2008). The coproduction of organizational presence: A study of médecins sans frontières in action. *Human Relations*, 61(10), 1339–1370.

Cooren, F., Fairhurst, G., & Huët, R. (2012). Why matter always matters in (organizational) communication. In P. M. Leonardi, B. A. Nardi, and J. Kallinikos (Eds.), *Materiality and Organizing: Social Interaction in a Technological World* (pp.296–314). Oxford University Press.

Cooren, F., Kuhn, T., Cornelissen, J. P., & Clark, T. (2011). Communication, organizing and organization: An overview and introduction to the special issue. *Organization Studies*, 32(9), 1149–1170.

Cooren, F., Matte, F., Benoit-Barné, C., & Brummans, B. H. J. M. (2013). Communication as ventriloquism: A grounded-in-action approach to the study of organizational tensions. *Communication Monographs*, 80(3), 255–277.

Cooren, F., & Sandler, S. (2014). Polyphony, ventriloquism, and constitution: In dialogue with Bakhtin. *Communication Theory*, 24, 225–244.

Cooren, F. M., & Matte, F. (2010). For a constitutive pragmatics: Obama, médecins sans frontières and the measuring stick. *Pragmatics and Society*, 1(1), 9–31.

Cornelissen, J.P., Christensen, L. T., & Kinuthia, K. (2012). Corporate brands and identity: Developing stronger theory and a call for shifting the debate. *European Journal of Marketing*, 46(7/8), 1093–1102.

Cornelissen, J. P., Holt, R., & Zundel, M. (2011). The role of analogy and metaphor in the framing and legitimization of strategic change. *Organization Studies*, 32(12), 1701–1716.

Cornelissen, J. P., & Werner, M. D. (2014). Putting framing in perspective: A review of framing and frame analysis across the management and organizational literature. *The Academy of Management Annals*, 8(1), 181–235.

Culler, J. D. (1986). *Ferdinand de Saussure*. Cornell University Press.

Cunliffe, A. L. (2001). Managers as practical authors: Reconstructing our understanding of management practice. *Journal of Management Studies*, 38(3), 351–371.

Czarniawska, B. (2013) Organizations as obstacles to organizing. In D. Robichaud, & F. Cooren, (Eds.), *Organization and Organizing: Materiality, Agency and Discourse* (pp.3–22). Routledge.

Dameron, S., Lê, J. K., & LeBaron, C. (2015). Materializing strategy and strategizing material: Why matter matters. *British Journal of Management*, 26, 1–12.

Danesi, M. (2013). Semiotizing a product into a brand. *Social Semiotics*, 23(4), 464–476.

Dean, D., Arroyo-Gamez, R. E., Punjaisri, K., & Pich, C. (2016). Internal brand co-creation: The experiential brand meaning cycle in higher education. *Journal of Business Research*, 69(8), 3041–3048.

Degn, L. (2015). Sensemaking, sensegiving and strategic management in Danish higher education. *Higher Education*, 69(6), 901–913.

Edlinger, G. (2015). Employer brand management as boundary-work: A grounded theory analysis of employer brand managers' narrative accounts: Employer brand management as boundary-work. *Human Resource Management Journal*, 25(4), 443–457.

Edwards, M. R., & Edwards, T. (2013). Employee responses to changing aspects of the employer brand following a multinational acquisition: A longitudinal study. *Human Resource Management*, 52(1), 27–54.

Entman, R. M. (1993). Framing: Toward clarification of a fractured paradigm. *Journal of Communication*, 43(4), 51–58.

Fairhurst, G. T., & Putnam, L. (2004). Organizations as discursive constructions. *Communication Theory*, 14(1), 5–26.

Fairhurst, G. T., & Cooren, F. (2009). Leadership as the hybrid production of presence (s). *Leadership*, 5(4), 469–490.

Fayard, A.-L., & Weeks, J. (2014). Affordances for practice. *Information and Organization*, 24(4), 236–249.

Flick, U. (Ed.) (2014). *The SAGE Handbook of Qualitative Data Analysis*. Sage.

Foster, C., Punjaisri, K., & Cheng, R. (2010). Exploring the relationship between corporate, internal and employer branding. *Journal of Product & Brand Management*, 19(6), 401–409.

Gioia, D. A., & Chittipeddi, K. (1991). Sensemaking and sensegiving in strategic change initiation. *Strategic Management Journal*, 12(6), 433–448.

Giuliani, M. (2016). Sensemaking, sensegiving and sensebreaking. *Journal of Intellectual Capital.* 17(2), 218–237

Golant, B. D. (2012). Bringing the corporate brand to life: The brand manager as practical author. *The Journal of Brand Management,* 20(2), 115–127.

Harris, F., & De Chernatony, L. (2001). Corporate branding and corporate brand performance. *European Journal of Marketing,* 35(3/4), 441–456.

Hart, S., & Murphy, J. (1998). *The New Wealth Creators.* Springer.

Hatch, M. J., & Schultz, M. (1997). Relations between organizational culture, identity and image. *European Journal of Marketing,* 31(5/6), 356–365.

Hatch, M. J., & Schultz, M. (2001). Are the strategic stars aligned for your corporate brand? *Harvard Business Review,* 79(2), 128–134.

Hatch, M. J., & Schultz, M. (2002). The dynamics of organizational identity. *Human Relations,* 55(8), 989–1018.

Hatch, M. J., & Schultz, M. (2003). Bringing the corporation into corporate branding. *European Journal of Marketing,* 37(7/8), 1041–1064.

Hatch, M. J., & Schultz, M. (2008). *Taking Brand Initiative: How Companies can Align Strategy, Culture, and Identity Through Corporate Branding.* John Wiley & Sons.

Hatch, M. J., & Schultz, M. (2009). Of bricks and brands: From corporate to enterprise branding. *Organizational Dynamics,* 38(2), 117–130.

Hatch, M. J., & Schultz, M. (2010). Toward a theory of brand co-creation with implications for brand governance. *Journal of Brand Management,* 17(8), 590–604.

Holman, D., & Thorpe, R. (2003). *Management and Language: The Manager as a Practical Author.* London: Sage.

Holstein, J. A., & Gubrium, J. F. (Eds.) (2008). *Handbook of Constructionist Research.* The Guilford Press.

Huzzard, T., Benner, M., & Kärreman, D. (Eds.) (2017). *The Corporatization of the Business School: Minerva Meets the Market.* Taylor & Francis.

Iedema, R. (1999). Formalizing organizational meaning. *Discourse & Society,* 10(1), 49–65.

Iedema, R. A. (2001). Resemiotization. *Semiotica: Journal of the International Association for Semiotic Studies,* 2001(137), 23–39.

Iedema, R. (2003). Multimodality, resemiotization: Extending the analysis of discourse as multi-semiotic practice. *Visual Communication,* 2(1), 29–57.

Iedema, R. (2007). On the multi-modality, materially and contingency of organization discourse. *Organization Studies,* 28(6), 931–946.

Iedema, R., & Scheeres, H. (2003). From doing work to talking work: Renegotiating knowing, doing, and identity. *Applied Linguistics,* 24(3), 316–337.

Iedema, R., & Wodak, R. (1999). Introduction: Organizational discourses and practices. *Discourse & Society,* 10(1), 5–19.

Iglesias, O., & Bonet, E. (2012). Persuasive brand management: How managers can influence brand meaning when they are losing control over it. *Journal of Organizational Change Management,* 25(2), 251–264.

Iglesias, O., Ind, N., & Alfaro, M. (2013). The organic view of the brand: A brand value co-creation model. *Journal of Brand Management,* 20(8), 670–688.

Ind, N. (2014). How participation is changing the practice of managing brands. *Journal of Brand Management,* 21(9), 734–742.

Ind, N., Iglesias, O., & Markovic, S. (2017). The co-creation continuum: From tactical market research tool to strategic collaborative innovation method. *Journal of Brand Management,* 24(4), 310–321.

Ind, N., Iglesias, O., & Schultz, M. (2013). Building brands together: Emergence and outcomes of co-creation. *California Management Review, 55*(3), 5–26.

Ind, N., & Schmidt, H. J. (2019). *Co-creating Brands: Brand Management from a Co-creative Perspective.* Bloomsbury.

Ivory (2021). *Our heritage.* Retrieved March 13, 2021, from https://ivory.com/our-her itage/

Jevons, C. (2005). Names, brands, branding: Beyond the signs, symbols, products and services. *Journal of Product & Brand Management, 14*(2), 117–118.

Jørgensen, M. W., & Phillips, L. J. (2002). *Discourse Analysis as Theory and Method.* Sage.

Kärreman, D., & Rylander, A. (2008). Managing meaning through branding: The case of a consulting firm. *Organization Studies, 29*(1), 103–125.

Keller, K. L., Heckler, S. E., & Houston, M. J. (1998). The effects of brand name suggestiveness on advertising recall. *Journal of Marketing, 62*(1), 48–57.

King, C., & Grace, D. (2005). Exploring the role of employees in the delivery of the brand: A case study approach. *Qualitative Market Research: An International Journal, 8*(3), 277–295.

Kippenberger, T. (2000). Remember the USP? (unique selling proposition). *The Antidote, 5*(6), 6–8.

Knox, S., & Bickerton, D. (2003). The six conventions of corporate branding. *European Journal of Marketing, 37*(7/8), 998–1016.

Kornberger, M. (2015). Think different: On studying the brand as organizing device. *International Studies of Management & Organization, 45*(2), 105–113.

Kornberger, M., Clegg, S. R., & Carter, C. (2006). Rethinking the polyphonic organization: Managing as discursive practice. *Scandinavian Journal of Management, 22*(1), 3–30.

Koschmann, M. A. (2013). The communicative constitution of collective identity in interorganizational collaboration. *Management Communication Quarterly, 27*(1), 61–89.

Kotler, P., & Keller, K. L. (2006). *Marketing Management,* 12th ed. Pearson.

Kuhn, T. (2008). A communicative theory of the firm: Developing an alternative perspective on intra-organizational power and stakeholder relationships. *Organization Studies, 29*(8–9), 1227–1254.

Kuhn, T. (2012). Negotiating the micro-macro divide: Thought leadership from organizational communication for theorizing organization. *Management Communication Quarterly, 26*(4), 543–584.

Lakoff, G., & Johnson, M. (1980). *Metaphors We Live By.* University of Chicago Press.

Latour, B. (1996). On Interobjectivity. *Mind, Culture, and Activity, 3*(4), 228–245.

Latour, B. (2013). "What's the story?" Organizing as a mode of existence. In D. Robichaud, & F. Cooren, (Eds.). *Organization and Organizing: Materiality, Agency and Discourse* (pp.66–89). Routledge.

Lee, B. (2012). Using documents in organizational research. In G. Symon & C. Cassell (Eds.), *Qualitative Organizational Research: Core Methods and Current Challenges* (pp.389–406). Sage.

Leitch, S., & Richardson, N. (2003). Corporate branding in the new economy. *European Journal of Marketing, 37*(7/8), 1065–1079.

Leonardi, P., & Barley, W. (2011). Materiality as organizational communication: Technology, intention, and delegation in the production of meaning. In T. R. Kuhn (Ed.) *Matters of Communication: Political, Cultural, and Technological Challenges to Communication Theorizing* (pp.101–124). Hampton Press.

Levy, S. J. (1959). Symbols for sale. *Harvard Business Review, 37*(4), 117–124.

Linders, A. (2008). Documents, texts and archives in constructionist research. In J. A. Holstein & J.F. Gubrium (Eds.) *Handbook of Constructionist Research* (pp.467–492). The Guilford Press.

Lowrie, A. (2007). Branding higher education: Equivalence and difference in developing identity. *Journal of Business Research*, 60(9), 990–999.

Lowrie, A. (2018). *Understanding Branding in Higher Education*. Springer.

Loy, D. (1993). Indra's postmodern net. *Philosophy East and West*, 43(3), 481–510.

Lury, C. (2004). *Brands: The Logos of the Global Economy*. Routledge.

Maitlis, S. (2005). The social processes of organizational sensemaking. *Academy of Management Journal*, 48(1), 21–49.

Maitlis, S., & Christianson, M. (2014). Sensemaking in organizations: Taking stock and moving forward. *Academy of Management Annals*, 8(1), 57–125.

Maitlis, S., & Sonenshein, S. (2010). Sensemaking in crisis and change: Inspiration and insights from Weick (1988). *Journal of Management Studies*, 47(3), 551–580.

Maslow, A. H. (1943). A theory of human motivation. *Psychological Review*, 50(4), 370–396.

Mason, K., & Batch, A. (2009). What's in a (brand) name? *Proceedings of American Society of Business and Behavioral Sciences Annual Conference*, 16(1).

Melewar, T., Gotsi, M., & Andriopoulos, C. (2012). Shaping the research agenda for corporate branding: Avenues for future research. *European Journal of Marketing*, 46(5), 600–608.

Merz, M. A., He, Y., & Vargo, S. L. (2009). The evolving brand logic: A service-dominant logic perspective. *Journal of the Academy of Marketing Science*, 37(3), 328–344.

Mills, C. E. (2009). Making organisational communication meaningful: Reviewing the key features of a model of sensemaking about change communication. *Australian Journal of Communication*, 36(2), 111.

Mills, J. H., Thurlow, A., & Mills, A. J. (2010). Making sense of sensemaking: The critical sensemaking approach. *Qualitative Research in Organizations and Management: An International Journal*, 5(2), 182–195.

Morgan, A. (2000). *What is Narrative Therapy? An Easy-to-Read Introduction*. Dulwich Centre Publications.

Mosley, R. (2007). Customer experience, organisational culture and the employer brand. *Journal of Brand Management*, 15(2), 123–134.

Mumby, D. K. (2016). Organizing beyond organization: Branding, discourse, and communicative capitalism. *Organization*, 23(6), 884–907.

Muniz, A. M., & O'Guinn, T. C. (2001). Brand community. *Journal of Consumer Research*, 27(4), 412–432.

Nakassis, C. V. (2013). Materiality, materialization. *HAU: Journal of Ethnographic Theory*, 3(3), 399–406.

Nicolini, D. (2012). *Practice Theory, Work, and Organization: An Introduction*. Oxford University Press.

Nicotera, A.M. (2013). Organizations as entitative beings: Some ontological implications of communicative constitution. In D. Robichaud, & F. Cooren, (Eds.). *Organization and Organizing: Materiality, Agency and Discourse* (pp.66–89). Routledge.

Nijhof, A., & Jeurissen, R. (2006). Editorial: A sensemaking perspective on corporate social responsibility: Introduction to the special issue. *Business Ethics: A European Review*, 15(4), 316–322.

Nymark, S. (2000). *Value-based Management in Learning Organizations through "Hard" and "Soft" Managerial Approaches: The Case of Hewlett-Packard*. Department of Industrial Economics and Strategy, Copenhagen Business School.

Payne, A., Storbacka, K., Frow, P., & Knox, S. (2009). Co-creating brands: Diagnosing and designing the relationship experience. *Journal of Business Research*, 62(3), 379–389.

Prahalad, C. K., & Ramaswamy, V. (2004). Co-creation experiences: The next practice in value creation. *Journal of Interactive Marketing*, 18(3), 5–14.

Punjaisri, K., Evanschitzky, H., & Rudd, J. (2013). Aligning employee service recovery performance with brand values: The role of brand-specific leadership. *Journal of Marketing Management*, 29(9–10).

Putnam, L. L. (2013). Dialectics, contradictions, and the question of agency: A tribute to James R. Taylor. In D. Robichaud, & F. Cooren (Eds.). *Organization and Organizing: Materiality, Agency and Discourse* (pp.23–36). Routledge.

Putnam, L. L., & Nicotera, A. M. (Eds.) (2009). *Building Theories of Organization: The Constitutive Role of Communication*. Routledge.

Putnam, L. L., & Nicotera, A. M. (2010). Communicative constitution of organization is a question: Critical issues for addressing it. *Management Communication Quarterly*, 24(1), 158–165.

Robichaud, D., & Cooren, F. (Eds.) (2013). *Organization and Organizing: Materiality, Agency and Discourse*. Routledge.

Salzer-Mörling, M., & Strannegård, L. (2004). Silence of the brands. *European Journal of Marketing*, 38(1/2), 224–238.

Schau, H. J., Muñiz Jr., A. M., & Arnould, E. J. (2009). How brand community practices create value. *Journal of Marketing*, 73(5), 30–51.

Schoeneborn, D., Blaschke, S., Cooren, F., McPhee, R. D., Seidl, D., Taylor, J. R. (2014). The three schools of CCO thinking: Interactive dialogue and systematic comparison. *Management Communication Quarterly* 28(2)285–316

Selg, P., & Ventsel, A. (2008). Towards a semiotic theory of hegemony: Naming as hegemonic operation in Lotman and Laclau. *Sign Systems Studies*, 36(1), 167–182.

Selg, P., & Ventsel, A. (2010). An outline for a semiotic theory of hegemony. *Semiotica: Journal of the International Association for Semiotic Studies*, 182, 443–474.

Shotter, J. (1993). *Conversational Realities: Constructing Life through Language* (pp.148–159). Sage.

Shotter, J. (2008). *Conversational Realities Revisited: Life, Language, Body and World*. Taos Institute Publications.

Simmons, J. A. (2009). "Both sides now": Aligning external and internal branding for a socially responsible era. *Marketing Intelligence & Planning*, 27(5), 681–697.

Stern, B. B. (2006). What does brand mean? Historical-analysis method and construct definition. *Journal of the Academy of Marketing Science*, 34(2), 216.

Superbrands (2021) Levis (pp.108–109)*Superbrands UK 4*. Retrieved March 13, 2021, from https://library.superbrands.com/online-ebook-html5/UK%20Volume%204/index.html?_ga=2.70815186.390204890.1619353204-839378057.1615631319#page=108

Symon, G., & Cassell, C. (Eds.) (2012). *Qualitative Organizational Research: Core Methods and Current Challenges*. Sage.

Taylor, J. R. (1999). What is "organizational communication"? Communication as a dialogic of text and conversation. *The Communication Review*, 3(1/2),21–63.

Taylor, J. R. (2011). Organization as an (imbricated) configuring of transactions. *Organization Studies*, 32(9), 1273–1294.

Taylor, J. R. (2013). Organizational communication at the crossroads. In D. Robichaud, & F. Cooren (Eds.). *Organization and Organizing: Materiality, Agency and Discourse* (pp.207–221). Routledge

Taylor, J. R., & Cooren, F. (1997). What makes communication 'organizational'? How the many voices of a collectivity become the one voice of an organization. *Journal of Pragmatics*, 27(4), 409–438.

Taylor, J. R., Cooren, F., Giroux, N., & Robichaud, D. (1996). The communicational basis of organization: Between the conversation and the text. *Communication Theory*, 6(1), 1–39.

Taylor, J. R., & Van Every, E. J. (1999). *The Emergent Organization: Communication as Its Site and Surface*. Routledge.

Taylor, J. R., & Van Every, E. J. (2011). *The Situated Organization: Case Studies in the Pragmatics of Communication Research*. Routledge.

Vallaster, C., & von Wallpach, S. (2013). An online discursive inquiry into the social dynamics of multi-stakeholder brand meaning co-creation. *Journal of Business Research*, 66(9), 1505–1515.

Vargo, S. L., & Lusch, R. F. (2004). Evolving to a new dominant logic for marketing. *Journal of Marketing*, 68(1), 1–17.

Vásquez, C., Bencherki, N., Cooren, F., & Sergi, V. (2018). From 'matters of concern' to 'matters of authority': Studying the performativity of strategy from a communicative constitution of organization (CCO) approach. *Long Range Planning*, 51(3), 417–435.

Vásquez, C., Del Fa, S., Sergi, V., & Cordelier, B. (2017a). From consumer to brand: Exploring the commodification of the student in a university advertising campaign. In T. Huzzard, M. Benner, & D. Kärreman (Eds.), *The Corporatization of the Business School* (pp.146–164). Routledge.

Vásquez, C., Del Fa, S., Sergi, V., & Cordelier, B. (2017b). *What are brand and branding? Exploring the organizing properties of branding in higher education from a CCO approach*. Paper presented at the EGOS Colloquium, Copenhagen.

Vásquez, C., Sergi, V., & Cordelier, B. (2013). From being branded to doing branding: Studying representation practices from a communication-centered approach. *Scandinavian Journal of Management*, 29(2), 135–146.

Vigsø, O. (2010). Naming is framing: Swine flu, new flu, and A (H1N1). *Observatorio (OBS*)*, 4(3), 229–241.

Visser, W. (2014). *CSR 2.0: Transforming Corporate Sustainability and Responsibility*. Springer.

Weick, K. E. (1995). *Sensemaking in Organizations*. Sage.

Weick, K. E. (2001). *Making Sense of the Organization*. Blackwell.

Weick, K. E., Sutcliffe, K. M., & Obstfeld, D. (2005). Organizing and the process of sensemaking. *Organization Science*, 16(4), 409–421.

White, H. (1973). Interpretation in history. *New Literary History*, 4(2), 281–314.

Wilden, R., Gudergan, S., & Lings, I. (2010). Employer branding: Strategic implications for staff recruitment. *Journal of Marketing Management*, 26(1–2),56–73.

Yanow, D. (2012). Organizational ethnography between toolbox and world-making. *Journal of Organizational Ethnography*, 1(1), 31–42.

Index

Printed in the United States
by Baker & Taylor Publisher Services